Serial Vigilantes
of Paperback Fiction

Serial Vigilantes
of Paperback Fiction

*An Encyclopedia from
Able Team to Z-Comm*

BRADLEY MENGEL

McFarland & Company, Inc., Publishers
Jefferson, North Carolina, and London

Acknowledgments: I want to acknowledge and thank the following people for their support, advice, information and encouragement: David Aubrey, Matthew Baugh, Peter Coogan, Henry Covert, Chet Cunningham, Win Eckert, Lee Goldberg, Gillian Hallam, Andrew Henry, Keith Hetherington, Chuck Loridans, Patrick Lozito, John Mengel, Stephanie Mengel, Mike Newton, Dennis Power, John Small, Douglas Wojtowicz.

LIBRARY OF CONGRESS CATALOGUING-IN-PUBLICATION DATA

Mengel, Bradley, 1975–
Serial vigilantes of paperback fiction : an encyclopedia
from Able Team to Z-Comm / Bradley Mengel.
p.   cm.
Includes bibliographical references and index.

ISBN 978-0-7864-4165-5
softcover : 50# alkaline paper ∞

1. Vigilantes in literature — Encyclopedias.
2. Serialized fiction — United States — Encyclopedias.
3. Serialized fiction — United States — Bibliography.
I. Title.
PS374.V56M46   2009   813'.087203 — dc22
2009029370

British Library cataloguing data are available

Cover images ©2009 Shutterstock

Manufactured in the United States of America

McFarland & Company, Inc., Publishers
Box 611, Jefferson, North Carolina 28640
www.mcfarlandpub.com

To all the writers whose works
made this book possible

Table of Contents

Introduction

Some of my fondest memories from my childhood were staying up with my father and watching *The A-Team*, *Knight Rider*, *Airwolf*, *The Equalizer* and *MacGyver*. My first taste of what I came to call the serial vigilantes in a print format came a few years later, when I discovered **The Destroyer** series by Richard Sapir and Warren Murphy. Over time, I began to become curious about other similar characters. So I decided to find what information was available.

I found that there has been little written critically on this particular sub-genre of crime and mystery fiction. Critics like Julian Symons totally ignore the subgenre, it does not even rate a mention in any of the three editions of his crime fiction reference *Bloody Murder*.

I discovered an article by Alice K. Turner (1977) in the compilation *Murder Ink* and William Kittredge and Steven M. Krauser briefly discuss the type in the introduction of the anthology *The Great American Detective* (1978).

I also uncovered William H. Young's *A Study of Action-Adventure Fiction — **The Executioner** and Mack Bolan* (1996), which examined **The Executioner** series in great detail and contained a chapter on other series but never really looked at what defined these series.

The internet was of limited help. Some series, such as **The Butcher**, were virtually impossible to find information on. Some websites provided inaccurate information (one site suggested that **The Penetrator** was first published in 1991 based on the fact that eight books from that series were reprinted at that time). I did find some very good sites on the Executioner and the Destroyer.

With this partial information, I began to collect the various series referred to in the above texts, discovering new series through advertising material and searching through used bookstores.

With the books, I was able to discover what made these series unique as well as allowing me to:

- Name the sub-genre,
- Create a definition for the sub-genre,
- Identify and describe series belonging to the sub-genre.

Nomenclature

The nomenclature of the sub-genre is not consistent. The publishers of these books label them as fiction, novel, horror, crime, adventure, action/adventure and men's action. And the categories can be changed from book to book within the same series; for example, Pinnacle books labeled the Destroyer #55: *Master's Challenge* as fiction, the Destroyer #56: *Encounter Group* as men's action and the Destroyer #58: *Total Recall* as action/adventure. With this level of inconsistency there is a need to turn to critical sources to name the type.

Turner (1977) labels the type as "the paperback hero" or "paperback series hero," basing the name on the fact that nearly every series was published exclusively in the paperback format. While this is an accurate assessment, the label is too general; a number of spy, private eye, western and crime series were also published as paperback originals. Turner's list includes characters that do not fit the mold of what she is trying to describe.

Also Turner claims that the paperback hero started in 1969 with the publication of the first Executioner novel by Don Pendleton. The listing of series includes Jonas Ward's Buchanan, Donald Hamilton's Matt Helm, John D. MacDonald's Travis McGee and Gerard De Villiers' Prince Malko Linge series (see **Malko**), which made their debuts between 1956 and 1965.

While Turner does make some interesting comments on the sub-genre, she appears to be unclear on what does fit into the group, including western and private eye series as well as the revival of Kenneth Robeson's pulp hero, The Avenger, onto her list.

Young (1996) offers the name of action/adventure fiction; this has the advantage of being one of the terms used by the publishers but, like the title of the paperback hero, this is too broad. Also, Young does not define what he means by this term. Young adopts the view that these characters are the evolution of the dime and pulp novels of earlier times.

John Cawelti suggests the term the Enforcer in "Myths of Violence in American Popular Culture" (1975) and "The New Mythology of Crime" (1975). He defines the Enforcer as an individual who operates outside the regular system of the law to enforce justice. This may be a Mob Enforcer as seen in *The Godfather* and other gangster stories or it may be a vigilante against the Mafia and other lawlessness. However, the Enforcer — while narrower than paperback hero or action/adventure fiction — it is still too broad and has not been used in other critical sources. The Enforcer can also be a confusing term as Andrew Sugar wrote a series called **The Enforcer**.

Kittredge and Krauser (1978) suggest the title of the Aggressor. Pringle (1987) also uses this term in his description of the Executioner. The term has also been used in a brief biography of Don Pendleton, crediting him with the creation of the type, which appeared in the back of the Executioner #46: *Blood Sport*. Coogan (2006) uses the term "the Aggressor" in a discussion of The Punisher.

Critically, this is the most commonly used term for this type of book. Kittredge and Krauser describe the Aggressor as different from the classical detective (Sherlock Holmes or Ellery Queen) or the hardboiled dick (Sam Spade or Philip Marlowe). These detective types are reactionary in that each is "presented with a puzzle and he solves it" (Kittredge and Krauser, 1978, p. xxix) whereas the Aggressor is moved to change society and wipe out the sources of corruption.

Ultimately, the Aggressor is unsuitable for use in this book as an aggressor is anyone who acts in an aggressive manner. Also the term can be confusing as it possible for there to be a character calling himself the Aggressor.

This book will use the term serial vigilante. This term was used in "A Real Rain" episode of *Criminal Minds* to describe a killer who is targeting people who have escaped justice. This term highlights the fact that these characters are vigilantes, taking the law into their own hands, as well as the fact that their activities are organized in a serial fashion.

The Qualities of the Serial Vigilante

The serial vigilante is a crusader for moral order. This comes from a sudden realization, typically an act of violence, that society is not doing its job and protecting people. Philip Magellan, **The Marksman**, expresses his philosophy to an FBI agent in #19 *Icepick in the Spine*:

> Your thing is to catch criminals again and again and run them over and over through the courts, hoping they'll eventually be put out of circulation, and my thing is a hell of a lot more direct — my verdicts are final, because they come down the barrel of a nine millimeter automatic [Scarpetta 7].

The serial vigilante will determine the greatest threat against society and attack that threat. After thirty-eight books of battling the Mafia, the Executioner began to battle terrorists in the Executioner #39: *The New War*. Don Pendleton explains this in the introduction to the listing of terrorist organizations in the Executioner #63: *The New War Book* (1984):

> The Mafia is not nearly as strong now as when Bolan first began his one man vigilante war; but I would have reshaped the series even if this was not true because I believe that the hard challenge of today is not organized crime but the organized savagery that we see today as international terrorism [Pendleton 143].

There are many things that most of the serial vigilantes have in common, aside from the threat against society. Their attacks against these threats are aggressive and violent. Turner (1977) quotes Andy Ettinger, editor for Pinnacle books, the publisher of many of serial vigilante heroes, as saying "without violence these books wouldn't sell." For the Destroyer handbook *Inside Sinanju*, Will Murray (1985) interviewed Warren Murphy and Richard Sapir, creators of the Destroyer series who confirm this:

> MURPHY: ...we had a little fight with the publisher, who wanted us to do more of an Executioner....
> QUESTION: So they wanted another war against the Mafia series?
> SAPIR: No, what they wanted was bodies. Like the Roman arenas. They wanted more blood and more blood [Murray 146].

However, Sapir and Murphy did not increase the level of blood but instead created their own type of serial vigilante laced with humor and satire.

The typical serial vigilante character has served in Vietnam and learnt the skills used in his crusade. This can be seen in the history of the Executioner, the Destroyer, the **Penetrator** and **Able Team**, to name a few. Others gained this training in different ways. The Butcher was a high-ranking member of the Mafia who turned against it as an act of redemption for the evil he had committed. **Dagger** was a war correspondent, and Carl Lyons of Able Team was a police officer. Others, like **The Death Merchant**, offer no explanation as to how they gained their skills.

Kettredge and Krause (1978) point out that the serial vigilante's crusade is sparked by an incident, which alters their perception of society. It may be something that happened to loved ones: The Executioner's father killed his family after discovering that his daughter was prostituting herself to help pay off his debt to Mafia loan sharks; **The Satan Sleuth**'s wife was killed by Devil worshippers; Robert Briganti became **The Assassin** when his family was killed after he refused to help the Mafia; Dagger's fiancée was killed after he exposed a conspiracy.

Others will have the incident happen to them: the Penetrator was bashed and left for dead after tracking down some black marketers; the Destroyer was framed and went through a fake execution.

The incident does not need to physical. Nile Barrabas, leader of **The Soldiers of Barrabas**, was court marshaled and dishonorably discharged for crimes he did not commit.

Nearly all the serial vigilantes are male, though Cherry Delight, **The Sexecutioner**; Penelope St. John Orsini, **The Baroness**; and Su-Lin Kelly of **The Girl Factory** are some exceptions to this. Females are common in teams. **S-Com**, **Z-Comm**, the Soldiers of Barrabas, and **Black Ops** all have one female member, **Warhawks, Inc.** has two and **Codename** has three.

Generally, lone serial vigilantes are racially Caucasian, though Mark Hardin, the Penetrator, is part Cheyenne; John Eagle, **The Expeditor**, is raised as an Apache; Su-Lin Kelly (the Girl Factory), Mace (**Kung Fu**) and Chong Fei K'ing (**K'ing Kung Fu**) are half Chinese. A few, such as the Assassin (Robert Briganti) and **The Sharpshooter** (Johnny Rock/John Rocetti) are ethnically Italian.

True racial diversity can be seen in the series featuring teams. The 11 members of the Soldiers of Barrabas include a Hispanic, an African American, an Osage Indian, a Chinese, an Italian, a Greek, a Jew and an Irishman. **Phoenix Force** was devised as an international force and was made up originally of an Israeli, an Englishman, a Canadian, a Cuban and a Japanese. After the death of the Japanese member partway through the series, an African American replaced him. S-Com has an Australian, a Cuban and an Israeli. Warhawks, Inc., have an Australian, a German, a Frenchman and an Israeli.

What separates the serial vigilante from other sub-genres is the notion of sanctioning. The serial vigilante operates in two different ways. Either the crusade is totally personal, operating without the support or influence of any government agency, or any support received is unofficial.

In the personal crusade, we see the serial vigilante operating solely on his own agenda. He may have a support network but they have no connection to any official agency. **The Hitman**, the Penetrator, the Expeditor and the Assassin (Briganti) are all examples of this type of serial vigilante.

In the case of unofficial sanctioning, the serial vigilante is supported by a government agency that cannot admit to supporting the serial vigilante or the government agency itself is covert. **The Hard Corps** is often hired by the CIA to take on missions that the agency may wish deny any involvement with. Similar arrangements operate for the Death Merchant and the Soldiers of Barrabas. These serial vigilantes are able to take on other missions and, in the event of trouble, may be able to have assistance. The Destroyer on the other hand works for a covert agency known as CURE, which officially does not exist and is able to operate outside the limitations of the American Constitution. The Butcher, the Sexecutioner, Phoenix Force and Able Team operate under similar conditions.

Some serial vigilantes can operate in both fashions throughout their series. The Executioner started out on a personal crusade, but after thirty-eight books is pardoned and is unofficially sanctioned to fight international terrorism. **The MIA Hunter** seeks to find prisoners of war from the Vietnam conflict and is so effective that by the seventh book the CIA uses him to rescue operatives who have gone missing in action. In the tenth book, he returns to a private crusade to rescue an army buddy who went to work for the Drug Enforcement Agency and was kidnapped by a drug kingpin.

Due to this unofficial status conveyed upon the serial vigilante, he is often seen to achieve more than conventional agencies are able to. Every book in the Destroyer series points out that the agency he works for, CURE, was founded because America "can't handle crime.... If we live within the Constitution, we're losing all hope of parity with the criminals, or at least the organized ones. The laws don't work. The thugs are winning.... We [CURE] are going to stop the thugs. The only other options are a police state or a complete breakdown.... We are going to operate outside the law to break up organized crime" (Sapir and Murphy, 1971, p. 35–36).

Similarly, **The Black Ops** commandos were "created by an elite cadre of red-tape-cutting government officials, to avenge acts of terror" (ad for Black Op series). In MIA Hunter #10: *Miami War Zone*, the MIA Hunter and his team do more damage to the drug trade in a week than the DEA had done in many years. One of the drug barons acknowledges it is because they "are not playing by the rules" (Buchanan, 1988, p. 107).

The serial vigilante's adventures are contemporary, although there have been occasional flashback tales.

So as can be seen the serial vigilante has many of the following characteristics: After gaining skills in the Vietnam conflict, some event, usually of a violent nature, happens to the hero, causing him to become aware of a threat to society. A violent crusade against this threat is launched, which is either unsanctioned or partially authorized by various government agencies. Because the serial vigilante doesn't follow established rules he is often quite successful in his crusade. In most cases the serial vigilante works alone but teams of serial vigilantes do exist. The lone serial vigilante is predominantly Caucasian, with teams tending to be more multicultural. The events of the serial vigilante's crusade are contemporary.

History of the Serial Vigilante

All four sources agree that the serial vigilante started in 1969 with the publication of The Executioner #1: *War on the Mafia* by Don Pendleton. But Kettredge and Krauser

(1978) suggest that he is the evolution of the American detective. There is some merit in this especially since Pendleton acknowledged in an interview with *Mediascene* (1973) the writings of Mickey Spillane were an influence upon him as a writer and on the character of Mack Bolan. Sapir and Murphy in a joint interview for *Inside Sinanju* state that in the creation of The Destroyer, they were trying to do James Bond with the fun of Doc Savage.

In between the private eye and the serial vigilante is John D. MacDonald's Travis McGee. McGee operates unofficially in his salvage operations, where McGee recovers stolen property for a fee of half its value plus expenses. McGee can be seen as a precursor to the serial vigilante, with his unofficial activities, but, like the private eye, he operates on a case-by-case basis. He does not crusade to stop thefts.

In 1963, nine new adventures of the Shadow were published; these stories were contemporary and had the Shadow facing CYPHER, a spy agency not unlike SPECTRE or THRUSH from James Bond and the Man from U.N.C.L.E. respectively.

A year later, Bantam books started to reprint Doc Savage's adventures which were a resounding success. Warren Murphy and Richard Sapir acknowledge Doc Savage as an inspiration for the Destroyer (Murray, 1985, p. 158).

The same year saw the third incarnation of dime- and pulp-novel hero Nick Carter. No longer a private eye, this new Nick Carter was a spy, code-named "**The Killmaster**," and was granted an N3 rating, an American "license to kill." A number of authors worked on this series, hidden by the pseudonym of Nick Carter, and went on to work on serial vigilante series, either under their own names or other pseudonyms. It could then be argued that this incarnation of Nick Carter was the first instance of the serial vigilante and that the Executioner was the first serial vigilante with no links to earlier series.

With success of these revivals of pulp heroes, the way was paved for the introduction of a new series hero. If one looks through the different series, references can be found to various pulp heroes as if to acknowledge the debt they owe. In Executioner #1: *War on the Mafia* two mafia hoods compare the Executioner to the Shadow and the Phantom (Pendleton, 1969, p. 83) although Pendleton claimed in *The Executioner Speaks Out* that he had never read pulps and couldn't comment on the suggestion that the Executioner is a resurrection of the pulps.

But the popularity of the serial vigilante worked the other way, influencing reprints of the pulp heroes. In 1975, four adventures of **The Spider** were reprinted. Unlike the Doc Savage reprints, these were rewritten to make the adventures contemporary with the publication of the books. The re-writers kept the adventure but altered many of the small details. They changed The Spider to just Spider, perhaps to make it sound more like a codename. They removed his Spider disguise of a fright wig, fangs and hunchback, keeping him in plain clothes, as none of the serial vigilantes wear costumes like the pulp heroes. His background was also altered; no longer a veteran of World War I, he became a veteran of Korea. But what did stay intact was the violent crusade against crime.

They say that nothing breeds imitation like success and Turner (1977) reports that the success of the Executioner had brought forth more than forty original series by 1971. My research shows that new series continued to be developed after that until the present. There have been over 100 series developed with over 1,800 volumes published in that time.

In the explosion of these series there have been several series, though unrelated, that shared the same name. These include the Assassin (Robert Briganti) (1973), **The Assassin** (Justin Perry) (1983), the Hitman (Mike Ross) (1973), **The Hitman** (Dirk Spencer) (1984), **The Revenger** (John Stark) (1973) and **The Revenger** (Ben Martin) (1973).

However, most of 120 series ended after the publication of less than thirty books in the series. A few lasted longer; these are the Butcher (35), Soldiers of Barrabas (38), the Penetrator (53), Phoenix Force (55), Able Team (56), the Death Merchant (71) and **Nick Carter, The Killmaster** lasted 259 books.

Currently, there are several serial vigilante series in publication. The Executioner and its spinoffs, **Super Bolan** (longer length Executioners) and **Stony Man** (which continues the adventures of **Able Team** and **Phoenix Force**) are currently published by Gold Eagle. The Destroyer, starting with #146 *Guardian Angel* as **The New Destroyer** is published by Tor books with creator Warren Murphy returning to write the series and restarting as #1. Avon books are publishing the **Home Team** series and Gold Eagle has launched the **Rogue Angel** series.

Other Mediums

While the serial vigilante began in the novel format, he has been adapted into other mediums with varying degrees of success. The Destroyer and the Executioner have both been made into comics.

Death Wish (1974 and sequels 1982, 1985, 1987, 1994), **The Black Samurai** (1976), the Destroyer (*Remo: Unarmed and Dangerous* 1985 and *Remo Williams* 1987 television pilot), the Penetrator (*Firing Line* 1991); and **The Specialist** (1994) have all had movies made of their adventures.

New serial vigilantes were developed for other mediums. The Punisher (1974 in Amazing Spider-Man #129: *The Punisher Strikes Twice*) is Marvel Comics' version of the serial vigilante. Marvel's *New Universe* line featured the serial vigilante Marc Hazzard: *Merc* (1986). Charlton Comics had Vengeance Squad (1975), Atlas-Seaboard had Targitt (1975) (which became John Targitt, Man-stalker, with the second issue), DC comics created their own serial vigilante in Vigilante (1982, in New Teen Titans Annual #2: *The Murder Machine*) which all made use of the serial vigilante format.

Movies like *The Exterminator* and its sequel (1980 and 1984), *Jake Speed* (1986), *Dark Avenger* (1990) and *Darkman* and its sequels (1990, 1994 and 1996) give us cinematic versions of the serial vigilante. But it was television that made the most of the serial vigilante formula with series like *The Persuaders* (1971–72), *Knight Rider* (1982–86) and its spinoffs, *Dalton's Code of Vengeance* (1985–86) and *Team Knight Rider* (1997), *The A-Team* (1983–87), *Airwolf* (1984–87), *Street Hawk* (1985), *Equalizer* (1985–89), *MacGyver* (1985–92), *Stingray* (1986–87), *Soldier of Fortune, Inc./Special Ops Force* (1997–98), and *Vengeance Unlimited* (1998–99).

These new serial vigilantes were then, in turn, adapted into other media. Many television series and movies were novelized. These novelizations generally retold the plot of the movie or episode, although some, such as *MacGyver*, the *A-Team*, *Tomb Raider* and *Darkman*, had original exploits written for them. Many of the television series were the basis of original comic strip exploits in British magazines such as *Countdown*, *TV Action* and *Look-In.* Others were adapted into comic books in America.

Other Genres

With any successful formula, other genres will borrow the format for their own use. Three genres that borrowed the formula were the western, war and science fiction.

Western series, like the *Six-Gun Samurai*, *Edge* and *Steele*, adopt the serial vigilante and place him in the old West, taking cues from "spaghetti" westerns like *A Fistful of Dollars* (1964). The Punisher was re-imagined in the old West for Marvel Comics in *A Man Named Frank* (1994).

Serial vigilante-inspired war stories set in World War II include Jeff Rovin's Force: Five series and Klaus Netzen's The Killers series. Vietnam War series such as Eric Helm's Vietnam: Ground Zero and Jonathon Cain's Saigon Commandos took the serial vigilante back to the Vietnam War and told their tales. Marvel Comics' The 'Nam used this formula and featured Frank Castle in a cameo. Indeed there have been serial vigilante tales which tell of exploits of serial vigilantes in the Vietnam War such as the Punisher: *Born*, Super Bolan #4: *Dirty War* and the Soldiers of Barrabas/Executioner crossover "*Incident at Hoi Binh*" in Executioner #63: *The New War Book* where Mack Bolan clears Nile Barrabas of the charge of massacring civilians.

But the science-fiction serial vigilante who wanders a post-apocalyptic world is the most prolific. This type of serial vigilante include James Axler's Deathlands and Outlanders series, Richard Harding's Outrider series, Jerry Ahern's Survivalist and Defender series, and D.B. Drumm's Traveler. The Mad Max movie series utilizes this format.

The success of the serial vigilante format can be seen from the fact that different genres have utilized the format and it has influenced the way that these genres have expanded.

Conclusion

The serial vigilante genre, so named because of the aggressive qualities of its protagonists, was first named by Kittredge and Krauser in 1978. Since then it has been used many times in other critical works. The serial vigilante has come to the realization that society's system of justice is flawed, which is generally sparked by a tragedy, and has decided to level the playing field. Just as the criminals operate outside the law and utilize legal loopholes, the serial vigilante also operates outside the law — acting for justice rather than the law. The serial vigilante's actions are never formally sanctioned; either they operate totally alone or any authorization of their activities is unofficial. The serial vigilante's justice is final and swift — a speeding bullet cannot be bribed. The serial vigilante's adventures are contemporary. Most commonly the serial vigilante is a lone male, although he may work as part of a team.

A number of pulp revivals and reprints throughout the 1960s paved the way for the introduction of the serial vigilante. In 1969, Pinnacle Books published *War Against the Mafia*, the first Executioner novel, starting the serial vigilante genre. The success of the Executioner paved the way for more serial vigilante series, several of which continue to the present. The serial vigilante format was adapted across various mediums appearing in comics, film and television. It has also been modified for use in other genres, such as war, westerns and science fiction.

The purpose of this encyclopedia is to offer a source of information about the serial vigilante series that have appeared in the various mediums.

THE VIGILANTES

ABLE TEAM

Fifty-one books by "Dick Stivers"

To get the full history of this spinoff of **The Executioner** we have to go back to the Executioner #2: *Death Squad.* In that novel, Bolan decides to use some of his fellow Vietnam veterans in his war on the Mafia, his Death Squad. In the final assault everyone except Mack, Rosario "Pol" Blancanales and Herman "Gadgets" Schwartz were killed. The idea was to confirm to Mack that this had to be his personal crusade. Also introduced in that book was an LA cop by the name of Carl Lyons who was after the Executioner, but by the end of the book he became Bolan's ally.

These three characters appeared sporadically throughout the series as Pendleton continued writing. Pol and Gadgets set up a detective firm, Able Investigations, with Pol's sister Toni.

Then Pendleton sold the Executioner to Gold Eagle. Mack Bolan had been pardoned and given the new identity of John Phoenix, the base Stony Man Farm and a new war on terrorism. Pol, Gadgets and Lyons became Able Team, Mack's force to fight terrorism on American soil, although the team operated in other countries.

Carl "Ironman" Lyons was the team leader, Gadgets was responsible for the electronic equipment, and Pol, which is short for Politician, was the negotiator for the group. Over the series Able Team was aided by other warriors but these three remained the core.

Behind the Scenes

Initially, the series was written under the byline Don Pendleton and Dick Stivers, highlighting the series' connection to the Executioner series. The non-existent Stivers was given the biography that he was a volunteer for Vietnam but was too young to see any action. His first taste of battle came during a mugging in Los Angeles. A traveler and adventurer, Stivers travels the world tackling crime. In truth Stivers did not exist and the books were written by several writers using the house name. These writers include:

- Norman Winski, also the author of the novelization of *The Sword and the Sorcerer*, the Hitman series and several works on astrology. Winski was also a member of the Chicago Beat scene and Charles Bukowski (*Barfly*) was godfather to his son.

- Ron Renauld, who wrote five A-Team novelizations as Charles Heath and wrote book 7 under his own name. He has also written for the Executioner.

- Nicholas Cain — a former military police officer. Cain wrote the semi-autobiographical Saigon Commandoes series. Under the pen name Jonathon Cain, he wrote the Little Saigon series about a former MP turned LA police officer working in the Vietnamese community. As Sgt. Nik Uhernik, he wrote the War Dogs series; Uhernik also appears as a character in the Saigon Commandoes series.

- Steve Mertz, who, along with Mike Newton, got his start working with Don Pendleton on the Executioner for Pinnacle Books, later ghostwriting a number of Executioner novels for Gold Eagle books and plotting the MIA Hunter series for Jove books.

The Books

All books were published by Gold Eagle Books. Books 1 to 3 were attributed to Don Pendleton and Dick Stivers; all other books were attributed to Stivers alone.

1. *Tower of Terror*, 187 pages, 1982 (L.R. Payne)
2. *The Hostaged Island*, 186 pages, 1982 (Payne & Norman Winski)
3. *Texas Showdown*, 190 pages, 1982 (Larry Powell & Payne)
4. *Amazon Slaughter*, 190 pages, 1983 (C.J. Shiao)
5. *Cairo Countdown*, 186 pages, 1983 (Paul Hofrichter)
6. *Warlord of Azatlan*, 183 pages, 1983
7. *Justice by Fire*, 189 pages, 1983 (G.H. Frost)
8. *Army of Devils*, 186 pages, 1983 (Frost)
9. *Kill School*, 189 pages, 1983 (Frost)
10. *Royal Flush*, 182 pages, 1984 (Stephen Mertz)
11. *Five Rings of Fire*, 179 pages, 1984 (Tom Arnett)
12. *Deathbites*, 184 pages, 1984 (Arnett)
13. *Scorched Earth*, 190 pages, 1984 (Frost)
14. *Into the Maze*, 185 pages, 1984 (Frost)
15. *They Came to Kill*, 185 pages, 1984 (Frost)
16. *Rain of Doom*, 185 pages, 1985 (Frost)
17. *Fire and Maneuver*, 184 pages, 1985 (Frost & Chuck Rogers)
18. *Tech War*, 186 pages, 1985 (Frost & Ivan Chan)
19. *Ironman*, 188 pages, 1985 (Frost)
20. *Shot to Hell*, 187 pages, 1985 (Rogers)
21. *Death Strike*, 186 pages, 1985 (Frost)
22. *The World War III Game*, 189 pages, 1986 (Arnett)
23. *Fall Back and Kill*, 188 pages, 1986 (Rogers)
24. *Blood Gambit*, 186 pages, 1986 (Arnett)
25. *Hard Kill*, 218 pages, 1986 (Rogers)
26. *The Iron God*, 221 pages, 1986 (Arnett)
27. *Cajun Angel*, 219 pages, 1986 (Rogers)
28. *Miami Crush*, 219 pages, 1987 (Rogers)
29. *Death Ride*, 220 pages, 1987 (Arnett)
30. *Hit and Run*, 220 pages, 1987 (Rogers)
31. *Ghost Train*, 221 pages, 1987 (Rogers)
32. *Firecross*, 221 pages, 1987 (Arnett)
33. *Cowboy's Revenge*, 221 pages, 1987 (Ron Renauld)
34. *Clear Shot*, 220 pages, 1988 (Renauld)
35. *Strike Force*, 219 pages, 1988 (Renauld)
36. *Final Run*, 219 pages, 1988 (Renauld)

37. *Red Menace*, 218 pages, 1988 (Renauld)
38. *Cold Steel*, 220 pages, 1988 (Renauld)
39. *Death Code*, 221 pages, 1988 (Larry Lind)
40. *Blood Mark*, 219 pages, 1989 (Renauld)
41. *White Fire*, 218 pages, 1989 (Renauld)
42. *Dead Zone*, 218 pages, 1989 (Renauld)
43. *Kill Orbit*, 221 pages, 1989 (Sgt. Nik Uhernik [Nicholas Cain])
44. *Night Heat*, 220 pages, 1989 (Nicholas Cain)
45. *Lethal Trade*, 219 pages, 1989 (Pennington)
46. *Counterblow*, 221 pages, 1990 (Cain)
47. *Shadow Warriors*, 221 pages, 1990 (Ken Rose)
48. *Cult War*, 219 pages, 1990 (Rose)
49. *Dueling Missiles*, 218 pages, 1990 (David North)
50. *Death Hunt*, 221 pages, 1990 (Pennington)
51. *Skin Walker*, 221 pages, 1991 (Rose)

Gold Eagle attempted to utilize the Super Bolan format on Able Team with Super Able Team:
1. *Mean Streets*, 349 pages, 1989 (Rose)
2. *Hostile Fire*, 346 pages, 1990 (Rose)

Able Team also appeared in the Anthologies:
1. *Heroes I*, 588 pages, 1992. Contains *Razorback* by Dick Stivers (North)
2. *Heroes II*, 586 pages, 1992. Contains *Death Lash* by Dick Stivers (North)
3. *Heroes III*, 445 pages, 1992. Contains *Secret Justice* by Dick Stivers (Rose)

Members of Able Team have guest-starred in various Executioner, **Phoenix Force** and **Stony Man** books.

Other Media

Able Team, as such, has not been adapted into other media, though all three characters appeared in the comic adaptation of *Death Squad* (see the Executioner entry for more detail).

According to Mike Newton in his interview for Young's *Mack Bolan and The Executioner: A Study of Action-Adventure Fiction*, stated that NBC had access to the Able Team files in 1982, a year before NBC produced *The A-Team*, suggesting that the television series is an unauthorized version of the book series.

AGENT FOR COMINSEC (TAGGART)
Six books by Ralph Hayes

Taggart is a former Mafia executioner who became the top agent for COMINSEC

(Committee for International Security). Taggart and four other agents independently investigate various conspiracies that threaten world peace.

For example in #4: The *Hellfire Conspiracy* four billionaires put an impostor in place of the president to stir up trouble with the Soviets and Chinese so that they could make more money from the arms sales. Taggart determines that the president is an impostor and is able to assassinate him.

COMINSEC is run by five generals representing their member nations, America, Britain, France, Germany and Japan (called Generals A, B, F, G and J, respectively), who use violence to solve the world's problems. (Imagine CURE from the Destroyer on a more global scale.)

In the final book of the series, *Death Makers Conspiracy*, Taggart teams with the Japanese agent for COMINSEC, implying that all member nations of COMISEC have one agent and that Taggart is America's agent.

Behind the Scenes

Ralph Hayes was born in 1927 and served in the Air Force 1945–47. After leaving the Air Force he studied and became a lawyer, specializing in insurance. In 1969, Hayes became a freelance writer, writing a number of travel guides and individual novels as well as the Buffalo Hunter western series and **Stoner, The Hunter** and **Checkforce** series. Under the Nick Carter house name he wrote eight **Killmaster** books. Hayes traveled extensively and utilized that experience for his travel guides and the settings for his books (Contemporary Authors Online, 2002).

The Books

All books were published by Belmont Tower books:

1. *The Bloody Monday Conspiracy*, 188 pages, 1974
2. *Doomsday Conspiracy*, 171 pages, 1974
3. *Turkish Mafia Conspiracy*, 170 pages, 1974
4. *Hellfire Conspiracy*, 174 pages, 1974
5. *Nightmare Conspiracy*, 201 pages, 1974
6. *Death Makers Conspiracy*, 180 pages, 1975

APE SWAIN
Three books by Daniel Da Cruz

The man known as Ape Swain uses a variety of names; sometimes he is known as Alfred Paul or Anthony Phillip; on other occasions he is called Alan Patrick. All of his aliases have initials A.P., leading some to suggest that this is the source of his nickname Ape. Others suggest that his long arms and short legs and the pelt of hair that has covered his arms, chest and back since puberty may be the source of the name. Now at age thirty-four, Ape is used to the strange looks he gets and the fact that his appearance leads people to underestimate his intelligence, facts that Swain exploits to his advantage.

Unlike many other serial vigilantes, Ape Swain is not driven from any tragedy or any sense of ideology to operate outside the law, but rather Swain is a businessman exploiting these situations to make a profit.

Swain attempts to overthrow governments to install ones more open to negotiation and organizes a large scale pipeline to smuggle people from behind the Iron Curtain.

Behind the Scenes

Daniel Da Cruz was born in 1921 and he served in the Marines from 1941 to 1947. A long time correspondent for various news services based in the Middle East, Da Cruz was able to utilize his experience, setting several of his books in the Middle East. In 1977, he was awarded a special Edgar award by the Mystery Writers of America for *The Captive City*. Da Cruz also wrote the Jock Sargent series. He died January 5, 1991, in Falls Church, Virginia.

The Books

All books were published by Ballantine:

1. *Landfall Finesse*, 219 pages, 1975
2. *Pipedream Finesse*, 200 pages, 1975
3. *The Captive City*, 198 pages, 1976

ARROW (FRANK ARROW/FRANCO ARRONETTI)

Three books by Walter Deptula

Franco Arronetti was the son of Tony Arronetti, a tough and honest cop in New York's Italian Harlem. Franco followed in his father's footsteps and joined the force. Franco, unlike his father, felt that he was not rewarded enough for his services and when the opportunity presented itself he took four thousand dollars after stopping a bank robbery. When Tony discovered what his son was doing, he turned his own son in and disowned the boy.

Franco then moved to Los Angeles and changed his name to Frank Arrow. After a chance meeting with a childhood friend, Arrow discovered that his talent for police work and his desire for money could be put to good use retrieving stolen items for a fee. His first retrieval operation was stealing back paintings from a dishonest art collector and claiming the reward money from the insurance companies.

From there Arrow built his fortune and moved to Hawaii where he lived a life of luxury between jobs. Arrow had his own jet, a purpose-built XTE 126, complete with library, bathroom and galley and a rainbow-colored tail and a red arrow on the front. He was able to travel all over the world.

Behind the Scenes

Walter J. Deptula Jr. was born in 1934. The Arrow books were his only published work.

The Books

All books were published by Curtis Books:

1. *Wine, Women & Death*, 222 pages, 1974
2. *Naked Mistress*, 194 pages, 1974
3. *Death List of Rico Scalisi*, 224 pages, 1974

THE ASSASSIN (ROBERT BRIGANTI)

Three books by Peter McCurtin

Robert Briganti was born in New Orleans in 1935, the descendant of Tommo Briganti who arrived in America from Naples in 1892. At age sixteen Robert joined the Carnival and left New Orleans and become one of the best sharpshooters on the circuit, and he toured America for years, gaining friends and contacts. With the death of his mentor, Briganti joined the Marston Arms company, selling surplus arms throughout South America and gaining an expertise in nearly all weapons. After marrying, Briganti retired from Marston and opened a sporting goods store and had a son Michael in 1963.

In 1972, Briganti was approached by mobster Joe Coraldi to get him weapons for his current gang war and Briganti refused him. So the mobsters ordered that Briganti be killed; the attack killed Briganti's wife and son but left Briganti alive. After getting out of hospital, Briganti began his war against the Mafia, starting with Coraldi. Next, **The Assassin** took out a Mafia summit held in New Orleans and finally wiped out the Boston Mafia family after they tried to kill him. Briganti sends tapes recounting his exploits to the authorities and these tapes form the basis for his three books.

Behind the Scenes

Peter McCurtin was an editor for Belmont Towers books before becoming an author. McCurtin, under his own name, was the author of several western series such as Carmody and Sundance as well as the **Soldier of Fortune/Death Dealer** series; under various pen names he contributed to the **Sexecutioner** and **Marksman** series. McCurtin also novelized the movie *The Exterminator* as well as several exposés on organized crime, such as *Mafioso*, *The Syndicate* and *Omerta*.

The Books

The series was published by Dell Books

1. *Manhattan Massacre*, 140 pages, 1973
2. *New Orleans Holocaust*, 191 pages, 1973
3. *Boston Bust*, 140 pages, 1973

THE AVENGER (MATTHEW HAWKE)

Four books by Chet Cunningham

Matt Hawke had served in Vietnam and upon his return joined the San Diego Police Department, eventually joining the Narcotics squad. From there he was recruited by the DEA and became one of their top agents. Hawke left the agency after finding his wife dead and tortured; she had been tortured for three days and made into what the Mafia called "turkey meat" (Mafia slang created by Don Pendleton for **The Executioner** series). Hawke, who had been on a stakeout for three days, discovered the remains of his wife and immediately shot and killed the Colombian responsible for the death and mutilation of his wife.

At that moment Hawke resigned from the DEA and began to wage a one-man war on drugs. His war took him from San Diego to Mexico, Houston, Miami and Columbia and Manhattan. Hawke would destroy all the drugs and use the money as his war chest. Hawke is aided by teenage prostitute Brandy who provides him with intelligence and he maintains his base in San Diego. The press dubs Hawke "The Avenger" and it's a title he adopts in his war on drugs.

Behind the Scenes

The Avenger was written by Chet Cunningham, who lives in San Diego, the setting for the first novel in The Avenger series. Cunningham has also written numerous western novels both under his own name and pseudonyms. Under his own name, Cunningham wrote **The Specialists** and, as Lionel Derrick, he wrote the even numbered books in **The Penetrator** series. A veteran of the Korean War, Cunningham has also written several volumes of military history. The Avenger series was ended due to a change in editorial staff and policy, with Cunningham planning a fifth novel where Matt Hawke took his war on drugs to Hollywood.

The series has no connection to the earlier pulp novel series, the Avenger by Kenneth Robeson (Paul Ernst), which was reprinted by Warner Books during the 1970s with Ron Goulart adopting the Robeson pen name and adding several new adventures to that series when the pulp adventures ran out.

The Books

All four books were published by Warner Books:

1. *The Avenger*, 204 pages, 1987
2. *Houston Hellground*, 187 pages, 1988
3. *Columbian Crackdown*, 183 pages, 1988
4. *Manhattan Massacre*, 170 pages, 1988

THE BARONESS (PENELOPE ST. JOHN ORSINI)

Eight books by Paul Kenyon

The National Security Agency (NSA) has a secret operative code-named "Coin." This operative's identity is so secret that it is only known to a man codenamed Key and Key's identity is only known to very few in the NSA. Coin is in reality Baroness

Penelope St. John Orsini. **The Baroness** is one of the world's top models, her face gracing the covers of Vogue and other fashion magazines.

Born Penelope Worthington, she married John Stanton Marlowe when she was young. Marlowe worked in espionage and died mysteriously, piloting his own Gulfstream. After his death, Penny married Baron Reynaldo St. John Orsini, a playboy who died in car crash in the Monte Carlo Grand Prix, leaving his widow wealthy and bored. Using the contacts she made during her time with both husbands, the Baroness began a freelance spy operation, using her cover as a top model to gain access anywhere in the world.

The Baroness is aided in her missions by her entourage from her modeling agency International Models:

• John Farnsworth: codename Key, former OSS agent and the Baroness' handler for the NSA under the cover of her business manager.

• Dan Wharton: Green Beret and master espionage agent trained by the CIA and NSA who poses as the Baroness' chauffeur and photographer.

• Joe Skytop: The Baroness' top photographer, a full-blood Cherokee and master of unarmed combat.

• Tom Sumo: First-generation Japanese American and electrical genius. Fashion consultant for the photo shoots.

• Paul and Yvette: two models in the Baroness' stable. Paul is adept in guerrilla warfare and is an explosives expert. Yvette is a mistress of disguise and costuming.

• Eric: Son of a Norwegian sailor, this blonde brawler is the top male model in the Baroness' agency.

• Fiona: The Baroness' top female model.

Behind the Scenes

The series was devised by Lyle Kenyon Engel. Engel was behind the creation of a number of series, including **The Killmaster, Blade,** and **The Butcher,** as well as packaging a number of historical family sagas such as those of Pearl S. Buck and John Jakes. Engel also wrote a number of nonfiction works many of which were about cars and car racing.

Engel founded the fiction factory Book Creations, Inc. (BCI), in 1973. This company conceived books and series, then hired writers to write the books and then sell the publication rights to paperback publishers. Engel passed away in 1986. Control of BCI went to Engel's brother George who ran the company until 1991, when it ceased business.

The Books

All books were published by Pocket Books:

1. *The Ecstasy Connection,* 223 pages, 1974
2. *Diamonds Are for Dying,* 173 pages, 1974
3. *Death Is a Ruby Light,* 207 pages, 1974
4. *Hard-Core Murder,* 223 pages, 1974
5. *Operation Doomsday,* 218 pages, 1974

6. *Sonic Slave*, 216 pages, 1974
7. *Flicker of Doom*, 222 pages, 1974
8. *Black Gold*, 217 pages, 1975

Several books were written but not published due to the cancellation. Those titles were:

9. "A Black Hole to Die In"
10. "Death Is a Copycat"
11. "Quicktime Death"

THE BIG BRAIN (COLIN GARRETT)

Three books by Gary Brandner

The Big Brain is Colin Garrett, the man with the highest IQ ever recorded. Garrett's parents, a professor of English and a PhD in biology, planned the birth of a genius child. Nothing was left to chance from diet to personal associates. The couple succeeded. Colin could read before he was two, argue logic at three and compose sonnets at four. But this genius came at a physical cost during periods of intense concentration: Colin's eyes glowed green, his temperature rose up to six degrees and his breathing and pulse rate slowed.

At age nine Colin was orphaned when his parents were killed in a car accident. The super genius child was adopted by his mother's sister and her husband, a childless couple in Boston who sent Colin to public school. It was at school that Colin learned to limit the amount of brain power he used, saving him from both ridicule and burnout.

Colin then attended college and, following that, joined the army and served in Vietnam. He showed a general the way to end the war, which led to his being tested by the Army, the results of which were so spectacular that he was offered any government post he wanted.

Sick of all the testing, he left the Army and went into private consulting. After three years, at age thirty, he was at the top of this field. It was then that Garrett was offered the opportunity to work for the very top-secret Agency Zero by the Army officer responsible for testing him.

Agency Zero is a highly covert agency that does not officially exist and has a budget taken from the official budgets of other departments. There are no records anywhere that relate to Agency Zero; this allows the agency to operate free from the normal laws, regulations and red tape that hinders other more official agencies. Agency Zero is on call to any government agency or department that requires its services.

Colin becomes a consultant for Agency Zero, tackling the cases that are too tough or unconventional for the normal agents. Garrett tackles brain-draining weapons, Satanic cults and energy weapons.

Behind the Scenes

Gary Brandner was born in 1933 and worked in a variety of writing careers, such as copy writing and technical writing, before he turned to fiction writing. He is the author of many books, including the Howling books, which were adapted to a number of movies. He has also written a number of other horror novels as well as nonfiction works. He has also edited a number of anthologies and submitted a number of mystery short stories to *Ellery Queen's Mystery Magazine*, *Alfred Hitchcock's Mystery Magazine* and *Mike Shayne Mystery Magazine*.

The Books

All books in this series were published by Zebra Books:

1. *The Aardvark Affair*, 160 pages, 1975
2. *The Beelzebub Business*, 159 pages, 1975
3. *Energy Zero*, 203 pages, 1976

BLACK OPS

Three books by Michael Kasner

When the war on terror became bogged down in red tape and diplomacy, a number of high-ranking people in elite positions in the American government couldn't stand by and see American citizens killed. So they created a black ops team that didn't exist, officially. This team was called the Clandestine Anti-terrorist Team or CAT.

The team's contact in the government is Winston T. Stedman, bureaucrat in the Pentagon who oversees all the team's missions and, through his cover in Defense Procurement Agency, is able to finance and equip the five-man team.

This clandestine team consists of:

• Judson Rykoff: ex-special forces major and team leader who served in the first Gulf War.
• Alexander Sendak: second-in-command ex–Delta Force invalided out of the army after serving in the first Gulf War.
• Melissa Bao: Chinese American whose family fled the fall of Saigon and former Seattle undercover police officer.
• Jacob "Big Jake" MacLeod: Former Navy SEAL.
• Erik Estevez: Ex-DEA pilot turned vigilante.

Each member was at a loss returning to civilian life after retiring until Judson offered them membership in CAT and an opportunity to make a difference — free from the rules.

Behind the Scenes

Michael Kasner is also the author of the futuristic Warkeep 2030 series also published by Gold Eagle Books.

The Books

All books were published by Gold Eagle books:

1. *Undercover War*, 349 pages, 1996

2. *Armageddon Now*, 349 pages, 1996

3. *Deep Terror*, 348 pages, 1996

BLACK SAMURAI (ROBERT SAND)

Eight books by Marc Olden

Robert Sand was an African-American soldier serving in Vietnam and while on leave in Japan came to the rescue of an old man being harassed by a group of racist soldiers. During the skirmish Sand was shot in the belly. The old man took Sand home and tended to his wounds and revealed that he was a Samurai Master and in gratitude for his help wanted to train Sand in the ways of the samurai. Seven years later, Sand had become the best pupil of the master, when a group of mercenaries attack the master's dojo, killing everyone except Sand.

The Black Samurai tracked down the men who killed his master and brother samurai, discovering a group of disgruntled soldiers intent on taking revenge on America for turning its back on them.

During his quest, Sand is contacted by a former United States president named Clarke. In many respects, Clarke bears a number of similarities to former President Lyndon Baines Johnson, including the fact that they both come from Texas.

Clarke offers to finance Sand's quest and gives him information on situations that suit Sand's unique talents, ranging from stopping a nuclear attack on New York, destroying a conspiracy, and fighting cults, slavery rings, right-wing takeovers of America and terrorist attacks.

Behind the Scenes

Marc Olden was born in Baltimore, Maryland, before his family moved to New York in the 1940s. He attended Queen's College and graduated with a degree in Creative Writing and Journalism. Initially working as a Broadway and entertainment publicist, he retired from that field to become a full-time writer.

One of his earliest nonfiction works, *Cocaine*, brought Olden into contact with a number of law enforcement personnel, which he used as the basis for his first series, Narc, about an undercover narcotics officer.

Olden was a lifelong student of the martial arts and the Orient and several of his thriller novels, such as *Kasieng*, *Giri* and *Oni*, explore the theme of Eastern culture.

Olden passed away in 2003.

The Books

All books were published by Signet Books:

1. *Black Samurai*, 167 pages, 1974

2. *Golden Kill*, 176 pages, 1974

3. *Killer Warrior*, 159 pages, 1974

4. *Deadly Peril*, 153 pages, 1974

5. *Inquisition*, 170 pages, 1974
6. *Warlock*, 153 pages, 1975
7. *Sword of Allah*, 152 pages,1975
8. *Katana*, 168 pages, 1975

The Movie

In 1976, Jim Kelly starred in *The Black Samurai: Agent for Dragon*. The film was directed by Al Adamson. In the film Robert Sand is an agent for DRAGON, but he works without interference from his fellow agents and he investigates the kidnapping of a former lover Tuki by the cult leader/slaver known as the Warlock. The movie takes several elements from several of the books and combines them into one story.

BLACK SWAN (SHAUNA BISHOP)

Four books by J.J. Montague

Shauna Bishop is a freelance operative for Section K of an unnamed agency. She receives a handsome check every month from Section K that pays the rent on her $450 penthouse suite in Newport, California, and has allowed her to save over $100,000 secured in three safety deposit boxes.

Code-named The Black Swan, Shauna's specialty is seduction and she has the body for the job. With long dark hair almost touching her buttocks, tall, in her twenties, her enormous breasts are jutting and firm with large nipples and while off duty Shauna rarely wears clothes.

The Black Swan is a nymphomaniac who has seduced numerous men on her missions and has killed four men with complete detachment and no remorse.

Section K has used her skills to obtain information from enemy agents or to cause them to defect to America. In other cases, Shauna uses her body as an extra inducement to sway independent nations to favor the United States, seducing rulers and politicians. Shauna is also a crack shot and worked with the Marines during a peacekeeping mission in the Middle East.

Shauna, on occasion, teams with male agents such as Mike Dark. The sexual chemistry often leads to pre- and post-mission sex.

When not staying at her Newport penthouse, Shauna travels the globe and has taken missions in France, Vietnam, China and the Middle East.

Behind the Scenes

J.J. Montague is the pen name of James Keenan. Keenan also writes under the names J.J. Savage and Bruce Brooks. Under his own name, he wrote the thriller *Run, Major, Run*.

The Books

All books were published by Canyon Books:

1. *Chinese Kiss*, 190 pages, 1974
2. *Cong Kiss*, 189 pages, 1974

3. *French Kiss*, 1974
4. *Judas Kiss*, 192 pages, 1975

BLOOD (MARK BLOOD)

Three books by Allan Morgan

Mark Blood was a hero during the Vietnam War, a war that desperately needed heroes. Returning from the hospital after being injured in his latest mission, Blood discovered that his wife Cynthia was killed during a plane hijacking and that his commander had kept this information from him for a week.

After a violent attack on his commander, Blood was discharged and returned to America where he was approached by the CIA to act as their unofficial agent. Rejecting their offer, Blood instead decided to investigate the death of his wife, a file clerk for the CIA.

Blood discovered that the official story that his wife was accidentally shot by the hijackers was false and that her throat had been slit. As the hijackers wanted to be taken to Cuba, Blood headed there and became involved in an anti–Castro group who had access to a new chemical weapon.

Blood discovered that this was the group who killed his wife and who the CIA wanted him to hunt down. After wiping out this group and the woman responsible for his wife's death, Blood reconsiders the CIA offer and undertakes two further missions for the CIA.

Behind the Scenes

Allan Morgan is the pen name of Marilyn Ruth Henderson. Henderson was a research chemist, but a back injury left her unable to stand for a lengthy periods and she began writing. Henderson is a keen traveler and uses her trips as research for her books. Henderson is one of the few female writers in the field and wrote *Assignment Intercept* for **The Killmaster** series under the name Nick Carter. Henderson also wrote a number of young adult books published by Scholastic as M.R. Henderson.

Under the name Adam Hamilton, Henderson wrote the **Peacekeeper** series.

The Books

All books were published by Award Books:

1. *Blood*, 188 pages, 1974
2. *The Spandau Warrant*, 173 pages, 1974
3. *The Cat Cay Warrant*, 203 pages, 1974

BRONSON: STREET VIGILANTE (RICHARD BRONSON)

Three books by Philip Rawls

Richard Bronson was a knee-jerk liberal with a wife and children in Cincinnati. But that all ended when criminals led by twins Bennie and Bernie raped his wife and murdered his children. The courts set his family's killers free. Bronson raged about this and he decided to arm himself and take out the criminals who killed his family. Bronson became even more savage than the street scum he fought, using their own violent tactics against them, dousing one female victim in kerosene and lighting her up, and feeding another victim to hungry rats. Bronson initially didn't care if innocent bystanders were killed and even contemplated killing a police officer if he got in his road.

As the series progresses, Bronson follows Bennie and Bernie to California and then to New York and the rage and violence begin to ebb as Bronson stops torturing people and is much more concerned about innocent bystanders.

Behind the Scenes

This series shows its inspiration with the main character Richard Bronson taking his name from the lead actor in the **Death Wish** films, Charles Bronson. Philip Rawls is a house name.

Leonard Levinson used the Philip Rawls pen name for this series. Levinson was born in 1935 and served the U.S. Army from 1954 to 1957. Under a number of pseudonyms and house names, he has contributed to a number of series, including **Kung Fu, Butler, The Sharpshooter,** and **The Sexecutioner.**

The Books

All books were published by Manor Books:

1. *Blind Rage*, 1975
2. *Streets of Blood*, 200 pages, 1975
3. *Switchblade*, 191 pages, 1975

BUNDUKI (JAMES ALLENVALE GUNN)

Four books by J.T. Edson

During the Mau Mau revolution, the Gunn family's plantation was attacked by the rebels. The only survivor was two-year-old son James Allenvale Gunn, who was found by John Clayton, Lord Greystoke.

The Greystokes lived in the next plantation and were friends with Gunns and they adopted James. James was raised with his adoptive cousin Dawn Drummond-Clayton. As James grew up he was trained at the jungle Ambagasali Game Preserve. James was given the nickname Bunduki, the Swahili word for gun.

Dawn often visited her cousin during her vacations and during one of those visits Bunduki and Dawn were on a routine patrol of the Game Preserve when their Land Rover was attacked by poachers and the Rover went over a cliff.

The pair awoke on the planet Zillikan, where aliens calling themselves the Suppliers had populated the planet with a number of rare and endangered animals and several tribes from Earth and needed someone to be their enforcer to keep law and order.

Bunduki and Dawn are not your typical serial vigilantes but they have not been sanctioned by the tribes of Zillikan but rather appointed by the God-like Suppliers to act as the judge and jury for all of Zillikan. This unofficial arrangement places them as serial vigilantes. Bunduki and Dawn battle warring factions of the Quagga tribe bent on conquering all of Zillikan.

Behind the Scenes

J.T. Edson was a dog trainer for the British army who served in Kenya. After leaving the army, he turned his hand to writing and started writing westerns, creating the Floating Outfit, Civil War, Ole Devil Hardin, and Waco series. With this success Edson was able to branch out into less conventional westerns with female protagonists (Calamity Jane), and different time periods (Company Z in the 1920s and Rockabye County in contemporary times).

Edson explains in his introduction to the Bunduki story in *J.T.'s Hundredth* that he was a fan of Edgar Rice Burroughs' Tarzan series and created a new Tarzan story. The story was rejected by Edgar Rice Burroughs, Inc., as it had been Burroughs' wish that no one else write his most famous creation. It was not until Edson read Philip Jose Farmer's *Tarzan Alive* that he saw a way to use his story and created Tarzan's adopted son Bunduki.

The Books

All books were published by Corgi Books:

1. *Bunduki*, 204 pages, 1975
2. *Bunduki and Dawn*, 190 pages, 1976
3. *Sacrifice for the Quagga God*, 194 pages, 1976
4. *Fearless Master of the Jungle*, 211 pages, 1980

Edson had written a fifth novel, "The Amazons of Zillikan," but due to ongoing issues with Edgar Rice Burroughs, Inc., this novel was never published.

Edson also wrote several short stories featuring Bunduki and Dawn set prior to their transportation to Zillikan:

• "The Mchawi's Powers," *J.T.'s Hundredth*, 41 pages, 1979
• "Death to Simba Nyeuse," *J.T.'s Ladies*, 40 pages, 1980
• "Accident — or Murder?" *More J.T.'s Ladies*, 59 pages, 1987
• "A Good Time Was Had by All," *Mark Counter's Kin*, 13 pages, 1990

BUTLER

Twelve books by Philip Kirk

Butler (no first name is ever given) is a former CIA agent, fired for being too critical of the Agency. He discovered that rather than being part of the solution to the world's problems, the CIA was part of the problem, being part of the military industrial complex and the secret society dedicated to taking over the world known as Hydra. Hydra is responsible for the assassination and removal of world leaders, including the assassination of President Kennedy.

Butler is not alone in his battle against Hydra as he is quickly recruited by the Bancroft Institute. The institute is known around the world as a leader in scientific research but its true mission is protecting the world against Hydra.

Butler is the Bancroft Institute's top agent, called on to tackle the hardest jobs, such as stopping assassination attempts, stealing military secrets, preventing the release of deadly viruses, stopping rogue satellites and ending other threats to world security and freedom.

One of the more unusual aspects with Butler is his relationships with women. Like many other secret agents and serial vigilantes, he has a number of sexual encounters with women but while the sex is fantastic, the women all seem to turn on him and accuse him of forcing them. In one instance Butler was forced to perform at gunpoint and the woman, a fellow agent of the Bancroft Institute, still accused him of rape.

Behind the Scenes

Leonard Levinson born in 1935 served the US Army from 1954 to 1957. Under a number of pseudonyms and house names, he has contributed to a number of series, including **Bronson**, **Kung Fu (Mace)**, **The Sharpshooter** and **The Sexecutioner**.

The Books

All books were published by Leisure Books:

1. *Hydra Conspiracy*, 201 pages, 1979 (Levinson)
2. *Smart Bombs*, 207 pages, 1979 (Levinson)
3. *Slayboys*, 203 pages, 1979 (Levinson)
4. *Chinese Roulette*, 204 pages, 1979 (Levinson)
5. *Love Me to Death*, 224 pages, 1980 (Levinson)
6. *Paris Kill*, 239 pages, 1980
7. *Killer Virus*, 1980
8. *Dead Fail*, 1980
9. *Laser Shuttle*, 1980
10. *Killer Satellites*, 235 pages, 1980 (Levinson)
11. *Q Factor*, 1984
12. *Midas Kill*, 239 pages, 1984

THE BUTCHER (BUCHER)

Thirty-five books by Stuart Jason (house name)

In November 1948, a newborn baby was left on the doorstep of St. Joseph's orphanage in Knoxville, Tennessee. The habitually drunk priest, Isham Green, and the overly tired Dr. Allen Adam from Child Welfare never realized that they had only given the child one name, Bucher.

Bucher ran away from the orphanage ten years later and eventually made his way to Chicago. There he met Luigi Orazio, who was dying of leukemia. Luigi and Bucher were the best of friends and after Luigi died, Luigi's parents, Tino and Maria Orazio, unofficially adopted Bucher.

Tino was high in the underworld circles in the post–Capone Chicago and when he realized his adopted son had lightning-swift reflexes and supersensitive survival instincts that bordered on magic and precognition, he allowed Bucher to become an enforcer for the syndicate.

Eleven years after the adoption, Tino was killed and Bucher, now nicknamed The Butcher, took over from his father. A decade later, The Butcher realized that what he was doing was wrong and he decided to leave. The Syndicate, realizing how much he knew, refused to let him go and put a price on his head.

The Butcher then joined a group known as White Hat and started working to destroy the Syndicate as well as taking other assignments, like tackling terrorists who have taken over the United Nations Building (*The UN Affair*) or tracking a murderer (*The Judas Judge*).

Behind the Scenes

Created by Lyle Kenyon Engel for Pinnacle Books, this series featured Michael Avallone, James "Doc" Dockery and Lee Floren behind the Stuart Jason pen name.

James "Doc" Dockery originated the Stuart Jason name for a series of Plantation novels: *Black Lord*, *Black Master*, *Black Hercules* and *Black Rebel*.

Avallone is most famous as author of the private eye Ed Noon as well as writing tie-in novels for the *Man from U.N.C.L.E.*, *I-Spy* and the *Partridge Family* television series. Avallone also wrote several **Killmaster** novels as Nick Carter.

Lee Floren also wrote several books in the Killmaster series.

The Books

All books were published by Pinnacle books:

1. *Kill Quick or Die*, 188 pages, 1971 (Dockery)
2. *Come Watch Him Die*, 188 pages, 1971 (Dockery)
3. *Keepers of Death*, 188 pages, 1972 (Dockery)
4. *Blood Debt*, 187 pages, 1972 (Dockery)
5. *Deadly Deal*, 188 pages, 1973 (Dockery)
6. *Kill Time*, 192 pages, 1973 (Dockery)
7. *Death Race*, 184 pages, 1973 (Dockery)
8. *Fire Bomb*, 181 pages, 1973 (Dockery)
9. *Sealed with Blood*, 183 pages, 1973 (Dockery)
10. *The Deadly Doctor*, 186 pages, 1974 (Floren)
11. *Valley of Death*, 178 pages, 1974 (Floren)
12. *Killer's Cargo*, 179 pages, 1974
13. *Blood Vengeance*, 180 pages, 1975

14. *African Contract*, 180 pages, 1975
15. *Kill Gently but Sure*, 1975
16. *Suicide in San Juan*, 186 pages, 1975
17. *The Cubano Caper*, 186 pages, 1976
18. *UN Affair*, 182 pages, 1976
19. *Mayday over Manhattan*, 184 pages, 1976
20. *The Hollywood Assassin*, 182 pages, 1976
21. *Instant Dead*, 179 pages, 1976
22. *Grecian Bloodbath*, 183 pages, 1976
23. *Appointment in Iran*, 150 pages, 1977
24. *Venetian Vendetta*, 183 pages, 1977
25. *Corporate Caper*, 166 pages, 1977
26. *The Terror Truckers*, 180 pages, 1977
27. *Judas Judge*, 184 pages, 1979 (Avallone)
28. *Kill Them Silently*, 181 pages, 1980 (Avallone)
29. *Slaughter in September*, 178 pages, 1980 (Avallone)
30. *Coffin Corner USA*, 1981 (Avallone)
31. *Death in Yellow*, 179 pages, 1981 (Avallone)
32. *Hoodoo Horror*, 177 pages, 1981 (Avallone)
33. *Go Die in Afghanistan*, 196 pages, 1982 (Avallone)
34. *The Man from White Hat*, 198 pages, 1982 (Avallone)
35. *Gotham Gore*, 194 pages, 1982 (Avallone)

Parodies

The Butcher was parodied as Al Baker, the Baker in **The Destroyer #38**: *Bay City Blast*, where he is portrayed as a low-level numbers runner who makes up information about the Mafia to get money from his backer.

CABOT CAIN

Six books by Alan Caillou

Independently wealthy, Cain tackles tough jobs for Interpol in an unofficial and unpaid role, if he thinks that the situation warrants his intervention. Cain's liaison with Interpol is Inspector Fenrek.

Highly educated, Cain has taught numerous courses at the Sorbonne and Stanford but more than that, this 6ft, 7in giant is a physical marvel, running between five and ten miles at a time and exercising at every opportunity. This regime is not a result of vanity; rather it is the practical realism of the dangerous nature of his freelance work and the fact that his size makes him stand out as a target. His physical prowess means that he is as prepared as he can be for any danger.

Cain travels all over the world for his missions, tracking down Communist assassins hiding in Brazilian Nazi strongholds, acting as a bodyguard for a tong leader's daughter in Macao, fighting mercenaries in Portugal, rescuing kidnap victims from white slavers in the Middle East, battling mad scientists seeking to unleash a plague of insects and rescuing Inspector Fenrek when he is captured by a criminal he had been hunting for twenty years.

Behind the Scenes

Allan Caillou was a screen writer and actor. As a script writer for the *Man from U.N.C.L.E.*, he is credited for developing the character of Ilya Kuryakin. His novel writing included the series, the Private Army of Colonel Tobin, also known as Tobin's Commando and Tobin's Army.

The Books

1. *Assault on Kolchak*, 221 pages, 1969
2. *Assault on Loveless*, 224 pages, 1969
3. *Assault on Ming*, 192 pages, 1970
4. *Assault on Fellawi*, 192 pages, 1972
5. *Assault on Agathon*, 191 pages, 1972
6. *Assault on Aimata*, 190 pages, 1975

The Movie

In 1975, Allan Caillou adapted his own novel as the screenplay for the Greek/British Channel 9* production of *Assault on Agathon*. Directed by Laszlo Benedek and starring Nico Minardos as Cabot Cain, the film took advantage of the Greek scenery to make Caillou's vision a reality. Released theatrically in 1976 throughout Europe, the movie has never been released theatrically in Greece.

CAGE (Huntington and Hadley Cage)

Six books by Alan Riefe

Huntington "Hunt" Cage is a successful private investigator, one of the best operating in New York City. Nobody knows about his secret weapon, his identical twin brother Hadley.

The brothers have no family except for their father, a recluse who lives in Canada, and the brothers have no friends in common. Hadley, Lee for short, is an artist who lives across the river in New Jersey. Lee, when he has to travel to New York, wears a disguise to avoid being recognized.

This gives Hunt the ability to be in two places at once and the brothers can call for

---

Not Channel 9 Australia as many sources including The Internet Movie Database claim. There is no record of Australian involvement in the film.

help with a specially made radio watch. While Hunt is a licensed private investigator, his contact in the DA office, Richard Giordano, frequently uses Hunt's skills to unofficially obtain evidence for matters.

But while Hunt is prepared to work within the law, Lee is more inclined to take the law into his own hands. Lee often kills the people his brother is investigating, such as the mobster who ordered a hit on Hunt and nearly killed his brother.

It is Hadley who makes this a serial vigilante series. He operates in an unofficial capacity and takes the law into his own hands. This is a source of friction between the brothers but it does make them an effective team.

Behind the Scenes

Alan Riefe is also the author of the Tyger Decker series. Under the pen name of Barbara Riefe, he has written a number of Gothic romances.

The Books

All books were published by Popular Library:

1. *The Lady Killer*, 126 pages, 1975
2. *The Conspirators*, 141 pages, 1975
3. *The Black Widower*, 176 pages, 1975
4. *Silver Puma*, 176 pages, 1975
5. *Bullet Proof Man*, 175 pages, 1975
6. *Killer with the Golden Touch*, 174 pages, 1975

CHAMELEON (Vince Garde)

Three books by Jerry LaPlante

Vince Garde was a lucky man; he had a genius-level intellect that allowed him to graduate from MIT with a PhD at age nineteen. His father had left him a small fortune and he was the founder and owner of Garde Scientific Associates (GSA), a scientific research firm that worked in all scientific areas, from undersea mining and medicine to space exploration and meteorology.

When Garde's younger half-sister, a runaway, turned up dead — the victim of an overdose — Garde changed his focus from scientific advancement to the pursuit of justice, starting a new firm VIBES. VIBES was an acronym chosen before the meaning, but it eventually came to stand for Vindication against Injustice, Bureaucracy and Ensconced Stupidity.

Garde used this new firm to bring justice to those who prey on others and have escaped conventional law enforcement. Garde's justice is like his temper, quick and deadly.

Initially investigating the drug trade and taking down the Anaconda, the drug kingpin responsible for his sister's addiction, Garde then brought his wrath against a cult leader, Sol Luna, using low frequency radio waves to brainwash his followers to unspeakable crimes so that Luna could take over the world. Garde's final recorded mission brought him against the feminist group DELILAH and DELILAH's plot to steal plutonium from the American Energy Commission (AEC) in a plot to rule the world.

Behind the Scenes

The Chameleon series is Jerry LaPlante's only writing credit.

The Books

All books were published by Zebra Books:

1. *Wrath of Garde*, 192 pages, 1979
2. *In Garde We Trust*, 240 pages, 1979
3. *Garde Save the World*, 224 pages, 1979

CHANT (JOHN SINCLAIR)

Three books by David Cross

Arthur Sinclair was a career diplomat who was posted to Japan, where he absorbed the culture. His son, John, was born in Japan and the older Sinclair had his son trained in the martial arts. At the age of sixteen, John was sent for training with the Black Flame Ninja master, Master Bai. John was to be trained as a weapon for good but Master Bai believed that he could corrupt his apprentice to the ways of the Black Flame, which burns away all humanity and allows Black Flame ninjas to be the ultimate assassins. John, however, walked away before the final test and Master Bai killed Arthur Sinclair.

John Sinclair then joined the American Army and so impressed his trainers that he was immediately offered an instructing job. But Sinclair wanted to serve in Vietnam and refused the job.

In Vietnam, Sinclair was able to quickly rise through the ranks to become the youngest captain in the Army, but his criticism of a top-secret operation code-named Cooked Goose led to attempts made on his life. Sinclair deserted the Army and lived with the Hmong in Laos. It was during his time in Vietnam that he acquired the nickname Chant, from the sound his victims made.

Sinclair then made his way back to America and began using his skills in martial arts, disguise and forgery to take on criminals and those who exploit others. Chant tackles slavers, prostitution and pornography rings, torturers and dictators.

Behind the Scenes

David Cross was the pseudonym used by George C. Chesbro. Chesbro initially wrote another book as the first Chant novel but the only thing the publisher liked was the name Chant, and so that novel was reworked and became the first novel in the Veil Kendry series published under his own name. Chesbro is also the author of the Mongo mystery series.

The Books

All books were published by Jove Books:

1. *Chant*, 231 pages, 1986
2. *Silent Killer*, 217 pages, 1986
3. *Code of Blood*, 212 pages, 1987

Other Appearances

Both Chant and Veil Kendry appear in the Mongo novel *Dark Chant in a Crimson Key* (Mysterious Press, 217 pages, 1992).

CHECK FORCE
Seven books by Ralph Hayes

Check Force is two men: Chane, a fugitive CIA agent, and Karlov, a disaffected KGB agent. The two men discovered a conspiracy known as Force III, an ultra-secret cabal set on taking over the world by forcing the United States and the Soviet Union into a nuclear war. The pair is often forced to work against their own governments as Force III manipulates world powers.

The awareness of this conspiracy has forced these former enemies to work together to stop Force III's sinister plans. Force III's plans involve them infiltrating and utilizing any group they feel will aid their plans, such as Israeli extremist groups and ambitious Chinese generals. The pair travels the globe, preventing assassinations and foiling terrorists and other warmongers.

Behind the Scenes

Ralph Hayes was born in 1927 and served in the Air Force 1945–47. After leaving the Air Force he studied and became a lawyer specializing in insurance. In 1969, Hayes became a freelance writer writing a number of travel guides and individual novels as well as the Buffalo Hunter western series and **Stoner, the Hunter** and **Agent for COMINSEC** series. Under the Nick Carter house name, he wrote eight **Killmaster** books. Hayes travelled extensively and utilized that experience for his travel guides and the settings for his books (Contemporary Authors Online, 2002).

The Books

All books were published by Manor books

1. *100 Megaton Kill*, 208 pages, 1975
2. *Clouds of War*, 188 pages, 1975
3. *Judgment Day*, 186 pages, 1975
4. *The Peking Plot*, 189 pages, 1975
5. *Nightmare Island*, 186 pages, 1975
6. *Seeds of Doom*, 192 pages, 1976
7. *Fires of Hell*, 1976

CHILL (DR. RUSSELL V. CHILLDERS)

Seven books by Jory Sherman

Dr. Russell V. Chillders is a world-renowned expert of supernatural phenomena. Born into a farming family to Judson and Carrie Chillders, he was an active boy and was sent by his mother to live and study under her brother Martin in Vienna.

Martin trained his nephew in the occult and performed rituals to raise the spirits. After the death of his Uncle Martin, Chill continued his studies, writing several works on the occult such as *Modern Occultism, Dark Mysteries, The Case for Reincarnation* and *Steps Beyond the Veil.* The fame from these works brought him public attention and he appeared on Johnny Carson and spoke at many public events.

With the funds, Chill bought an estate in Chamblee, Georgia. The estate was cheap, as it was reported haunted, and it gave Chill enough room to grow all his own vegetables, make wine and store all of his books.

But Chill doesn't just write about the occult, he also investigates paranormal events. Chill is assisted by Laura Littlefawn, a sensitive Indian telepath; the pair shares a psychic bond which alerts them when the other is in danger.

Chill's other assistant is Hal Strong, a fellow psychic investigator who assists Chill with research and as a sounding board for ideas and theories.

Together they have investigated vampires, possessions, haunting, demons and werewolves. Chill is called to investigate these events by fellow paranormal scholars, law enforcement and the victims.

Behind the Scenes

Jory Sherman (born 1932) started his career as a writer by writing poems that appeared in many different magazines and journals. His books of poetry went into multiple printings and received critical acclaim. Sherman then branched off into writing westerns and other series fiction for many publishers. Currently residing in Texas, Sherman is experimenting with the e-book format and reissued the first two Chill novels through Hard Shell Word Factory.

The Books

All books were published by Pinnacle Books:

1. *Satan's Seed*, 213 pages, 1978
2. *Chill: The Sepulture*, 244 pages, 1978
3. *Bamboo Demons*, 182 pages, 1979
4. *Vegas Vampire*, 176 pages, 1980
5. *Phoenix Man*, 175 pages, 1980
6. *House of Scorpions*, 176 pages, 1980
7. *Shadows*, 181 pages, 1980

C.O.B.R.A. (JON SKUL)

Six books by Joseph Rosenberger

There are times when the rules prevent official government agencies from operating effectively. In situations such as this, the CIA, DIA, FBI and NSA send their problem to C.O.B.R.A.

C.O.B.R.A. was founded by the highest authority in America. In consultation with the five top men of the NSA, he placed Jonas Barron to head this agency. A small agency, it has only 250 agents, 165 male agents called Eagles and 85 female agents called Doves. The top agent of C.O.B.R.A. is Jonathon Skul. Skul is cut from the same cloth as Richard Camellion, **the Death Merchant**, and he gets the toughest of the toughest missions that C.O.B.R.A. has to offer.

Not surprisingly, given that the missions directed to C.O.B.R.A. come from the intelligence community of the United States during the Cold War, the majority of their problems were created by the Soviet Union and in particular by the KGB.

Skul travels the world tackling threats to world security, such as drug operations run as a joint Mob-KGB operation, plugging security leaks in other intelligence agencies, and stopping terrorist attacks as well as protecting defectors.

Behind the Scenes

Joseph Rosenberger became a professional writer at the age of twenty-one after selling an article. After working a series of jobs including Korean Karate instructor, circus pitchman and private eye, he became a full-time writer in 1961. Rosenberger was the author of the **Murder Master** and Death Merchant series and, under the pseudonym Lee Chang, created and wrote the first martial arts series **Kung Fu (Mace)**.

The Books

All books were published by Critic's Choice:

1. *Heroin Connection*, 253 pages, 1986
2. *Paris Kill-Ground*, 224 pages, 1987
3. *Red Dragon*, 256 pages, 1987
4. *Nightmare in Panama*, 249 pages, 1987
5. *Project Andromeda*, 250 pages, 1988
6. *Belgrade Battleground*, 240 pages, 1989

CODENAME

Six books by William Johnstone

The Codename team was formed by a consortium of wealthy men and those in the government who felt that the laws protected the criminals, as a secret strike force to combat America's enemies. The team was rigorously tested and drawn from many departments of American law enforcement.

The team consists of:

- John Barrone (CIA), team leader
- Don Yee (CIA), computers
- Mike Rojas (IRS Internal security)
- Jenny Barnes (FBI), explosives
- Chris Farmer (Secret Service), sniper
- Al Durstman (FBI)
- Linda Marsh (LAPD)
- Paul Brewer (Border Patrol)
- Lana Henry (ATF)
- Bob Garrett (NSA)

In the second book (*Codename Survival*) Al Durstman is killed. Typically each book involves the Codename team being called into action by their backers and split into teams of three or four. Typically, we follow John's team, which generally includes Jenny Barnes.

In *Codename Death*, one of the team's backers, Marist J. Quinncannon, hires Barrone for a private mission to find his granddaughter's killers when she is killed in a snuff porn film.

Behind the Scenes

The series was created by William W. Johnstone, author of numerous horror, adventure and western novels. Johnstone is the author of the **Rig Warrior** series. Johnstone was discharged from the French Foreign Legion for being underage, then worked in a carnival, became a deputy sheriff and did a stint in the army. He started writing in 1970 but did not make his first sale until 1979 with *The Devil's Kiss*. Johnstone died in 2004 in Shreveport, Louisiana.

The Books

All books were published by Kensington Pinnacle Books:

1. *Codename Payback*, 335 pages, 2000
2. *Codename Survival*, 333 pages, 2000
3. *Codename Death*, 253 pages, 2001
4. *Codename Coldfire*, 253 pages, 2002
5. *Codename Quickstrike*, 256 pages, 2003
6. *Codename Extreme Prejudice*, 256 pages, 2004

CONFIRMED KILL

Four books by Mike Morris

The Confirmed Kill Team is the top-secret anti-terrorist sniper team answerable only to the president of the United States.

The field team consists of two men:

- Con Duggan — the twenty-year veteran sniper and team leader.
- Steven Dye — the red-headed freckle-faced spotter, just as lethal as his commander.
  The field team is augmented by two unofficial members:
- Penelope James — This fiery Englishwoman, after joining the team during their first mission in England, is an expert infiltrator and information gatherer.
- The team is transported by Ivan Tescher in his advanced Whisper Helicopter.

The Confirmed Kill Team is supported by an intelligence-gathering team working with a super computer known as SCAR (Security Caretaker and Research) that is able to analyze and evaluate threats and determine that a mission is unable to be handled by conventional forces and requires the specialized skills of the team.

The team's liaison with the president is Michael Burns, a cigar-smoking Special Forces veteran who organized the team.

Their first mission took them to London to eliminate a terrorist cell; this was followed by a mission in Japan to tackle a gangster threatening the bullet train. The team's next mission was personal when rogue sniper Peter Coy Booker kidnapped Duggan's lover Maggie Stuart. Their fourth and final mission was the infiltration and elimination of an American terrorist cell that had stolen a shipment of biological weapons.

Behind the Scenes

Mike Morris is a former Marine sniper, according to the brief biography on the back of the books. In reality, Morris was the pseudonym of Gregory Vanhee. Vanhee was the author of two other action novels, *Night Strike* and *The Shooter*. Vanhee lived in Seattle and served as a rifleman in the Marines. In 1992, at fifty-five Vanhee died of a heart attack after completing the four books in the Confirmed Kill series.

The Books

All books were published by Diamond Books:

1. *Confirmed Kill*, 183 pages, 1992
2. *Sniper Shot*, 185 pages, 1992
3. *Direct Hit*, 171 pages, 1993
4. *Point Blank*, 199 pages, 1993

CONTRACT (COLIN LYNCH)

Four books by Paul Mann

Colin Lynch served in the Special Boat Squadron (SBS) of the British naval service during the Falklands War. The SBS trained Lynch in all forms of warfare, such as reconnaissance, sabotage, infiltration and assassination. After that war finished, Lynch joined the Counter Terrorism Command drawn from all arms of the British Service. Quickly rising through the ranks, he became a squad leader.

It was Christmas 1988 when Lynch's squad had duty at Heathrow airport when a major terrorist attack took place. Sickened and disheartened, Lynch resigned from the service. It was then that he was offered the chance to take on the terrorists using their own tactics by American Jack Halloran. Halloran, a former Marine who served in Korea, is a wealthy businessman who is sick of the foreign policy of the United States and Great Britain in dealing with terrorists.

Lynch signed on with Halloran to tackle various terrorist threats around the world with a rotating group of mercenaries, starting with an assassination attempt on Colonel Muammar al-Gaddafi.

The assassination attempt only killed a look-alike decoy but Lynch signed on to rescue hostages in Beirut, ferret out traitors and to rescue Queen Elizabeth and Prince Phillip when the IRA captured the *Britannia*.

Behind the Scenes

Paul Mann was born in England and worked as a journalist for many years in London, New York, various parts of Canada and Sydney, eventually settling in South Australia. Working as a freelance writer, much of his journalist work appeared in leading newspapers and magazines in Australia.

The Books

All books were published by Pan Books:

1. *The Libyan Contract*, 260 pages, 1988
2. *The Beirut Contract*, 349 pages, 1989
3. *The Traitor's Contract*, 370 pages, 1991
4. *The Britannia Contract*, 443 pages, 1993

COUNTER FORCE (STEVE CROWN)

Nine books by Dan Streib

Billionaire Adam Crown was unimpressed with the way that the United States government was fighting communism, especially after his only child, an aerospace engineer, defected to the Soviet Union after the death of his wife in childbirth. As Adam Crown was establishing his own private agency Counter Force, he was also raising his only grandchild and heir Steve Crown.

In time Counter Force became the agency that the official agencies such as the CIA and NSA came to when the situations became too much for them. At age twenty-nine, Steve Crown was not only one of the directors of Counter Force but also the top agent.

Crown and Counter Force tackle missions such as assisting defectors, stopping assassins, fighting terrorists and hijackers and preventing the use of super weapons as well as fighting gangs and hit men hired to kill members of Counter Force.

Behind the Scenes

Dan Streib, born in 1928, served in the U.S. Army during the Korean War (1950–53) and died in 1996 of a heart attack. An extensive traveler for both work and pleasure, San Diego based Streib used the locales he visited in his works, which include the **Hawk** series under his own name **The Death Squad** series under the name Frank Colter, romances under the names of Louise Grandville and Lee Davis Whilloughby, and westerns under the names Jonathan Schofield and J. Faragut Jones.

The Books

All books were published by Fawcett Publishing:

1. *Counter Force*, 192 pages, 1983
2. *Trident Hijacking*, 208 pages, 1983
3. *Death Shuttle*, 192 pages, 1983
4. *Karate Killers*, 199 pages, 1983
5. *Terror for Sale*, 170 pages, 1983
6. *Titan's Duel*, 208 pages, 1984
7. *Mind Breakers*, 208 pages, 1984
8. *Body Hunters*, 224 pages, 1984
9. *Bloody Rose*, 224 pages, 1985

CRIME MINISTER (RICHARD DARTLEY)

Five books by Ian Barclay

Richard Woodgate was the son of upper-middle-class parents, people so sure in their superiority that for a variety of reasons they considered every president since Truman to be an idiot.

Richard hardly lived up to this superiority, coasting through school with a C average and no ambition or drive. This aimlessness continued even when he was drafted to Vietnam; Richard learned to kill but he never applied himself and wasn't very good at it.

Woodgate discovered his purpose in life when his father, supposedly on a business trip to Miami, was found dead in Rio. With this Richard discovered that his father had been an agent for the CIA, fighting to keep America safe from her enemies. Suddenly, Woodgate had a goal and with his new focus he began to train to join the CIA. After a year of training with his uncle, a gunsmith for hire, Woodley applied to the CIA. The CIA, looking at his record and not understanding his motives, rejected his application.

Changing his name to Richard Dartley, he became a freelance operator, eventually building a reputation that commanded a one-million-dollar fee for his services. Dartley carefully selects his jobs, fighting against those he considers evil and only killing the people he imagines that his father would have killed.

Dartley is hired by business consortiums to kill drug dealers, eliminate dictators, stop rival assassins, and eliminate political rivals. On one occasion Dartley was even hired by the CIA.

Behind the Scenes

Ian Barclay is the pen name of George Ryan. Under his own name, Ryan wrote the 1997 novelization of the movie *Speed 2*. As Spike Andrews, he wrote the C.A.T. Crisis Aversion Team series for Warner Books. Ryan also wrote under the names Chad Calhoun and Lee Davis Willoughby.

The Books

All books were published by Warner Books:

1. *Crime Minister*, 395 pages, 1984
2. *Reprisal*, 313 pages, 1985
3. *Rebound*, 310 pages, 1986
4. *Reckoning*, 220 pages, 1987
5. *Retribution*, 188 pages, 1987

CROSS

Two books by Andrew Vachss

Cross and his team of mercenaries offer a revenge-for-hire service to those people who can find them at their headquarters, the red 71 located in the worst area of Chicago, or at the Double X bar, which the team owns and operates. The various missions they undertake can take just Cross himself or various members of his team.

The team consists of:

- Cross: The product of reform schools, Cross was given the choice between jail and the Army to serve in Vietnam. He joined the Army and eventually became a mercenary serving in Africa. Cross never cared if he lived or died and has a bullseye tattooed on his right hand.
- Buddha: This chubby, Asian, money-hungry Vietnam veteran met Cross during the war. He is the only member of the team who has legal status and all assets are in his name. His wife, So Long, is constantly nagging him to make even more money.
- Rhino: This giant of a man met Cross in reform school where his voice was permanently damaged by being force-fed Drano.
- Princess: This giant body builder has the intellect of a child. He was captured as a youth and forced into cage fights. Rescued by Cross and his crew, he joined the team and is looked after by Rhino. So named because he wears makeup and pink tutus, Princess will not start a fight but he will finish it.
- Ace: This African American hit man met Cross in reform school and joined his crew after the war. He got his name from the death card, the Ace of Spades.
- Falcon: A Chickasaw Indian who is a freelance operator working with the crew as

needed. Falcon operates primarily in the city and he has a tribe who he looks after. Falcon met Cross during the war.

• Tiger: another freelance operator and the only female member of the team. Her name comes from her striped hair and vicious streak.

• Luis and Maddox: former team members, who are no longer available.

The crew helps people who have been wronged, targeting stalkers, dog killers and pedophiles, freeing kidnap victims and on occasion acting as assassins for hire.

Behind the Scenes

This series of short stories are written by Andrew Vachss, an attorney who specialized in child abuse cases. Before that Vachss worked for a relief agency in Biafra and for children's services. He is the author the Burke series as well as *Batman: The Ultimate Evil*.

The Stories

Both story collections were published by Vintage Crime/Black Lizard: *Born Bad*, 1994, featuring "Bandit" (3 pages), "Cripple" (2 pages), "Mad Dog" (5 pages), "Statute of Limitation" (8 pages), "Crossfire" (27 pages), "Value Received" (2 pages), "Head Case" (12 pages), "Kidnap" (32 pages), "Stone Magic" (6 pages).

The following stories are not identified as part of the Cross series but the nameless protagonist of these stories might be Cross: "Cain" (5 pages) and "White Alligator" (3 pages). A character named Falcon appears in "Anytime I want" (5 pages).

Everybody Pays, 1999, featuring "The Concrete Puppy" (12 pages), "Harvest Time" (17 pages), "Pigeon Drop" (9 pages), "Two-Way Radio" (3 pages), and "Everybody Pays" (114 pages).

Three Cross novels have been written but have not been published to date.

The Comics

Between 1992 and 1993, Dark Horse comics adapted a number of Vachss' stories as comics in a ten-issue series Hard Looks. Most issues adapt various Cross stories as outlined below. The stories are adapted by a number of writers and artists, including Tim Bradstreet, Gary Pleece, Warren Pleece, James Colbert and Phil Hester.

Issue 1: "Statute of Limitations"

Issue 2: "Value Received"

Issue 3: "Cripple"; "Anytime I Want"

Issue 6: "Bandit"; "Mad Dog"

Issue 7: "Stone Magic"; "White Alligator"

Issue 8: "Head Case"

Issue 9: "Cain"

Cross also appeared in original comic stories published by Dark Horse:
Cross hunted the alien Predators in the following titles:

Dark Horse Presents #67–69
(collected as *Predator: Race War Ground Zero*), 1993
Predator Race War #1–4, 1993

The complete series was collected in trade paperback in 1995.

Then in 1995 and 1996 Dark Horse also published a seven-issue series *Cross* based on a story by Vachss with James Colbert with script by Chet Williamson and art by Geofrey Darrow. This adapted the first of three unpublished Cross novels, *Genesis*.

DAGGER (CHRISTIAN DAGGUERRE)

Two books by Carl Stephens

Christian Dagguerre, despite his youth, was a veteran war correspondent, having covered conflicts all over the world, including Vietnam. With danger such a part of his work he did not expect any problems during a vacation in Mexico with his fiancée.

But his employer, Hannibal S. Kydd, nicknamed Captain Kydd, leaked a rumor that his star reporter was hot on the trail of a dangerous terrorist. The terrorist, fearing capture, decided to strike first, killing Dagguerre's fiancée. Kydd, a multimillionaire, realized that such a personal vendetta makes for great reporting and even better ratings.

Dagger is unaware of the machinations of his employer and suddenly finds himself hunted and on the run. Dagger uses his investigative and survival skills to track and destroy those responsible for the attack.

After taking revenge on the terrorists who killed his fiancée, Dagger becomes a willing participant in Kydd's rating-grabbing war on terrorism, traveling the world investigating and fighting terrorism with his first assignment taking him to Japan to fight the Red Army.

Behind the Scenes

Carl Stephens was a pseudonym used by Roy Obstfeld. Obstfeld is an associate professor of English at Orange Coast College and is the author of more than forty books, including several writing guides. Under the Don Pendleton house name, Obstfeld has written four novels for **The Executioner** series. In 1982, Obstfeld was nominated for the Edgar award for his thriller, *Dead Heat*, published by Charter Books.

The Books

Both books were published by Gold Eagle Books:

1. *Centaur Conspiracy*, 1983
2. *Ride of the Razorback*, 1984

A third book was written but, due to poor sales, the series was cancelled before its publication.

DC MAN (BRIAN PETERSON)

Four books by James P. Cody

Brian Peterson was a former military intelligence agent who retired and became a successful lobbyist. He was married to a senator's daughter and had a small daughter. When his father-in-law lost his seat, Peterson helped him to pack up his office. It was then that he got the call that changed his life. Two teenage joyriders had caused an accident that killed his wife and child. Peterson was devastated and moved to the bottom of a bottle in Key West. The Senator found him and helped him to dry out and return to his old life.

Then one day, one of Peterson's clients comes to him with a problem, which is dealt with quickly and quietly. This is followed by a series of problems solved discreetly and it becomes common knowledge throughout Washington that Brian Peterson is the man to see if you have a situation that needs to be taken care of quietly. Peterson is able to use his military and intelligence contacts and on occasion can call in a favor from those who he has helped in the past. Peterson is called on to investigate security leaks, suspicious deaths, assassinations and kidnappings.

Behind the Scenes

James P. Cody is the pseudonym of Peter Thomas Rohrbach. Rohrbach born in 1926 is a former Catholic priest. Under his own name he is the author of several religious books such as *Conversation with Christ* and *Dynamic Preaching* as well as several film and television scripts.

The Books

All books were published by Berkley:

1. *Top Secret Kill*, 190 pages, 1974
2. *Search and Destroy*, 192 pages, 1974
3. *French Killing*, 172 pages, 1975
4. *Your Daughter Will Die*, 188 pages, 1975

DEADLY FORCE

Seven books by Mark Dixon

Deadly Force was founded by Vietnam vet, ex-cop, former CIA agent, inventor and genius — Luke Simpson. After earning six million from one of his inventions, a computer patrol car uplink, Simpson decided to form Deadly Force, Inc. Simpson had been hampered by the rules and regulations all through his career and Deadly Force was the chance to make his own rules. Simpson built his headquarters in the Superstition Mountains of Arizona (Phoenix is the nearest town) and then formed Deadly Force, Inc., a mercenary group frequently used by the CIA.

The rest of the team consists of:

- Jake O'Bannion: thirty year vet of the NYPD. The team's management and services expert.
- Ben Sanchez: part Apache, ex-Army Ranger, part-time cop and mercenary.
- Calvin Steeples: pilot in Vietnam and part-time crop duster.
- Tran Cao "Frags": South Vietnamese master of science and technology.

Deadly Force, Inc., tackles the tough and dirty jobs, like a crime ring threatening Chicago, sponsored by the Soviets to weaken America. Deadly Force takes the job because the Chicago police department and FBI are busy passing the buck and claiming the problem is someone else's responsibility. Not bogged down in bureaucracy, the force is able to stop the crime wave. In other cases, Deadly Force fights mobsters and fends off assassins and rogue mercenaries.

Behind the Scenes

Mark Dixon is the pen name of Charlie McDade, who has written several books for the Executioner series and, under the name of Bill Duggan, wrote several western novels.

The Books

All books were published by Berkley Books:

1. *Deadly Force*, 282 pages, 1987
2. *Special Delivery*, 216 pages, 1987
3. *Heartlanders*, 219 pages, 1988
4. *Crimewave*, 202 pages, 1988
5. *Battlezone*, 187 pages, 1989
6. *Blood Cult*, 187 pages, 1989
7. *Body Count*, 203 pages, 1989

DEATH MERCHANT (RICHARD JOSEPH CAMELLION)

Seventy-one books by Joseph Rosenberger

The Death Merchant is one of the most enigmatic serial vigilantes; we never discover what drove the man known as Richard Camellion to become the Death Merchant, but there are hints throughout the series.

In the first book, we find out that Camellion is considered the best freelance agent in the world. The back cover of the Corgi edition (1971) is suggestive: "Richard Camellion had not been born to a life of crime and killing but circumstance had led him to become a master of murder and cunning disguises." But it never reveals just what those circumstances were. Camellion is hired by the Mafia to kill an informer and kills several other Mafia hoods as well. Oddly, after that first book the Mafia does not appear again as Camellion is hired by the CIA.

In #9: *The Laser War*, it is revealed that Richard Joseph Algernon Camellion was an ex-school teacher from St. Louis. In #62: *The Soul Search Project*, when asked if he is Camellion, he lies and says that Richard Joseph Camellion is the name on his baptismal record, suggesting that it is not his real name. Ultimately there is no revelation; Camellion is just the best at what he does as both a master of disguise and murder and no explanation is needed as he get results.

The first book of the series had Camellion hired by the Mafia to clean house, but later books had Camellion working for the CIA in adventures that became increasingly incredible, living up to the full series title, The Incredible Adventures of the Death Merchant.

The Death Merchant has faced the unusual situations of retrieving a laser invented by the Nazis, scrolls written by Judas Iscariot, and locating Shamballa, which is a base built by aliens that Camellion had previously encountered. More mundane assignments have included saving Fidel Castro from assassination by the Soviets, preventing a Cuban takeover of the Panama Canal, retrieving downed satellites and foiling a plot to overthrow America.

One feature of the series is that Rosenberger frequently inserted lengthy footnotes into his stories to explain the factual basis for his characters assertions.

Behind the Scenes

Joseph Rosenberger became a professional writer at the age of twenty-one after selling an article. After working a series of jobs including Korean karate instructor, circus pitchman and private eye, he became a full-time writer in 1961. Rosenberger was the author of the **Murder Master** and **C.O.B.R.A.** series and, under the pseudonym Lee Chang, created and wrote the first martial arts series **Kung Fu (Mace).**

The Books

Books 1—64 were published by Pinnacle Books, books 65–70 and Super Death Merchant by Dell Books.

1. *The Death Merchant*, 188 pages, 1971
2. *Operation Overkill*, 187 pages, 1972
3. *Psychotron Plot*, 157 pages, 1972
4. *Chinese Conspiracy*, 190 pages, 1973
5. *Satan Strike*, 189 pages, 1973
6. *Albanian Connection*, 191 pages, 1973
7. *Castro File*, 218 pages, 1974
8. *Billionaire Mission*, 213 pages, 1974
9. *Laser War*, 187 pages, 1974
10. *Mainline Plot*, 184 pages, 1974
11. *Manhattan Wipeout*, 179 pages, 1975
12. *KGB Frame*, 180 pages, 1975
13. *Mato Grosso Horror*, 180 pages, 1975
14. *Vengeance of the Golden Hawk*, 180 pages, 1976
15. *Iron Swastika Plot*, 178 pages, 1976
16. *Invasion of the Clones*, 181 pages, 1976
17. *Zemlya Expedition*, 177 pages, 1976
18. *Nightmare in Algeria*, 182 pages, 1976
19. *Armageddon USA*, 183 pages, 1976

20. *Hell in Hindu Land*, 198 pages, 1976
21. *Pole Star Secret*, 195 pages, 1977
22. *Kondrashev Chase*, 210 pages, 1977
23. *Budapest Action*, 202 pages, 1977
24. *Kronos Plot*, 200 pages, 1977
25. *Enigma Project*, 196 pages, 1977
26. *Mexican Hit*, 184 pages, 1978
27. *Surinam Affair*, 182 pages, 1978
28. *Nipponese Nightmare*, 198 pages, 1978
29. *Fatal Formula*, 181 pages, 1978
30. *Shamballa Strike*, 208 pages, 1978
31. *Operation Thunderbolt*, 180 pages, 1978
32. *Deadly Manhunt*, 180 pages, 1979
33. *Alaska Conspiracy*, 220 pages, 1979
34. *Operation Mind Murder*, 184 pages, 1979
35. *Massacre in Rome*, 173 pages, 1979
36. *Cosmic Reality Kill*, 169 pages, 1979
37. *Bermuda Triangle Action*, 177 pages, 1980
38. *Burning Blue Death*, 183 pages, 1980
39. *Fourth Reich*, 183 pages, 1980
40. *Blueprint Invisibility*, 181 pages, 1980
41. *Shamrock Smash*, 180 pages, 1980
42. *High Command Murder*, 187 pages, 1980
43. *Devil's Trashcan*, 184 pages, 1981
44. *Island of the Damned*, 185 pages, 1981
45. *Rim of Fire Conspiracy*, 184 pages, 1981
46. *Bloodbath*, 183 pages, 1981
47. *Operation Skyhook*, 202 pages, 1981
48. *The Psionics War*, 185 pages, 1982
49. *Night of the Peacock*, 197 pages, 1982
50. *Hellbomb Theft*, 202 pages, 1982
51. *Inca File*, 202 pages, 1982
52. *Flight of the Phoenix*, 198 pages, 1982
53. *Judas Scrolls*, 200 pages, 1982
54. *Apocalypse USA*, 201 pages, 1983
55. *Slaughter in El Salvador*, 201 pages, 1983
56. *Afghanistan Crashout*, 200 pages, 1983

57. *Rumanian Operation*, 200 pages, 1983
58. *Silicon Valley Connection*, 218 pages, 1984
59. *Burma Probe*, 215 pages, 1984
60. *Methuselah Factor*, 216 pages, 1984
61. *Bulgarian Termination*, 215 pages, 1984
62. *Soul Search Project*, 260 pages, 1985
63. *Atlantean Horror*, 242 pages, 1985
64. *Pakistan Mission*, 231 pages, 1985
65. *Mission Deadly Snow*, 182 pages, 1986
66. *Cobra Chase*, 183 pages, 1984
67. *Escape from Gulag Taria*, 188 pages, 1986
68. *Hindu Trinity Caper*, 187 pages, 1987
69. *Miracle Mission*, 188 pages, 1987
70. *Greenland Mystery*, 188 pages, 1988

Super Death Merchant

1. *Apocalypse*, 398 pages, 1987

Parodies

The Death Merchant was parodied as Nicholas Lizzard in **Destroyer** 38 *Bay City Blast*. Lizzard is not as adept at the art of disguise as he thinks, appearing as a women while he still has a three-day growth. Eventually, he is killed by Remo and Chuin.

Spinoffs

In 1977 and 1978, *Assassination: Theory and Practice* (161 pages) and *Mind Murder: The Art of Behavior Modification* (129 pages) by Richard Camellion were published by Paladin Press. These books are nonfiction examinations of the espionage skills of assassination and behavior modification, with Camellion essentially acting as narrator for these documentary books.

DEATH SQUAD
Two books by Frank Colter

The Death Squad is three San Diego police officers who have had enough. Enough of the stupid regulations that bleeding-heart judges place on the police and the criminal lawyers who use every loophole of the law to get their clients back on the street. Regulations that got police officers killed. During a routine call, a rookie cop was killed because these officers played by the rules, unable to draw their weapons. The death pushed the three officers too far, ready to take immediate action. The three police officers were:

- Mark Sanders: police sergeant with six years of experience on the police force. The six-foot-three, muscular thirty-one-year-old partner to the rookie cop.
- Sam Durham: A six-foot-four twenty-six-year-old African American police officer with a body of rock-hard muscle. Durham had to fight all through his childhood as the first African American in an all-white neighborhood. The rookie cop was a friend who followed him onto the force.
- Raul Gomez: A five-foot-ten Chicano, a tough and stocky twenty-eight-year-old officer.

The trio takes down cop killers, rapists, rich kids who think their wealth and connections mean they can flout the law, contract killers and others who openly operate outside the law.

Behind the Scenes

Frank Colter is the pen name used by Dan Streib. Streib, born in 1928, served in the U.S. Army during the Korean War (1950–53) and died in 1996 of a heart attack. An extensive traveler for both work and pleasure, San Diego–based Streib used the locales he visited in his works, which include the **Hawk** and **Counter Force** series under his own name, romances under the names of Louise Grandville and Lee Davis Whilloughby, and westerns under the names Jonathan Schofield and J. Faragut Jones.

The Books

Both books were published by Belmont Tower:

1. *Gang War*, 168 pages, 1975
2. *Killers for Hire*, 1975

DEATH WISH (PAUL BENJAMIN)

Two books by Brian Garfield

Paul Benjamin was an accountant who had liberal political views until the death of his wife and the rape of his daughter during an invasion of his apartment. Paul was forty-seven years old, slightly overweight with freckles. After the attack, he became restless knowing that the men who killed his wife and victimized his daughter would never be caught. Walking the streets one night, he was attacked by a mugger and fought him off with a roll of quarters in a sock. In an effort to help him get over the death of his wife, his firm sent him to Arizona for a pre-takeover audit. During that time Benjamin bought a gun and, on his return to New York, began killing criminals, often baiting them, setting himself up as a target or staking out a car for car thieves. In his final gun battle Benjamin is seriously wounded and fears capture by police but the police officer turns a blind eye in a show of support.

In the second book, Paul has been transferred to the Chicago office and begins his vigilante hunting again. This time there is a rival vigilante and Benjamin's secret has been discovered by a friend of his new girlfriend.

Behind the Scenes

Brian Wynne Garfield was a writer of westerns and thrillers. He tells of an incident in 1971 where the roof of his convertible was slashed and some minor items stolen that inspired *Death Wish*. Garfield was so disappointed with the movie version missing the point of his story that he wrote *Death Sentence*. There was a plan to novelize *Death Wish III,* published by Heroic Press, but it was discovered that only Garfield had rights to produce sequel novels.

The Books

1. *Death Wish*, 189 pages, 1972, McKay (US) Hodder & Stoughton (UK)
2. *Death Sentence*, 157 pages, 1976, M. Evans & Co.

The Movies

When Garfield's novel was adapted to the screen, several changes were made. The hero's name and occupation was changed from Paul Benjamin, accountant, to Paul Kersey, architect. Kersey was played by Charles Bronson, who was not overweight and didn't have freckles. The plot played out the same, although when Kersey was sent to Arizona to redesign a housing estate, he was given a gun as a gift. The police were actively hunting Kersey for his vigilante action and there was a conspiracy to cover the effectiveness of his actions. Indeed the police capture Kersey and tell him to get out of town.

This spawned four sequels where Kersey returns to his vigilante ways when either his friends or family have been attacked. These films form a separate continuity from the novels with none of the films adapting *Death Sentence*.

1. *Death Wish*, 93 min, 1974, producers: Hal Landers & Bobby Roberts
2. *Death Wish II*, 88 min, 1982, producers: Menahem Golan & Yoram Globus
3. *Death Wish III*, 91 min, 1985, producers: Menahem Golan & Yoram Globus
4. *Death Wish IV: The Crackdown*, 99 min, 1987, producer: Poncho Kohner
5. *Death Wish V: The Face of Death*, 95 min, 1994, producer: Damian Lee

According to *Bronson's Loose: The Making of the Death Wish Films.* There were plans for a sixth movie, "Death Wish VI: The New Vigilante," but this never came to fruition, although Talbot suggests that the 2001 vigilante movie *Death Game* from the same production company deliberately touted itself as from the producer of *Death Wish*.

Death Sentence by Brian Garfield was the basis for the 2007 movie *Death Sentence*; however, the lead character played by Kevin Bacon is now named Nick Hume. Hume witnesses the murder of his son and feels that the justice system is not doing enough and takes the law into his own hands.

Related Books

Talbot P. (2006). *Bronson's Loose!: The Making of the Death Wish Films.* New York: iUniverse, Inc.

THE DESTROYER (REMO WILLIAMS)

Ongoing series created by Richard Sapir and Warren Murphy

His name was Remo and he was dead. Many years ago a secret government agency known as CURE framed him for a crime he did not commit and had him executed on an electric chair that did not work. When he awoke Remo was offered the chance to work as the enforcement arm of CURE. He was selected because he was an orphan with no ties and his record in both the Marines in Vietnam and the Police in Newark showed that he was a patriot.

CURE then assigned him to be trained by "karate" instructor Chuin. Chuin was in reality the Master of Sinanju, the source of all martial arts. When Chuin saw that Remo was absorbing the basics of Sinanju, he left off with karate tricks and began to make the man he considered his adopted son the next Master of Sinanju.

Over the years Remo and Chuin, at the bequest of Harold W. Smith, former OSS and CIA agent and head of CURE, saved America from many different foes, such as Niuhc (Chuin's nephew and renegade master), the Dutchman (Niuhc's pupil), Mr. Gordons (an android built for survival), and many others.

The Destroyer series is arguably the most successful of the serial vigilantes with continuing publication and forays into other media.

Behind the Scenes

The Destroyer was created in 1963 by New Jersey reporters Richard Ben Sapir and Warren Murphy. The pair initially conceived the character in the James Bond mold as a psychiatrist who fought crime, but eventually settled on the idea of a dead man framed for a crime he didn't commit and sent to work for a secret agency (Murray, 1985). Both Murphy and Sapir left the series at various periods to try other books.

Richard Sapir wrote a number of books as Richard Ben Sapir, such as *The Far Arena*, *Spies*, *Bressio*, *The Quest* and *The Body*. Sapir lived in Boston, Massachusetts, with his wife Patricia Chute. Sapir passed away in 1987; this was revealed in Warren Murphy's introduction to Destroyer #75.

Warren Murphy's efforts outside of the Destroyer have included the Digger/Trace series, the Razoni & Jackson series, the screenplays for *Lethal Weapon 2* and *The Eiger Sanction*, the Grandmaster series and an Arthurian fantasy series, *The Forever King* and *The Broken Sword*; the latter two series were co-written with his wife Molly Cochran. Cochran also served as ghostwriter for the Destroyer books, making her one of the few female writers of serial-vigilante fiction.

Over the course of the series, a number of ghostwriters wrote for the series, including Ric Meyers, Robert Randisi, William Joy, Ed Hunsburger, Mike Newton, Alan Philipson, Will Murray, James Mullaney and Tim Somheil.

Will Murray is a pulp historian and the author of numerous articles and books on the pulps. He has written a number of short stories that have appeared in Batman, Wonder Woman and Cthulhu anthologies. Under the name Kenneth Robeson, he has written seven new Doc Savage novels based on notes and outlines left by Doc's creator, Lester Dent.

James Mullaney has also written an Iron Fist mini-series Breathless for Marvel Comics in 2004. Tim Somheil has written several books for **the Executioner** series.

The Books

Books 1–58 were published by Pinnacle Books; 59–94 were published by Signet Books; 95–145 were published by Gold Eagle. The New Destroyer was published by Tor Books. Unless otherwise attributed, all books were written by Richard Sapir and Warren Murphy:

1. *Created, The Destroyer*, 187 pages, 1971
2. *Death Check*, 190 pages, 1972
3. *Chinese Puzzle*, 187 pages, 1972
4. *Mafia Fix*, 184 pages, 1972
5. *Dr. Quake*, 187 pages, 1972
6. *Death Therapy*, 188 pages, 1972
7. *Union Bust*, 190 pages, 1973 (Sapir)
8. *Summit Chase*, 158 pages, 1973 (Murphy)
9. *Murder's Shield*, 190 pages, 1973
10. *Terror Squad*, 188 pages, 1973
11. *Kill or Cure*, 191 pages, 1973
12. *Slave Safari*, 186 pages, 1973
13. *Acid Rock*, 187 pages, 1973
14. *Judgment Day*, 184 pages, 1974
15. *Murder Ward*, 176 pages, 1974
16. *Oil Slick*, 179 pages, 1974
17. *Last War Dance*, 178 pages, 1974
18. *Funny Money*, 180 pages, 1975
19. *Holy Terror*, 182 pages, 1975
20. *Assassin's Playoff*, 178 pages, 1975
21. *Deadly Seeds*, 180 pages, 1975
22. *Brain Drain*, 180 pages, 1976
23. *Child's Play*, 183 pages, 1976
24. *King's Curse*, 178 pages, 1976
25. *Sweet Dreams*, 174 pages, 1976
26. *In Enemy Hands*, 178 pages, 1976
27. *The Last Temple*, 180 pages, 1977 (Murphy & Meyers)
28. *Ship of Death*, 179 pages, 1977
29. *The Final Death*, 177 pages, 1977 (Sapir, Murphy & Meyers)
30. *Mugger Blood*, 182 pages, 1977
31. *The Head Men*, 197 pages, 1977
32. *Killer Chromosomes*, 181 pages, 1978
33. *Voodoo Die*, 181 pages, 1978

34. *Chained Reaction*, 178 pages, 1978
35. *Last Call*, 182 pages, 1978
36. *Power Play*, 180 pages, 1979
37. *Bottom Line*, 178 pages, 1979
38. *Bay City Blast*, 179 pages, 1979
39. *Missing Link*, 172 pages, 1980
40. *Dangerous Games*, 188 pages, 1980 (Murphy & Randisi)
41. *Firing Line*, 180 pages, 1980 (Murphy)
42. *Timber Line*, 181 pages, 1980 (Murphy & Joy)
43. *Midnight Man*, 162 pages, 1981 (Murphy & Randisi)
44. *Balance of Power*, 183 pages, 1981 (Murphy, Sapir & Cochran)
45. *Spoils of War*, 192 pages, 1981
46. *Next of Kin*, 183 pages, 1981 (Cochran)
47. *Dying Space*, 196 pages, 1982 (Cochran)
48. *Profit Motive*, 256 pages, 1982
49. *Skin Deep*, 199 pages, 1982 (Cochran)
50. *Killing Time*, 199 pages, 1982 (Cochran)
51. *Shock Value*, 199 pages, 1983 (Cochran)
52. *Fool's Gold*, 245 pages, 1983
53. *Time Trial*, 201 pages, 1983 (Cochran)
54. *Last Drop*, 199 pages, 1983 (Cochran)
55. *Master's Challenge*, 245 pages, 1984 (Sapir, Murphy & Cochran)
56. *Encounter Group*, 185 pages, 1984
57. *Date with Death*, 186 pages, 1984 (Murphy, Cochran & Hunsburger)
58. *Total Recall*, 185 pages, 1984 (Murphy & Randisi)
59. *The Arms of Kali*, 253 pages, 1984
60. *The End of the Game*, 205 pages, 1985
61. *Lords of the Earth*, 254 pages, 1985
62. *The Seventh Stone*, 223 pages, 1985 (Sapir, Murphy & Hunburger)
63. *The Sky Is Falling*, 255 pages, 1985 (Sapir & Murray)
64. *The Last Alchemist*, 221 pages, 1986 (Sapir & Murray)
65. *Lost Yesterday*, 255 pages, 1986 (Sapir & Murray)
66. *Sue Me*, 221 pages, 1986 (Sapir)
67. *Look into My Eyes*, 253 pages, 1987 (Sapir)
68. *An Old-Fashioned War*, 224 pages, 1987 (Sapir)
69. *Blood Ties*, 252 pages, 1987 (Murphy & Murray)
70. *The Eleventh Hour*, 222 pages, 1987 (Murphy, Murray & Cochran)
71. *Return Engagement*, 253 pages, 1987 (Murphy & Murray)

72. *Sole Survivor*, 222 pages, 1988 (Murphy & Murray)
73. *Line of Succession*, 252 pages, 1988 (Murphy & Murray)
74. *Walking Wounded*, 224 pages, 1988 (Murray)
75. *Rain of Terror*, 256 pages, 1988 (Murray)
76. *The Final Crusade*, 223 pages, 1989 (Murray)
77. *Coin of the Realm*, 256 pages, 1989 (Murray)
78. *Blue Smoke and Mirrors*, 224 pages, 1989 (Murray)
79. *Shooting Schedule*, 255 pages, 1990 (Murray)
80. *Death Sentence*, 221 pages, 1990 (Murray)
81. *Hostile Takeover*, 252 pages, 1990 (Murray)
82. *Survival Course*, 253 pages, 1990 (Murray)
83. *Skull Duggery*, 256 pages, 1991 (Murray)
84. *Ground Zero*, 253 pages, 1991 (Murray)
85. *Blood Lust*, 256 pages, 1991 (Murray)
86. *Arabian Nightmare*, 237 pages, 1991 (Murray)
87. *Mob Psychology*, 250 pages, 1992 (Murray)
88. *The Ultimate Death*, 255 pages, 1992 (Murray, Meyers & Mullaney)
89. *Dark Horse*, 256 pages, 1992 (Murray)
90. *Ghost in the Machine*, 256 pages, 1992 (Murray)
91. *Cold Warrior*, 255 pages, 1993 (Murray)
92. *The Last Dragon*, 251 pages, 1993 (Murray)
93. *Terminal Transmission*, 256 pages, 1993 (Murray)
94. *Feeding Frenzy*, 250 pages, 1993 (Murphy & Murray)
95. *High Priestess*, 349 pages, 1994 (Murray)
96. *Infernal Revenue*, 349 pages, 1994 (Murray)
97. *Identity Crisis*, 349 pages, 1994 (Murray)
98. *Target of Opportunity*, 349 pages, 1995 (Murray)
99. *The Color of Fear*, 346 pages, 1995 (Murray)
100. *Last Rites*, 349 pages, 1995 (Murray)
101. *Bidding War*, 347 pages, 1995 (Murray)
102. *Unite and Conquer*, 346 pages, 1996 (Murray)
103. *Engines of Destruction*, 349 pages, 1996 (Murray)
104. *Angry White Mailmen*, 348 pages, 1996 (Murray)
105. *Scorched Earth*, 349 pages, 1996 (Murray)
106. *White Water*, 349 pages, 1997 (Murray)
107. *Feast or Famine*, 348 pages, 1997 (Murray)
108. *Bamboo Dragon*, 349 pages, 1997 (Newton)

109. *American Obsession*, 348 pages, 1997 (Philipson)

110. *Never Say Die*, 347 pages, 1998 (Newton)

111. *Prophet of Doom*, 347 pages, 1998 (Mullaney & Snaggers)

112. *Brain Storm*, 347 pages, 1998 (Mullaney & Snaggers)

113. *The Empire Dreams*, 347 pages, 1998 (Mullaney)

114. *Falling Marks*, 348 pages, 1999 (Mullaney)

115. *Misfortune Teller*, 348 pages, 1999 (Mullaney)

116. *The Final Reel*, 349 pages, 1999 (Mullaney)

117. *Deadly Genes*, 349 pages, 1999 (Mullaney)

118. *Killer Watts*, 348 pages, 2000 (Mullaney)

119. *Fade to Black*, 348 pages, 2000 (Mullaney)

120. *The Last Monarch*, 347 pages, 2000 (Mullaney)

121. *A Pound of Prevention*, 346 pages, 2000 (Mullaney)

122. *Syndication Rites*, 352 pages, 2001 (Mullaney)

123. *Disloyal Opposition*, 347 pages, 2001 (Mullaney)

124. *By Eminent Domain*, 346 pages, 2001 (Mullaney)

125. *The Wrong Stuff*, 349 pages, 2001 (Mullaney)

126. *Air Raid*, 346 pages, 2002 (Mullaney)

127. *Market Force*, 348 pages, 2002 (Mullaney)

128. *The End of the Beginning*, 346 pages, 2002 (Mullaney)

129. *Father to Son*, 349 pages, 2002 (Mullaney)

130. *Waste Not, Want Not*, 346 pages, 2003 (Mullancy)

131. *Unnatural Selection*, 352 pages, 2003 (Mullaney)

132. *Wolf's Bane*, 349 pages, 2003 (Newton)

133. *Troubled Waters*, 348 pages, 2003 (Newton)

134. *Bloody Tourists*, 346 pages, 2004 (Somheil)

135. *Political Pressure*, 346 pages, 2004 (Somheil)

136. *Unpopular Science*, 347 pages, 2004 (Somheil)

137. *Industrial Evolution*, 347 pages, 2004 (Somheil)

138. *No Contest*, 352 pages, 2005 (Somheil)

139. *Dream Thing*, 349 pages, 2005 (Somheil)

140. *Dark Ages*, 352 pages, 2005 (Somheil)

141. *Frightening Strikes*, 348 pages, 2005 (Somheil)

142. *Mind Blower*, 347 pages, 2006 (Somheil)

143. *Bad Dog*, 352 pages, 2006 (Somheil)

144. *Holy Mother*, 347 pages, 2006 (Somheil)

145. *Dragon Bones*, 352 pages, 2006 (Somheil)

The New Destroyer

All titles by Warren Murphy and James Mullaney:

146. *Guardian Angel*, 260 pages, 2007

147. *Choke Hold*, 250 pages, 2007

148. *Dead Reckoning*, 256 pages, 2008

149. *Killer Ratings*, 279 pages, 2008

In the Corgi reprints, the numbering is changed slightly as #13: *Acid Rock* was published as #11, #11: *Kill Or Cure* became #12 and #12: *Slave Safari* became #13. Warren Murphy has declared that books 108–110 and 132–145 (written by Mike Newton, Allan Philipson and Tim Somheil) are not part of the Destroyer canon.

Related Works

There are also the companion books:

- The Assassin's Handbook, *Pinnacle, 285 pages, 1982 (Murphy & Sapir)*
- Inside Sinanju *(which is a revised and expanded version of* The Assassin's Handbook*), Pinnacle, 268 pages, 1985 (Murray)*
- The Assassin's Handbook 2: Chuin's Big Book of Rainy Day Fun!, *Ballybunnion Books, 263 pages, 2003 (Murphy & Mullaney)*
- Remo Williams: The Adventure Begins *(the movie novelization; also titled* Remo: Unarmed and Dangerous*), Signet, 253 pages, 1985 (Murphy & Sapir from a screenplay by Christopher Wood)*
- New Blood *(a collection of short stories written by fans of the series), Ballybunnion Books, 265 pages, 2005 (edited by Murphy)*

The short story "Terminal Philosophy" appeared in the magazine *All-Star Action Heroes* #1: (1989).

The Comics

Marvel Comics over the years has published three different series of the Destroyer:

- Vol. 1 (1989–90): Nine issues in the larger magazine format in black and white, the stories featured were a mixture of adaptations and original stories. In 1991, the first three issues were reissued in trade paperback and colored.
- Vol. 2 (1991): One issue in comic book format.
- Vol 3 (1991–92): Four-issue mini-series in comic book format.

The comics and the novels shared a symbiotic relationship; the comics adapted some of the books and later some of the books were based on the plots of the comics (for example, Vol. 3, no. 4 became #92: *The Last Dragon*) as Will Murray wrote both the comics and some of the later novels.

Film and Television

The Destroyer has been filmed twice.

The first film was released in 1985 and starred Fred Ward as Remo, Joel Gray as Chuin, and Wilford Brimley as Harold W. Smith. Titled *Remo Williams: The Adventure*

Begins (*Remo: Unarmed and Dangerous*) it takes liberties with the premise of the series but manages to capture something of the magic that is the Destroyer. In this, Remo is Ed Macon, a cop who was believed killed and became part of CURE. The portrayal of Smith was way off base but Remo and Chuin interact well. This was novelized by Sapir and Murphy.

There was a pilot to a television series aired once and never seen again. It starred Jeffery Meek as Remo and Roddy McDowall as Chuin. The movie was based on the novella "The Day Remo Died" by Sapir and Murphy which appeared in *The Assassin's Handbook*.

DEXTER (DEXTER MORGAN)

Four books by Jeff Lindsay

Dexter Morgan is a serial killer who preys on other killers. At the age of three, Dexter was witness to the brutal murder of his mother and he and his four-year-old brother, Brian, were left in the blood-drenched room for days. Dexter was adopted by one of the police officers who found him, Harry Morgan, and Brian was placed in foster care.

As Dexter grew older, Harry noticed that Dexter was exhibiting signs of sociopathic tendencies and so Harry instilled in his son what Dexter calls the Code of Harry. Harry trained Dexter to fake emotions, blend in and kill only other killers. Dexter's first kill was a nurse killing her patients with morphine overdoses and who was treating Harry.

Dexter became a blood splatter expert with the Miami-Dade police department. He uses his access to police records to track other serial killers, having claimed over forty victims and keeping a drop of their blood as a trophy. In each book Dexter is called to assist his adopted sister Deborah in tracking down other killers such as the Ice Truck Killer and Dr. Danco. In *Dearly Devoted Dexter*, Dexter notices that his girlfriend's children, previously traumatized by their abusive father, are starting to display the same tendencies as himself and he resolves to teach them the Code of Harry.

Behind the Scenes

Jeff Lindsay lives in southern Florida with his wife and three daughters. Lindsay is the pen name of Jeffry Freundlish. Born in 1952, he is married to Ernest Hemmingway's niece. *Darkly Dreaming Dexter* was nominated for the best first novel in the 2005 Edgar Awards until it was discovered that Freundlish had previously published several crime novels as Jeffrey Lindsay and the nomination was vacated.

The Books

All books were published by Doubleday:

1. *Darkly Dreaming Dexter*, 288 pages, 2004
2. *Dearly Devoted Dexter*, 292 pages, 2005
3. *Dexter in the Dark*, 320 pages, 2007
4. *Dexter by Design*, 320 pages, 2008.

The Show

In 2006, Showtime launched *Dexter,* the first season adapting the first novel, starring Michael T. Hall as Dexter. The show does vary from the novel, the television format allowing for more character interaction.

Season 1:
1. "Dexter"
2. "Crocodile"
3. "Popping Cherry"
4. "Let's Give the Boy a Hand"
5. "Love American Style"
6. "Return to Sender"
7. "Circle of Friends"
8. "Shrink Wrap"
9. "Father Knows Best"
10. "Seeing Red"
11. "Truth Be Told"
12. "Born Free"

With the second season the show began to take its own path, only borrowing elements of *Dearly Devoted Dexter.*

Season 2:
1. "It's Alive"
2. "Waiting to Exhale"
3. "An Inconvenient Lie"
4. "See-Through"
5. "The Dark Defender"
6. "Dex, Lies and Videotape"
7. "That Night, a Forest Grew"
8. "Morning Come"
9. "Resistance Is Futile"
10. "There's Something about Harry"
11. "Left Turn Ahead"
12. "The British Invasion"

DOG TEAM

Two books by William Johnstone

The first book follows the adventures, both military and sexual, of Terry Kovak, starting with his sexual initiation with his sister-in-law at fifteen, then his first kill on his sixteenth birthday in 1954.

Kovak is recruited into the Dog Teams — the elite of the elite military — who operate by taking out the targets that are too sensitive and tough for anyone else. After the disbanding of the Dog Teams in 1965, Kovak became a mercenary fighting in Africa for freedom as he saw it.

After Kovak's death and funeral in the late 1970s, we discover that the Dog Teams have been reactivated and that Kovak's son from one of his earlier relationships is to be one of the members of the new Dog Teams. We see the reactivated Dog Teams tackle terrorist and other threats to America around the world.

Behind the Scenes

The series was created by William W. Johnstone, author of numerous horror, adventure and western novels. Johnstone was discharged from the French Foreign Legion for being underage, then worked in a carnival, became a deputy sheriff and did a stint in the army. He started writing in 1970 but did not make his first sale until 1979 with *The Devil's Kiss*. Johnstone died in 2004 in Shreveport, Louisiana.

The Books

Book 1 was published by Zebra Books; Pinnacle reprinted book 1 in 1997 and printed book 2:

1. *The Last of the Dog Teams*, 252 pages, 1981
2. *The Return of the Dog Teams*, 304 pages, 2005

Connections

Barry Rivers, **the Rig Warrior**, took the codename Dog because he had read a book about the Dog Teams. In his second adventure Rivers met the president, who confirmed that there were Dog Teams.

DRACULA

Nine books by Robert Lory

In 1883, a group of unnamed vampire hunters, implicitly Van Helsing and his band, drive a stake through the heart of Dracula. The master vampire remains dormant until he is revived by Professor Damien Harmon in the present day to fight crime, very much against his will. Harmon used to be a criminologist and in 1938 he was in the field on a case and he was beaten severely and confined to a wheelchair. Since then he has fought crime with the help of various agents, most recently Cam Sanchez. Cam is the only agent to share Harmon's interest in the occult and so he has become the longest serving.

Harmon has a limited psychic ability and has implanted a mentally controlled device in Dracula's chest which will drive a sliver of the stake through his heart if the vampire does not comply with Harmon's requests. Harmon has developed a synthetic blood substitute to prevent the vampire from attacking humans. Dracula is not very happy that Harmon is making him drink fake blood.

Added into this mix is Ktara, who can change from human to cat form, an agent of Dracula who lead Harmon and Cam to the vampire's resting place. Throughout the series it is hinted that both Ktara and Dracula are from Atlantis.

Harman blackmails Dracula into being his ultimate agent and together they fight other vampires, mad men who set vampire bats attacking New York, and voodoo doctors as well as take on more personal crusades, such as retrieving gold stolen from Castle Dracula and rescuing Harmon's niece Jenny.

Behind the Scenes

This series was written by Robert Lory. Lory was also the author of the Horrorscopes series under his own name as well as the writing several books in **the Expeditor** series. It is interesting to compare the Dracula and the Expeditor series as both involve wheelchair bound crime fighters who utilize field agents to fight crime.

The Books

All books were published by Pinnacle Books:

1. *Dracula Returns*, 124 pages, 1973
2. *The Hand of Dracula*, 127 pages, 1973
3. *Dracula's Brothers*, 140 pages, 1973
4. *Dracula's Gold*, 142 pages, 1973
5. *The Drums of Dracula*, 128 pages, 1974
6. *The Witching of Dracula*, 126 pages, 1974
7. *Dracula's Lost World*, 181 pages, 1974
8. *Dracula's Disciples*, 179 pages, 1975
9. *Challenge to Dracula*, 180 pages, 1975

   Dracula Returns should be considered a sequel to *Dracula* (1897) by Bram Stoker.

   To this list I should add an unofficial entry. The American editions were published by Pinnacle Books but the British reprints were by the New English Library. New English Library brought out another Dracula book, *Dracula and the Virgins of the Undead* (124 pages, 1974), by Etienne Aubin, which has the number 3 on the front cover and pictures of *Dracula Returns* and *The Hand of Dracula* on the back cover, implying that it is part of Lory's series.

   The book has nothing to do with Lory's series at all and is set in Wiltshire, London, where local squire Adam Cochrane investigates strange events and discovers that Dracula is behind it all.

EAGLE ATTACK TEAM

Six books by Larry Hicks

In 1988, the president of the United States decided that he needed a small rapid-deployment team to quickly and quietly eliminate potential threats to world safety. Code-named Fire Storm, this highly classified and covert twenty-one man team operated six helicopters including Hueys, Blackhawks and Apaches. These machines are constantly being replaced and updated with the latest classified equipment, such as anti-radar and radiation sensors.

The Eagle Attack Team draws its members from retired and active personnel from the Army, Navy, Air Force and Marines with service in every war and operation theatre from Korea to the Gulf War. Each copter has a pilot, a co-pilot and a gunner. The rest of the unit consists of maintenance personnel. With the dangerous nature of the mission undertaken by the team, new members are often joining to replace injured and deceased members.

The core of the team consists of:

- Lt. Col. Mack "Truck" Grundy: retired US Army Special Forces who served in Korea and Vietnam. Commander and lead pilot of the team. His daughter Linn served as helicopter pilot flying support out of Saudi Arabia during Desert Storm.
- Chief Warrant Officer Cliff "Bad Bear" Sate-Zalebay: retired US Army Special Forces in Vietnam. This Kiowa Indian is second in command and a demolitions expert.
- Lt. Col. Stewart "Stu" Barringer: US Army retired, veteran of Korea and Vietnam as well as POW raids on Laos and northern Vietnam. The operational expert of the team, he organizes transport and support for the team on their missions.
- Warrant Officer Jackson "Push" Okahara: US Army and the head of the maintenance team, nicknamed Push because he can drop and do 200 pushups at any time.
- Warrant Officer Stanton "Belch" Fullove: US Army, electronics and computer expert.

The team is able to travel all around the world, undertaking missions such as rescuing freedom fighters in Albania, destroying Neo-Nazi bases in the Bavarian Alps, eliminating rogue Soviet forces in Armenia and even undertaking a mission during Desert Storm.

Behind the Scenes

Larry Hicks is a veteran of operations in Vietnam, Cambodia and Laos.

The Books

All books were published by Diamond Books:

1. *Eagle Attack Team*, 210 pages, 1991
2. *Debt of Honor*, 212 pages, 1991
3. *Tank Killers*, 196 pages, 1991
4. *Desert Fire*, 198 pages, 1992
5. *Night Strike*, 194 pages, 1992
6. *Force Red*, 178 pages, 1993

EAGLE FORCE
Nine books by Dan Schmidt

Commander Vic Gabriel was the son of Colonel Charles Gabriel, one of the founders of the Special Forces. After following his father into the Special Forces, Vic left when his brother died from a drug overdose and began a vigilante campaign against the drug lords. The Angel of Death, as Gabriel became known, wound down his war on drugs and established the commando team — Eagle Force.

Eagle Force consists of:
• Vic Gabriel: Team leader.
• Bad Zac Dillinger: former Miami Private Eye.
• Henry Van Boolwarke: Former member of the South African Reconnaissance Commando.
• Johnny Simms: tough commando from the streets of Washington.

This mercenary force is based out the Pyrenees, France, until *Ring of Fire* when their base is attacked by their greatest enemy, Michael Saunders, the man who murdered Gabriel's father. The team doesn't get their revenge until *Hell's March* and begins rebuilding in *Armageddon USA*. The team tackles rouge law enforcement agents, drug dealers, satanic cults and other mercenary groups.

Eagle Force's motto is "Hit First, Hit Hard, Hit Last."

Behind the Scenes
Dan Schmidt is the author of a number of horror novels as well as writing several **Executioners** as Don Pendleton and, as Frank Garrett, he wrote the **Killsquad** series.

The Books
All books were published by Bantam books:
1. *Contract for Slaughter*, 156 pages, 1989
2. *Death Camp Columbia*, 148 pages, 1989
3. *Flight 666*, 149 pages, 1989
4. *Red Firestorm*, 148 pages, 1989
5. *Ring of Fire*, 166 pages, 1990
6. *Berserker*, 132 pages, 1990
7. *Edge of the Blade*, 156 pages, 1990
8. *Hell's March*, 263 pages, 1990
9. *Armageddon, USA*, 192 pages, 1991

THE ENFORCER (ALEX JASON)
Seven books by Andrew Sugar

Alexander Graham Bell Jason's father worked for the phone company. Alex Jason became an investigative reporter and was a master martial artist. Then he found out that he was dying of stomach cancer.

Approached by the John Anryn Institute, he was offered the chance to survive. His brain would be transferred to a new body, a cloned body. The clones, however, only last for ninety days, a feature that ensures loyalty in all the Institute's agents. Jason became one of the Enforcers for the Institute, which not only develops scientific marvels such as cloning and laser weapons but actively fights against crime and collectivists.

For several books Jason and the Institute are pitted against the criminal mastermind Lochner, who operates under many aliases and is trying to take over the Institute. Lochner is responsible for the death of many Institute operatives, including Dr. Janet Evans, who was pregnant with Jason's child. The hunt for Lochner ended in *Bio Blitz* where Lochner used mutated insects to attack the Institute. The arch criminal was not killed by Jason but rather by his boss Mortimer Flack, whose fiancée Ellen was also murdered by Lochner. The Institute tackles all forms of crime from cop killings to mutated insects.

Behind the Scenes

Andrew Sugar is also the author of the Israeli Commando series as well as several nonfiction books on camping. Sugar also served as editor for the two issues of the Argosy Annual.

The Books

All books were published by Manor Books:

1. *The Enforcer*, 222 pages, 1973
2. *Calling Dr. Kill*, 221 pages, 1973
3. *Kill City*, 221 pages, 1973
4. *Kill Deadline*, 221 pages, 1974
5. *Steel Trap*, 188 pages, 1974
6. *Bio Blitz*, 188 pages, 1975
7. *Caribbean Kill*, 222 pages, 1975

THE EXECUTIONER (MACK BOLAN) (ALSO SUPER BOLAN)

Ongoing series created by Don Pendleton

This is arguably the first and most successful of all the serial vigilantes. In 1969, Beeline Books, perhaps to capitalize on the success of Bantam's **Doc Savage** reprints and the Nick Carter, **Killmaster** series, created the Pinnacle line to publish similar types of books. Their first effort was by a relatively unknown author, Don Pendleton, and the novel *War Against the Mafia*.

It was the story of Sgt. Mack Bolan, who was called home from Vietnam to look after his brother, Johnny, after the death of the rest of his family. It turns out that his father, Sam Bolan, had gotten into debt with some Mafia loan sharks and got behind in the payments. Sam's daughter, Cindy, unknown to her father tried to help and ended up as a prostitute for the Mafia. When Sam found this out he shot and killed his wife and daughter and seriously wounded Johnny before killing himself.

Bolan came home and found this out from his brother and decided to kill those he felt responsible for his family's tragedy or, rather, he discovered that instead of fighting communism in Vietnam, he should have been at home fighting the Mafia who corrupted society. So Bolan launched his war against the Mafia, in a cross-country blitz.

The first thirty-eight books (with the exception of #16: *Sicilian Slaughter*) were written by Don Pendleton. Number 16 was written under the house name of "Jim Peterson," during a dispute between Pendleton and Pinnacle.

After book #38 Pendleton made a number of changes to the Executioner; firstly, he changed the publisher to Gold Eagle, an imprint created by Harlequin Books for their action/adventure line. He then changed Mack's focus to terrorism and gave him the new identity of Col. John Macklin Phoenix (Ret.) and handed the writing over to a number of ghosts, including Chet Cunningham, Ron Renauld, Rich Rainey, Will Murray, Mike Newton and Mel Odom.

The terrorist wars lasted until the Day of Morning Trilogy: #62: *Day of Mourning*, *Terminal Velocity* (a Super Bolan), and #64: *Dead Man Running*, where Bolan loses his unofficial status and returns to fighting any evil anywhere, a situation that continues to today.

Gold Eagle created four spinoffs of the Executioner series: **Able Team**, **Phoenix Force**, **Stony Man** and **Super Bolan**. (The first three series are all discussed in their own articles.) The Super Bolan series was created to tell longer stories featuring the Executioner and are not counted as part of the regular Executioner series (they have different numbering) though the two series do intersect, as several trilogies start in the Executioner and are continued through Super Bolan, as can be seen from the Day of Mourning Trilogy mentioned above.

Behind the Scenes

Don Pendleton (1927–1995) lied about his age and joined the Navy at age 14. After leaving the Navy, Pendleton worked for the FAA as an air traffic controller and then became an aeronautical engineer. In 1966, Pendleton left his engineering to become a full-time writer. Initially writing sexy paperbacks, Pendleton then developed the Executioner for Beeline Books, the new Pinnacle imprint. The series was a success, leading to the creation of many similar characters. After a number of disputed disagreements with Pinnacle, Pendleton licensed both the Executioner and his name to Gold Eagle. Pendleton is also the creator of the Ashton Ford psychic detective and the private eye series Joe Copp.

During a dispute between Pendleton and Pinnacle, Pinnacle commissioned one Executioner (#16: *Sicilian Slaughter*) published under the house name of Jim Peterson. The man behind the Peterson name was William Crawford. Crawford was born in 1929 and served in the US Border Patrol as well as the El Paso Police Department. Crawford wrote the Stryker series for Pinnacle, detailing the violent exploits of police officer Colin Stryker, as well as numerous articles and short stories for law enforcement, sports and rodeo journals.

Notable ghosts who have written the Gold Eagle Executioners include:

• Mike Newton trained with Don Pendleton, co-writing several Executioners with Pendleton for Pinnacle books and writing numerous books for that series for Gold Eagle, making him the most prolific writer of Executioner novels. Newton has also written several western series under the pen name Lyle Brandt as well as four entries in the **Destroyer** series. Newton is also the author or several nonfiction works, including *How to Write Action-Adventure Fiction*, and several reference works on serial killers and cryptozoology.

- Chet Cunningham lives in San Diego, the setting for the first novel in his series, **the Avenger**. He is also the author of **the Specialists** under his own name and, as Lionel Derrick, he wrote the even numbered books in **the Penetrator** series. Cunningham has also written numerous western novels both under his own name and pseudonyms. A veteran of the Korean War, Cunningham has also written several volumes of military history.

- Steve Mertz, along with Mike Newton, got his start working with Don Pendleton on the Executioner for Pinnacle Books, later ghostwriting a number of Executioner and Able Team novels for Gold Eagle Books and plotted the **MIA Hunter** series for Jove Books.

- Ron Renauld wrote five A-Team novelizations as Charles Heath and wrote book 7 under his own name. He has also written for Able Team.

- Rich Rainey, under his full name Richard Rainey, has written several nonfiction works on the occult and the horror genre. Rainey has also produced several books in the Executioner franchise and contributed to the SOB (**Soldiers of Barrabas**) series as Jack Hild and the final book in the post-apocalyptic Warlord series as Jason Frost as well as writing **the Protector** series under his own name.

- Mel Odom is the author of a number of children's books, including the junior novelization of the first Tomb Raider movie, as well as writing a number of books for the Executioner and its spinoff series. Under the Alex Archer pen name, he contributes to the **Rogue Angel** series.

- Will Murray is a pulp historian and the author of numerous articles and books on the pulps. He has written a number of short stories that have appeared in Batman, Wonder Woman and Cthulhu anthologies. Under the name Kenneth Robeson, he has written seven new Doc Savage novels based on notes and outlines left by Doc's creator, Lester Dent. He has also written many books in the Destroyer series.

- Dan Schmidt is the author of a number of horror novels and the **Eagle Force** series under his own name and the **Killsquad** series under the pseudonym Frank Garrett.

- Steven Krauzer, graduate of both Yale and University of New Hampshire, wrote his graduate thesis on the hardboiled detective. He was co-editor of the anthology *The Great American Detective*, which contained a critical examination of the Executioner and a short story by Don Pendleton featuring the Executioner.

- William Fieldhouse has written a number of books in the Executioner franchise, including Phoenix Force and Stony Man. Under his own name, Fieldhouse has written several westerns including *Klaw* and *Gun Lust*. As Chuck Bainbridge, he wrote several books in the **Hard Corps** series.

The Novels

Books 1–38 were published by Pinnacle Books and written by Don Pendleton, with the exception of 16. Books 38 onwards and Super Bolan were published by Gold Eagle Books and written by ghostwriters under the byline Don Pendleton.

The Executioner

1. *War Against the Mafia*, 170 pages, 1969 (Pendleton)
2. *Death Squad*, 185 pages, 1969 (Pendleton)
3. *Battle Mask*, 155 pages, 1970 (Pendleton)
4. *Miami Massacre*, 158 pages, 1970 (Pendleton)
5. *Continental Contract*, 188 pages, 1971 (Pendleton)
6. *Assault on Soho*, 187 pages, 1971 (Pendleton)
7. *Nightmare in New York*, 185 pages, 1971 (Pendleton)
8. *Chicago Wipeout*, 160 pages, 1971 (Pendleton)
9. *Vegas Vendetta*, 159 pages, 1971 (Pendleton)
10. *Caribbean Kill*, 160 pages, 1972 (Pendleton)
11. *California Hit*, 187 pages, 1972 (Pendleton)
12. *Boston Blitz*, 187 pages, 1972 (Pendleton)
13. *Washington I.O.U.*, 158 pages, 1972 (Pendleton)
14. *San Diego Siege*, 174 pages, 1972 (Pendleton)
15. *Panic in Philly*, 190 pages, 1973 (Pendleton)
16. *Sicilian Slaughter*, 187 pages, 1973 (Jim Peterson)
17. *Jersey Guns*, 169 pages, 1974 (Pendleton)
18. *Texas Storm*, 188 pages, 1974 (Pendleton)
19. *Detroit Deathwatch*, 182 pages, 1974 (Pendleton)
20. *New Orleans Knockout*, 178 pages, 1974 (Pendleton)
21. *Firebase Seattle*, 184 pages, 1975 (Pendleton)
22. *Hawaiian Hellground*, 177 pages, 1975 (Pendleton)
23. *St. Louis Showdown*, 181 pages, 1975 (Pendleton)
24. *Canadian Crisis*, 181 pages, 1975 (Pendleton)
25. *Colorado Kill-Zone*, 180 pages, 1976 (Pendleton)
26. *Acapulco Rampage*, 184 pages, 1976 (Pendleton)
27. *Dixie Convoy*, 177 pages, 1976 (Pendleton)
28. *Savage Fire*, 179 pages, 1977 (Pendleton)
29. *Command Strike*, 177 pages, 1977 (Pendleton with Mike Newton & Stephen Mertz)
30. *Cleveland Pipeline*, 176 pages, 1977 (Pendleton with Newton)
31. *Arizona Ambush*, 176 pages, 1977 (Pendleton with Newton)
32. *Tennessee Smash*, 179 pages, 1977 (Pendleton with Newton)
33. *Monday's Mob*, 178 pages, 1978 (Pendleton)

34. *Terrible Tuesday*, 178 pages, 1979 (Pendleton)

35. *Wednesday's Wrath*, 156 pages, 1979 (Pendleton)

36. *Thermal Thursday*, 176 pages, 1979 (Pendleton)

37. *Friday's Feast*, 181 pages, 1979 (Pendleton)

38. *Satan's Sabbath*, 175 pages, 1980 (Pendleton)

39. *The New War*, 183 pages, 1981 (Saul Wernick)

40. *Double Crossfire*, 189 pages, 1982 (Steven Krauser)

41. *The Violent Streets*, 187 pages, 1982 (Newton)

42. *The Iranian Hit*, 185 pages, 1982 (Mertz)

43. *Return to Vietnam*, 185 pages, 1982 (Mertz)

44. *Terrorist Summit*, 182 pages, 1982 (Krauser)

45. *Paramilitary Plot*, 188 pages, 1982 (Newton)

46. *Bloodsport*, 188 pages, 1982 (Ray Obstfeld)

47. *Renegade Agent*, 188 pages, 1982 (Krauser)

48. *The Libya Connection*, 185 pages, 1982 (Mertz)

49. *Doomsday Disciples*, 188 pages, 1983 (Newton)

50. *Brothers in Blood*, 188 pages, 1983 (Krauser)

51. *Vulture's Vengeance*, 186 pages, 1983 (Patrick Neary)

52. *Tuscany Terror*, 162 pages, 1983 (Mertz)

53. *The Invisible Assassins*, 185 pages, 1983 (Alan Bomack)

54. *Mountain Rampage*, 173 pages, 1983 (E. Richard Churchill)

55. *Paradine's Gauntlet*, 183 pages, 1983 (Newton)

56. *Island Deathtrap*, 189 pages, 1983 (Churchill)

57. *Flesh Wounds*, 184 pages, 1983 (Obstfeld)

58. *Ambush on Blood River*, 188 pages, 1983 (Bomack)

59. *Crude Kill*, 186 pages, 1983 (Chet Cunningham)

60. *Sold for Slaughter*, 189 pages, 1983 (Newton)

61. *Tiger War*, 186 pages, 1984 (Tom Jagninski)

62. *Day of Mourning*, 185 pages, 1984 (Mertz)

63. *The New War Book*, 187 pages, 1984 (Pendleton with Wiley Slade, Aaron Hill & Judy Newton)

64. *Dead Man Running*, 185 pages, 1984 (Mertz)

65. *Cambodia Clash*, 186 pages, 1984 (Jagninski)

66. *Orbiting Omega*, 187 pages, 1984 (Cunningham)

67. *Beirut Payback*, 186 pages, 1984 (Mertz)

68. *Prairie Fire*, 185 pages, 1984 (Newton)

69. *Skysweeper*, 184 pages, 1984 (Cunningham)

70. *Ice Cold Kill*, 186 pages, 1984 (Peter Leslie)

71. *Blood Dues*, 186 pages, 1984 (Newton)
72. *Hellbinder*, 185 pages, 1984 (Cunningham)
73. *Appointment in Kabul*, 185 pages, 1985 (Mertz)
74. *Savannah Swingsaw*, 186 pages, 1985 (Obstfeld)
75. *The Bone Yard*, 184 pages, 1985 (Newton)
76. *Teheran Wipeout*, 185 pages, 1985 (Mertz)
77. *Hollywood Hell*, 186 pages, 1985 (Newton)
78. *Death Games*, 187 pages, 1985 (Tom Arnett)
79. *Council of Kings*, 185 pages, 1985 (Cunningham & Les Danforth)
80. *Running Hot*, 184 pages, 1985
81. *Shock Waves*, 185 pages, 1985 (Newton)
82. *Hammerhead Reef*, 187 pages, 1985 (Bomack)
83. *Missouri Deathwatch*, 189 pages, 1985 (Newton)
84. *Fastburn*, 186 pages, 1985 (James Lord)
85. *Sunscream*, 186 pages, 1986 (Leslie)
86. *Hell's Gate*, 187 pages, 1986 (Arnett)
87. *Hellfire Crusade*, 189 pages, 1986 (Bomack)
88. *Baltimore Trackdown*, 189 pages, 1986 (Cunningham)
89. *Defenders and Believers*, 186 pages, 1986 (Newton)
90. *Blood Heat Zero*, 185 pages, 1986 (Leslie)
91. *The Trial*, 249 pages, 1986 (Newton)
92. *Moscow Massacre*, 252 pages, 1986 (Mertz)
93. *The Fire Eaters*, 252 pages, 1986 (Obstfeld)
94. *Save the Children*, 253 pages, 1986 (Mertz)
95. *Blood and Thunder*, 252 pages, 1986 (Schmidt)
96. *Death Has a Name*, 253 pages, 1986 (Mike McQuay)
97. *Meltdown*, 252 pages, 1986 (Charlie McDade)
98. *Black Dice*, 252 pages, 1987 (Dan Schmidt)
99. *Code of Dishonor*, 250 pages, 1987 (McQuay)
100. *Blood Testament*, 250 pages, 1987 (Newton)
101. *Eternal Triangle*, 250 pages, (Newton)
102. *Split Image*, 252 pages, 1987 (McDade)
103. *Assault on Rome*, 252 pages, 1987 (Newton)
104. *Devil's Horn*, 251 pages, 1987 (Schmidt)
105. *Countdown to Chaos*, 252 pages, 1987 (Kent Delaney)
106. *Run to Ground*, 252 pages, 1987 (Newton)
107. *American Nightmare*, 252 pages, 1987 (McQuay)
108. *Time to Kill*, 251 pages, 1987 (Newton)

109. *Hong Kong Hit List*, 251 pages, 1988 (Leslie)

110. *Trojan Horse*, 251 pages, 1988 (Schmidt)

111. *The Fiery Cross*, 251 pages, 1988 (Newton)

112. *Blood of the Lion*, 251 pages, 1988 (Schmidt)

113. *Vietnam Fallout*, 251 pages, 1988 (McDade)

114. *Cold Judgment*, 252 pages, 1988 (Newton)

115. *Circle of Steel*, 253 pages, 1988 (Schmidt)

116. *The Killing Urge*, 251 pages, 1988 (McQuay)

117. *Vendetta in Venice*, 251 pages, 1988 (Leslie)

118. *Warrior's Revenge*, 252 pages, 1988 (Kevin Randle)

119. *Line of Fire*, 253 pages, 1988 (Newton)

120. *Border Sweep*, 251 pages, 1988 (McDade)

121. *Twisted Path*, 250 pages, 1989 (Kirk Sanson)

122. *Desert Strike*, 253 pages, 1989 (Jack Garside)

123. *War Born*, 253 pages, 1989 (Mel Odom)

124. *Night Kill*, 253 pages, 1989 (Newton)

125. *Dead Man's Tale*, 251 pages, 1989 (Leslie)

126. *Death Wind*, 251 pages, 1989 (Odom)

127. *Kill Zone*, 250 pages, 1989 (Carl Furst)

128. *Sudan Slaughter*, 221 pages, 1989 (Sanson)

129. *Haitian Hit*, 218 pages, 1989 (Newton)

130. *Dead Line*, 220 pages, 1989 (Furst)

131. *Ice Wolf*, 219 pages, 1989 (Odom)

132. *The Big Kill*, 221 pages, 1989 (McDade)

133. *Blood Run*, 219 pages, 1990 (Newton)

134. *White Line War*, 219 pages, 1990 (Sanson)

135. *Devil Force*, 219 pages, 1990 (Odom)

136. *Down and Dirty*, 221 pages, 1990 (Furst)

137. *Battle Lines*, 220 pages, 1990 (Leslie)

138. *Kill Trap*, 221 pages, 1990 (Sanson)

139. *Cutting Edge*, 218 pages, 1990 (Jerry Van Cook)

140. *Wild Card*, 221 pages, 1990 (Odom)

141. *Direct Hit*, 221 pages, 1990 (Furst)

142. *Fatal Error*, 220 pages, 1990 (Newton)

143. *Helldust Cruise*, 221 pages, 1990 (Leslie)

144. *Whipsaw*, 218 pages, 1990 (McDade)

145. *Chicago Payoff*, 218 pages, 1991 (Roland Green)

146. *Deadly Tactics*, 219 pages, 1991 (Rich Rainey)

147. *Payback Game*, 218 pages, 1991 (Van Cook)
148. *Deep and Swift*, 219 pages, 1991 (Furst)
149. *Blood Rules*, 218 pages, 1991 (Newton)
150. *Death Load*, 221 pages, 1991 (McDade)
151. *Message to Medellin*, 221 pages, 1991 (Newton)
152. *Combat Stretch*, 219 pages, 1991 (Van Cook)
153. *Firebase Florida*, 220 pages, 1991 (Furst)
154. *Night Hit*, 219 pages, 1991 (Odom)
155. *Hawaiian Heat*, 221 pages, 1991 (Newton)
156. *Phantom Force*, 218 pages, 1991 (Rainey)
157. *Cayman Strike*, 220 pages, 1992 (Van Cook)
158. *Firing Line*, 220 pages, 1992 (Green)
159. *Steel and Flame*, 218 pages, 1992 (Furst)
160. *Storm Warning*, 219 pages, 1992 (Odom)
161. *Eye of the Storm*, 220 pages, 1992 (Odom)
162. *Colors of Hell*, 219 pages, 1992 (Newton)
163. *Warrior's Edge*, 218 pages, 1992 (Rainey)
164. *Death Trail*, 220 pages, 1992 (Van Cook)
165. *Fire Sweep*, 221 pages, 1992 (Newton)
166. *Assassin's Creed*, 219 pages, 1992 (William Fieldhouse)
167. *Double Action*, 219 pages, 1992 (Ron Renauld)
168. *Blood Price*, 219 pages, 1992 (Furst)
169. *White Heat*, 218 pages, 1993 (David Robbins)
170. *Baja Blitz*, 220 pages, 1993 (Newton)
171. *Deadly Force*, 218 pages, 1993 (McDade)
172. *Fast Strike*, 220 pages, 1993 (Odom)
173. *Capital Hit*, 221 pages, 1993 (Green)
174. *Battle Plan*, 221 pages, 1993 (Van Cook)
175. *Battle Ground*, 221 pages, 1993 (Van Cook)
176. *Ransom Run*, 220 pages, 1993 (Rainey)
177. *Evil Code*, 220 pages, 1993 (Fieldhouse)
178. *Black Hand*, 218 pages, 1993 (Robbins)
179. *War Hammer*, 218 pages, (Mike Linaker)
180. *Force Down*, 219 pages, 1993 (Rainey)
181. *Shifting Target*, 221 pages, 1994 (Renauld)
182. *Lethal Agent*, 220 pages, 1994 (Odom)
183. *Clean Sweep*, 218 pages, 1994 (Green)
184. *Death Warrant*, 219 pages, 1994 (Van Cook)

185. *Sudden Fury*, 219 pages, 1994 (Linaker)

186. *Fire Burst*, 218 pages, 1994 (Newton)

187. *Cleansing Flame*, 221 pages, 1994 (Newton)

188. *War Paint*, 218 pages, 1994 (Odom)

189. *Wellfire*, 218 pages, 1994 (Van Cook)

190. *Killing Range*, 218 pages, 1994 (Newton)

191. *Extreme Force*, 220 pages, 1994 (Robbins)

192. *Maximum Impact*, 219 pages, 1994 (Rainey)

193. *Hostile Action*, 218 pages, 1994 (Linaker)

194. *Deadly Contest*, 218 pages, 1995 (Newton)

195. *Select Fire*, 218 pages, 1995 (Odom)

196. *Triburst*, 221 pages, 1995 (Van Cook)

197. *Armed Force*, 219 pages, 1995 (Odom)

198. *Shoot Down*, 220 pages, 1995 (Michael Kasner)

199. *Rogue Agent*, 219 pages, 1995 (Robbins)

200. *Crisis Point*, 220 pages, 1995 (Newton)

201. *Prime Target*, 219 pages, 1995 (Rick Price)

202. *Combat Zone*, 219 pages, 1995 (Fieldhouse)

203. *Hard Contact*, 221 pages, 1995 (Linaker)

204. *Rescue Run*, 221 pages, 1995 (Van Cook)

205. *Hell Road*, 218 pages, 1996 (Schmidt)

206. *Hunting Cry*, 219 pages, 1996 (Newton)

207. *Freedom Strike*, 221 pages, 1996 (David Rice)

208. *Death Whisper*, 219 pages, 1996 (Chuck Rogers)

209. *Asian Crucible*, 218 pages, 1996 (Fieldhouse)

210. *Fire Lash*, 220 pages, 1996 (Newton)

211. *Steel Claws*, 219 pages, 1996 (Newton)

212. *Ride the Beast*, 218 pages, 1996 (Newton)

213. *Blood Harvest*, 219 pages, 1996 (Odom)

214. *Fission Fury*, 221 pages, 1996 (David North)

215. *Fire Hammer*, 218 pages, 1996 (Tim Somheil)

216. *Death Force*, 218 pages, 1996 (Schmidt)

217. *Fight or Die*, 221 pages, 1997 (Kasner)

218. *End Game*, 220 pages, 1997 (Linaker)

219. *Terror Intent*, 219 pages, 1997 (Somheil)

220. *Tiger Stalk*, 219 pages, 1997 (North)

221. *Blood and Fire*, 220 pages, 1997 (Rogers)

222. *Patriot Gambit*, 220 pages, 1997 (Newton)

223. *Hour of Conflict*, 220 pages, 1997 (Newton)

224. *Call to Arms*, 219 pages, 1997 (Newton)

225. *Body Armor*, 220 pages, 1997 (Fieldhouse)

226. *Red Horse*, 221 pages, 1997 (Will Murray)

227. *Blood Circle*, 220 pages, 1997 (Rogers)

228. *Terminal Option*, 218 pages, 1997 (Schmidt)

229. *Zero Tolerance*, 220 pages, 1998 (Newton)

230. *Deep Attack*, 219 pages, 1998 (Robbins)

231. *Slaughter Squad*, 219 pages, 1998 (Alan Philipson)

232. *Jackal Hunt*, 219 pages, 1998 (North)

233. *Tough Justice*, 221 pages, 1998 (Newton)

234. *Target Command*, 221 pages, 1998 (Rogers)

235. *Plague Wind*, 220 pages, 1998 (Rogers)

236. *Vengeance Rising*, 220 pages, 1998 (Rogers)

237. *Hellfire Trigger*, 220 pages, 1998 (Mark Ellis)

238. *Crimson Tide*, 218 pages, 1998 (Odom)

239. *Hostile Proximity*, 219 pages, 1998 (Somheil)

240. *Devil's Guard*, 219 pages, 1998 (Ellis)

241. *Evil Reborn*, 219 pages, 1999 (Schmidt)

242. *Doomsday Conspiracy*, 220 pages, 1999 (Schmidt)

243. *Assault Reflex*, 220 pages, 1999 (Schmidt)

244. *Judas Kill*, 220 pages, 1999 (Rainey)

245. *Virtual Destruction*, 221 pages, 1999 (Fieldhouse)

246. *Blood of the Earth*, 221 pages, 1999 (Rogers)

247. *Black Dawn Rising*, 220 pages, 1999 (Linaker)

248. *Rolling Death*, 220 pages, 1999 (Schmidt)

249. *Shadow Target*, 218 pages, 1999 (Newton)

250. *Warning Shot*, 221 pages, 1999 (Van Cook)

251. *Kill Radius*, 219 pages, 1999 (Van Cook)

252. *Death Line*, 219 pages, 1999 (Van Cook)

253. *Risk Factor*, 221 pages, 2000 (Schmidt)

254. *Chill Effect*, 219 pages, 2000 (Rogers)

255. *War Bird*, 218 pages, 2000 (Jon Guenther)

256. *Point of Impact*, 218 pages, 2000 (Schmidt)

257. *Precision Play*, 221 pages, 2000 (Van Cook)

258. *Target Lock*, 221 pages, 2000 (Newton)

259. *Nightfire*, 218 pages, 2000 (Philipson)

260. *Dayhunt*, 221 pages, 2000 (Philipson)

261. *Dawnkill*, 219 pages, 2000 (Philipson)

262. *Trigger Point*, 221 pages, 2000 (Gerald Montgomery)

263. *Skysniper*, 218 pages, 2000 (Rogers)

264. *Iron Fist*, 219 pages, 2000 (Montgomery)

265. *Freedom Force*, 218 pages, 2000 (Van Cook)

266. *Ultimate Price*, 218 pages, 2001 (Montgomery)

267. *Invisible Invader*, 220 pages, 2001 (Robbins)

268. *Shattered Trust*, 219 pages, 2001 (Newton)

269. *Shifting Shadows*, 220 pages, 2001 (Newton)

270. *Judgment Day*, 220 pages, 2001 (Newton)

271. *Cyberhunt*, 220 pages, 2001 (Guenther)

272. *Stealth Striker*, 219 pages, 2001 (Schmidt)

273. *Uforce*, 218 pages, 2001 (Rainey)

274. *Rogue Target*, 220 pages, 2001 (Van Cook)

275. *Crossed Borders*, 219 pages, 2001 (Rainey)

276. *Leviathan*, 220 pages, 2001 (Montgomery)

277. *Dirty Mission*, 218 pages, 2001 (Newton)

278. *Triple Reverse*, 219 pages, 2002 (Van Cook)

279. *Fire Wind*, 221 pages, 2002 (Schmidt)

280. *Fear Rally*, 221 pages, 2002 (Guenther)

281. *Blood Stone*, 221 pages, 2002 (Newton)

282. *Jungle Conflict*, 220 pages, 2002 (Van Cook)

283. *Ring of Retaliation*, 220 pages, 2002 (Guenther)

284. *Devil's Army*, 220 pages, 2002 (Schmidt)

285. *Final Strike*, 224 pages, 2002 (The Doomsday Trilogy #2)

286. *Armageddon Exit*, 218 pages, 2002 (Schmidt)

287. *Rogue Warrior*, 219 pages, 2002 (Newton)

288. *Arctic Blast*, 221 pages, 2002 (Guenther)

289. *Vendetta Force*, 221 pages, 2002 (Van Cook)

290. *Pursued*, 221 pages, 2003 (Newton)

291. *Blood Trade*, 218 pages, 2003 (Douglas P. Wojtowicz)

292. *Savage Game*, 220 pages, 2003 (Rogers)

293. *Death Merchants*, 221 pages, 2003 (Tresslar)

294. *Scorpion Rising*, 218 pages, 2003 (Robbins)

295. *Hostile Alliance*, 220 pages, 2003 (Van Cook)

296. *Nuclear Game*, 220 pages, 2003 (Odom)

297. *Deadly Pursuit*, 218 pages, 2003 (Odom)

298. *Final Play*, 221 pages, 2003 (Odom)

299. *Dangerous Encounter*, 220 pages, 2003 (Andy Boot)

300. *Warrior's Requiem*, 221 pages, 2003 (Newton)

301. *Blast Radius*, 219 pages, 2003 (Rogers)

302. *Shadow Search*, 220 pages, 2003 (Linaker)

303. *Sea of Terror*, 220 pages, 2003 (Newton)

304. *Soviet Specter*, 219 pages, 2004 (Van Cook)

305. *Point Position*, 220 pages, 2004 (Boot)

306. *Mercy Mission*, 219 pages, 2004 (Somheil)

307. *Hard Pursuit*, 218 pages, 2004 (Wojtowicz)

308. *Into the Fire*, 221 pages, 2004 (Newton)

309. *Flames of Fury*, 219 pages, 2004 (Newton)

310. *Killing Heat*, 220 pages, 2004 (Newton)

311. *Night of the Knives*, 220 pages, 2004 (Rogers)

312. *Death Gamble*, 220 pages, 2004 (Tresslar)

313. *Lockdown*, 220 pages, 2004 (Robbins)

314. *Lethal Payload*, 220 pages, 2005 (Rogers)

315. *Agent of Peril*, 219 pages, 2005 (Wojtowicz)

316. *Poison Justice*, 219 pages, 2005 (Schmidt)

317. *Hour of Judgment*, 220 pages, 2005 (Newton)

318. *Code of Resistance*, 221 pages, 2005 (Rogers)

319. *Entry Point*, 221 pages, 2005 (Guenther)

320. *Exit Code*, 219 pages, 2005 (Guenther)

321. *Suicide Highway*, 221 pages, 2005 (Wojtowicz)

322. *Time Bomb*, 219 pages, 2005 (Robbins)

323. *Soft Target*, 221 pages, 2005 (Van Cook)

324. *Terminal Zone*, 219 pages, 2005 (Rogers)

325. *Edge of Hell*, 219 pages, 2005 (Wojtowicz)

326. *Blood Tide*, 219 pages, 2006 (Rogers)

327. *Serpent's Lair*, 219 pages, 2006 (Wojtowicz)

328. *Triangle of Terror*, 219 pages, 2006 (Schmidt)

329. *Hostile Crossing*, 219 pages, 2006 (Van Cook)

330. *Dual Action*, 221 pages, 2006 (Newton)

331. *Assault Force*, 220 pages, 2006 (Schmidt)

332. *Slaughter House*, 221 pages, 2006 (Renauld)

333. *Aftershock*, 219 pages, 2006 (Wojtowicz)

334. *Jungle Justice*, 221 pages, 2006 (Newton)

335. *Blood Vector*, 220 pages, 2006 (Rogers)

336. *Homeland Terror*, 219 pages, 2006 (Renauld)

337. *Tropic Blast*, 220 pages, 2006 (Van Cook)

338. *Nuclear Reaction*, 220 pages, 2007 (Newton)

339. *Deadly Contact*, 219 pages, 2007 (Linaker)

340. *Splinter Cell*, 219 pages, 2007 (Van Cook)

341. *Rebel Force*, 219 pages, 2007 (Nathan Meyer)

342. *Double Play*, 221 pages, 2007 (Wojtowicz)

343. *Border War*, 221 pages, 2007 (Rogers)

344. *Primal Law*, 219 pages, 2007 (Newton)

345. *Orange Alert*, 220 pages, 2007 (Peter Spring)

346. *Vigilante Run*, 221 pages, 2007 (Phil Elmore)

347. *Dragon's Den*, 220 pages, 2007 (Guenther)

348. *Carnage Code*, 221 pages, 2007 (Van Cook)

349. *Firestorm*, 220 pages, 2007 (Tresslar)

350. *Volatile Agent*, 218 pages, 2008 (Meyer)

351. *Hell Night*, 221 pages, 2008 (Van Cook)

352. *Killing Trade*, 219 pages, 2008 (Elmore)

353. *Black Death Reprise*, 218 pages, 2008 (Spring)

354. *Ambush Force*, 221 pages, 2008 (Rogers)

355. *Outback Assault*, 218 pages, 2008 (Wojtowicz)

356. *Defense Breach*, 187 pages, 2008 (Spring)

357. *Extreme Justice*, 187 pages, 2008 (Newton)

Super Bolan

1. *Stonyman Doctrine*, 371 pages, 1983 (Dick Stivers)

2. *Terminal Velocity*, 380 pages, 1984 (Bomack)

3. *Resurrection Day*, 376 pages, 1985 (Cunningham)

4. *Dirty War*, 376 pages, 1985 (Mertz)

5. *Flight 741*, 378 pages, 1986 (Newton)

6. *Dead Easy*, 379 pages, 1986 (Leslie)

7. *Sudden Death*, 352 pages1987 (Leslie)

8. *Rogue Force*, 379 pages, 1987 (Newton)

9. *Tropic Heat*, 380 pages, 1987 (McDade)

10. *Fire in the Sky*, 347 pages, 1988 (McQuay)

11. *Anvil of Hell*, 348 pages, 1988 (Leslie)

12. *Flash Point*, 350 pages, 1988 (McDade)

13. *Flesh and Blood*, 349 pages, 1988 (Newton)

14. *Moving Target*, 349 pages, 1989 (Gayle Stone & Mark Sadler)

15. *Tightrope*, 349 pages, 1989 (Furst)

16. *Blowout*, 348 pages, 1989 (Leslie)
17. *Blood Fever*, 346 pages, 1989 (Stone & Sadler)
18. *Knockdown*, 347 pages, 1990 (Furst)
19. *Assault*, 349 pages, 1990 (Newton)
20. *Backlash*, 347 pages, 1990 (McDade)
21. *Siege*, 346 pages, 1990 (Odom)
22. *Blockade*, 352 pages, 1991 (Furst)
23. *Evil Kingdom*, 349 pages, 1991 (Odom)
24. *Counterblow*, 347 pages, 1991 (McDade)
25. *Hardline*, 348 pages, 1991 (Leslie)
26. *Firepower*, 349 pages, 1992 (Renauld)
27. *Storm Burst*, 349 pages, 1992 (Van Cook)
28. *Intercept*, 349 pages, 1992 (Furst)
29. *Lethal Impact*, 346 pages, 1992 (Newton)
30. *Deadfall*, 347 pages, 1993 (McDade)
31. *Onslaught*, 349 pages, 1993 (Van Cook)
32. *Battle Force*, 348 pages, 1993 (Odom)
33. *Rampage*, 347 pages, 1993 (Renauld)
34. *Takedown*, 347 pages, 1993 (Rainey)
35. *Death's Head*, 346 pages, 1994 (Green)
36. *Hellground*, 346 pages, 1994 (Newton)
37. *Inferno*, 348 pages, 1994 (Odom)
38. *Ambush*, 349 pages, 1994 (Van Cook)
39. *Blood Strike*, 348 pages, 1994 (Newton)
40. *Killpoint*, 349 pages, 1995 (Odom)
41. *Vendetta*, 346 pages, 1995 (Newton)
42. *Stalk Line*, 346 pages, 1995 (Van Cook)
43. *Omega Game*, 346 pages, 1995 (Newton)
44. *Shock Tactic*, 349 pages, 1995 (Robbins)
45. *Showdown*, 348 pages, 1995 (Van Cook)
46. *Precision Kill*, 349 pages, 1996 (Robbins)
47. *Jungle Law*, 349 pages, 1996 (Newton)
48. *Dead Center*, 349 pages, 1996 (Odom)
49. *Tooth and Claw*, 349 pages, 1996 (McQuay)
50. *Red Heat*, 349 pages, 1996 (Van Cook)
51. *Thermal Strike*, 349 pages, 1996 (Robbins)
52. *Day of the Vulture*, 348 pages, 1997 (McQuay)
53. *Flames of Wrath*, 349 pages, 1997 (Fieldhouse)

54. *High Aggression*, 346 pages, 1997 (Somheil)

55. *Code of Bushido*, 347 pages, 1997 (Schmidt)

56. *Terror Spin*, 348 pages, 1994 (Newton)

57. *Judgment in Stone*, 347 pages, 1997 (Rainey)

58. *Rage for Justice*, 346 pages, 1998 (Somheil)

59. *Rebels and Hostiles*, 346 pages, 1998 (Kasner)

60. *Ultimate Game*, 347 pages, 1998 (Philipson)

61. *Blood Feud*, 346 pages, 1998 (Robbins)

62. *Renegade Force*, 346 pages, 1998 (Schmidt)

63. *Retribution*, 347 pages, 1998 (Van Cook)

64. *Initiation*, 346 pages, 1999 (Newton)

65. *Cloud of Death*, 346 pages, 1999 (Newton)

66. *Termination Point*, 346 pages, 1999 (Newton)

67. *Hellfire Strike*, 346 pages, 1999 (North)

68. *Code of Conflict*, 348 pages, 1999 (Robbins)

69. *Vengeance*, 352 pages, 1999 (Newton)

70. *Executive Action*, 349 pages, 2000 (North)

71. *Killsport*, 348 pages, 2000 (Newton)

72. *Conflagration*, 347 pages, 2000 (Somheil)

73. *Storm Front*, 348 pages, 2000 (Rainey)

74. *War Season*, 348 pages, 2000 (Schmidt)

75. *Evil Alliance*, 346 pages, 2000 (Robbins)

76. *Scorched Earth*, 346 pages, 2001 (Schmidt)

77. *Deception*, 348 pages, 2001 (Guenther)

78. *Destiny's Hour*, 349 pages, 2001 (Newton)

79. *Power of the Lance*, 347 pages, 2001 (Newton)

80. *A Dying Evil*, 347 pages, 2001 (Newton)

81. *Deep Treachery*, 349 pages, 2001 (Schmidt)

82. *War Load*, 346 pages, 2002 (Robbins)

83. *Sworn Enemies*, 349 pages, 2002 (Renauld)

84. *Dark Truth*, 346 pages, 2002 (Schmidt)

85. *Breakaway*, 347 pages, 2002 (Rogers)

86. *Blood and Sand*, 347 pages, 2002 (Schmidt)

87. *Caged*, 347 pages, 2002 (Kasner)

88. *Sleepers*, 348 pages, 2003 (Newton)

89. *Strike and Retrieve*, 349 pages, 2003 (Renauld)

90. *Age of War*, 346 pages, 2003 (Robbins)

91. *Line of Control*, 347 pages, 2003 (Guenther)

92. *Breached*, 348 pages, 2003 (Guenther)
93. *Retaliation*, 349 pages, 2003 (Newton)
94. *Pressure Point*, 347 pages, 2004 (Renauld)
95. *Silent Running*, 348 pages, 2004 (Kasner)
96. *Stolen Arrows*, 347 pages, 2004 (Nick Pollotta)
97. *Zero Option*, 346 pages, 2004 (Linaker)
98. *Predator Paradise*, 346 pages, 2004 (Schmidt)
99. *Circle of Deception*, 346 pages, 2004 (Linaker)
100. *Devil's Bargain*, 349 pages, 2005 (Schmidt)
101. *False Front*, 346 pages, 2005 (Van Cook)
102. *Lethal Tribute*, 348 pages, 2005 (Rogers)
103. *Season of Slaughter*, 347 pages, 2005 (Wojtowicz)
104. *Point of Betrayal*, 349 pages, 2005 (Tresslar)
105. *Ballistic Force*, 347 pages, 2005 (Renauld)
106. *Renegade*, 347 pages, 2006 (Van Cook)
107. *Survival Reflex*, 346 pages, 2006 (Newton)
108. *Path to War*, 346 pages, 2006 (Schmidt)
109. *Blood Dynasty*, 349 pages, 2006 (Linaker)
110. *Ultimate Stakes*, 346 pages, 2006 (Guenther)
111. *State of Evil*, 348 pages, 2006 (Newton)
112. *Force Lines*, 347 pages, 2007 (Schmidt)
113. *Contagion Option*, 347 pages, 2007 (Wojtowicz)
114. *Hellfire Code*, 348 pages, 2007 (Guenther)
115. *War Drums*, 349 pages, 2007 (Linaker)
116. *Ripple Effect*, 349 pages, 2007 (Newton)
117. *Devil's Playground*, 348 pages, 2007 (Wojtowicz)
118. *The Killing Rule*, 346 pages, 2008 (Rogers)
119. *Patriot Play*, 346 pages, 2008 (Linaker)
120. *Appointment in Baghdad*, 347 pages, 2008 (Meyer)
121. *Havana Five*, 315 pages, 2008 (Guenther)

Related Works

A guide to the series *The War Book* came out during the Pinnacle run of the series in 1977, which was later revised as #63: *The New War Book*.

The Executioner has also appeared in the short story "Willing to Kill" by Don Pendleton, which appeared in the anthology *The Great American Detective* edited by William Kittredge and Steven M. Krauzer. In his introduction to the 1975 Ballentine edition of *Hound of the Baskervilles*, Pendleton recounts a dream where Bolan meets Sherlock Holmes.

Comics

In 1993, *War against the Mafia* was adapted as a four-part series by Innovation Comics, though only the first three parts were released. It was written by Don and Linda Pendleton and illustrated by Sandu Florea. The year 1996 saw that creative team reunited for a 128-page black and white graphic novel based on *Death Squad* (Executioner #2). In 2008, IDW comics published the five issue mini-series Devil's Tools, scripted by Douglas Wojtowicz, a frequent author of the Executioner novels. This series is an original adventure with Mack attempting to shut down an illegal weapons smuggling operation.

The Movies

While there have been at least four movies titled *The Executioner*, none of them is based on Mack Bolan series. The film *The Executioner: Part II* has no connection to any of the films or to the novels.

References and Parodies

In **Destroyer** #8: *Mafia Summit* Remo asks if anyone has seen Mack Bolan at a Mafia summit. In Destroyer #38: *Bay City Blast*, the Executioner is parodied as Mark Tolan, the Exterminator. In the 1984 film *The Exterminator*, the detective chasing John Eastland, the Exterminator, nearly refers to the vigilante as the Executioner.

Niles Barrabas recalls meeting Mack Bolan during the events of **Soldiers of Barrabas** #3: *The Ashes of Eden* although he refers to him as John Macklin Bolan. He mentions a patrol the pair went on in Vietnam, which took place prior to the events of "Incident at Hoi Bihn" (Executioner #63: *The New War Book*). Barrabas refers to Bolan's war on the Mafia and his supposed death. His use of John Macklin Bolan could hint at the fact that he knew Mack Bolan's new identity John Macklin Phoenix.

THE EXPEDITOR (JOHN EAGLE)

Fourteen books by Paul Edwards (house name)

John Eagle, an adopted Apache Indian, responded to an ad in the paper and after two years of rigorous training was eventually hired by a mysterious, wheelchair-bound man known as Merlin to fight crime.

Merlin was a wealthy man who, after being shot and his spine severed at the Battle of Argonne (1918), returned to the United States and mixed with other moneyed men and discovered the ones who would be likely to misuse their wealth. Merlin tried to fight these men and in 1943 an attempt was made on his life. Merlin then hired an actor to play him while he lived in Hawaii and, through his agents, called Expeditors, continued the fight. The actor meanwhile moved to Scotland. In *The Valley of Vultures* it is revealed that Merlin's real surname might be Frobisher. Eagle faces many different threats such as hunting the son of Hitler seeking to raise the Fourth Reich, Russian plots to steal brains and Arab plots to take over the world.

Behind the Scenes

This series was created Lyle Kenyon Engel. The series used a number of ghost writers including Robert Lory.

Robert Lory also wrote the **Dracula** series as well as the Horrorscope series. It is interesting to note that both Dracula and The Expeditor feature wheelchair-bound crime fighters (Professor Harmon in Dracula and Mr. Merlin in the Expeditor) directing operatives.

The Books

All books were published by Pyramid Books:

1. *Needles of Death*, 175 pages, 1973
2. *Brain Scavengers*, 176 pages, 1973
3. *Fist of Fatima*, 156 pages, 1973 (Lory)
4. *Valley of the Vultures*, 192 pages, 1973
5. *Laughing Death*, 142 pages, 1973 (Lory)
6. *Glyphs of Gold*, 174 pages, 1974 (Lory)
7. *Ice Goddess*, 172 pages, 1974
8. *Death Devils*, 191 pages, 1974 (Lory)
9. *Deadly Cyborgs*, 176 pages, 1975
10. *Holocaust Auction*, 158 pages, 1975 (Lory)
11. *Poppies of Death*, 159 pages, 1975
12. *Green Goddess*, 188 pages, 1975
13. *Operation Weather Kill*, 159 pages, 1975
14. *Silver Skull*, 191 pages, 1975

THE FORCE

Four books by Jake Decker

The Force is the field team for the covert agency the Association. Based in Washington, the Association is run by a man codenamed the Librarian and his top aide, Pamela. Pamela is the height of efficiency and she has a photographic memory. The Force operates out of Ma's Diner, run by retired agent Harv "Ma" Liscomb.

The Force consists of team members:

• Steve Sinclair: Vietnam veteran and team leader. Steve was about to retire when he was offered the chance to join the team and train Micah.

• Micah: Cajun agent with the ability to psychically influence people. This talent means that he can implant suggestions and quickly gain information.

• Jezebel "Jez" Cooke: Red-haired Senator's daughter and final member of the Force, she acts as the balance between the two male members of the team. Jez came across Steve and Micah during their first case together; the socialite was such a help to the pair that she was offered a job by the Association.

The Force tackles various threats to national security, such as drug trafficking, Soviet plots to replace the wives of high-level political figures with duplicates, and assassins.

Behind the Scenes

This series is the only credit for Jake Decker.

The Books

All books were published by Pinnacle Books:

1. *Deadly Snow*, 250 pages, 1984
2. *Death's Little Sister*, 216 pages, 1984
3. *Death's Gambit*, 220 pages, 1984
4. *Death Comes Home*, 215 pages, 1985

GANNON (JOHN GANNON)

Two books by John Whitlatch

John Gannon is an ordinary insurance adjuster whose life is thrown into turmoil when a gang of bikers breaks into his house and rapes and kills Gannon's wife. While there is much evidence against the gang, they hire a high-powered attorney. The district attorney, facing an election, decides not to take the matter to trial as the probable loss on such a high profile case would not look good for his campaign.

Gannon tries to take the law into his own hands but, being unused to physical combat, is badly beaten and left for dead in the desert. He survives and, after healing, gains skills with the bow and arrow. He gains support from a few people who believe in his cause, respecting his determination. He tracks the gang to their hideout.

The gang had been headquartered in a small Mexican village. The village turns a blind eye to the bikers' deeds as long as they are left alone and they offer no help to Gannon. That is, until an old man from the village is killed and the villagers join the fight. Gannon discovers that the gang is working with their lawyer and a prominent Mexican to smuggle drugs into America. This provides some extra motivation to the complete elimination of the gang.

Behind the Scenes

John Whitlatch is the author of eleven adventure books, such as *Stuntman's Holiday*, *Morgan's Rebellion*, *Cory's Losers* and *Frank T's Plan*. All of Whitlatch's novels revolve around the avenging of injuries to loved ones in a variety of settings, including the Old West.

The Books

Both books were published by Pocket Books:

1. *Gannon's Vendetta*, 249 pages, 1969
2. *Gannon's Line*, 253 pages, 1976

GANNON II (MIKE GANNON)
Three books by Dean Ballinger

Mike Gannon is a security expert, one of the best in the business, traveling the world, troubleshooting security problems. When Gannon finds out that his teenaged sister has been raped and beaten by some rich college boys, he returns home to Cleveland to bring his skills to avenge her.

Gannon quickly discovers that the boys responsible are the sons of wealthy and influential men: Men who are able to buy their sons out of trouble; men who do not like this security expert nosing around in their business and they hire local mobsters to stop him. Gannon is able to cut a bloody swath through the Cleveland underworld on his quest for justice and eventually get revenge for his sister's rape.

While Gannon can tackle the Mafia as well as the Executioner or other serial vigilantes, Gannon faces the corrupting power of money, facing off against wealthy men who believe that their money can buy them out of any situation and poor men can be bought off to help them cover their sins. After avenging his sister, Gannon creates a bloodbath to prevent a land grab.

Behind the Scenes
Dean W. Ballenger's first published works were the Gannon series. He is also the author of several westerns as well as several other adventure novels.

The Books
All books were published by Manor Books:

1. *Blood for Breakfast*, 191 pages, 1973
2. *Blood Fix*, 191 pages, 1974
3. *Blood Beast*, 191 pages, 1974

GIRL FACTORY (SU-LIN KELLY)
Two books by Robert Franklin Murphy

Su-Lin Kelly is the daughter of adventurer "Chinese" Kelly and Mata Wong. The six-foot Eurasian beauty inherited her husband's, Rene Cartes, espionage network after he died and she avenged his death. Su-Lin is a nymphomaniac and after the death of her father was trained in espionage and the love arts at Shan Tal Cloister (the Girl Factory of the title) by Mata Wong, where many of the wives and mistresses of many great men were trained. The Cloister is also home to many scientific secrets revealed to group called the Matsu Underground (MU). These scientific secrets include brain transfers and were revealed to the MU by visiting aliens.

Su-Lin works as a freelance operative with the cover that she is a jet-setting playgirl with her own fortune, maintained by her financial adviser Mack Gordon. Su-Lin takes her assignments from Sam Gruber and Ella Crumb, who operate the Nest, the best-informed intelligence agency. The Nest operates from a non-descript office in the bowels of Washington bureaucracy.

In her first adventure, Su-Lin discovers that the cloning technique Quantum Growth has been stolen from the Cloister and is going to be used to clone world leaders and replace them. Kelly stops this plot and blows up the Cloister to prevent any further secrets from falling into the wrong hands. In doing so she discovers that the real Su-Lin Kelly died with her father and that she is in fact a clone made by her grieving mother, Mata Wong, head of the Shan Tal Cloister.

Su-Lin is aided by Joe Zen, her right-hand man and occasional bed partner; Mala Key, her lesbian maid; and Zero, an expert cabbie who is on call for Su-Lin.

In the second book Su-Lin becomes involved in the case of a missing Russian biochemist who is also a chess master. It is feared that the Russian may be forced to make bio-weapons for a terrorist group. But she discovers that the true reason for the Russian's disappearance is far more unusual and Su-Lin becomes involved in a lethal chess match with living pieces.

During this case, she is again cloned using Quantum Growth; it appears that the process has been refined from the last time she was cloned. The Quantum Growth Generator is portable and Su-Lin is resurrected with nearly all her memories intact.

Behind the Scenes

It seems likely that Robert Franklin Murphy is a pseudonym, as the books are copyright to Script Representatives, Inc. Murphy has no other writing credits.

Zebra Books was founded in 1975 by Walter Zacherius and Roberta Grossman. Grossman was twenty-nine at the time and was the youngest president of a paperback house. The company published many paperback series, including William Johnstone's **Rig Warrior** and Jerry Ahern's Survivalist series, and expanded into many lines, such as romance, black fiction, and gay and lesbian fiction. In 1988, the company acquired Pinnacle Books and moved their action adventure line to that imprint and the Zebra Books line became a romance line.

The Books

The books were published by Zebra Books in America and Mews Books in the United Kingdom:

1. *The Girl Factory* (The Man-Made Woman), 160 pages, 1975
2. *King's Mate*, 142 pages, 1975

HANDYMAN (JEFFERSON BOONE)

Six books by Jon Messmann

Jefferson Boone was a diplomatic brat, the son of a career diplomat who followed his father around the world. Boone displayed a skill for languages which made him fit in anywhere in any situation. All of this made Boone a natural to follow into his father's footsteps in the diplomatic corps and father and son had many discussions about the nature of the diplomatic corps and modern diplomacy. Richard Boone expressed his frustration with the restrictions placed upon him and the need for a "handyman"—someone not bound by diplomatic regulations who could respond to threats and problems.

Shortly after, Robert Boone travelled to a small, troubled country and was killed in a riot. This small nation was struggling towards democracy and Jefferson Boone realized that had a handyman been in place his father might not have died. His official career with the State Department ended that day and his new unofficial position of handyman began.

Unlike others who operate outside the law, Boone is a good shot but not great and he is only an above-average fighter with some martial arts training. But what makes him an effective fixer is his determination; once Boone accepts a job he doesn't stop until it is done. Boone frequently leaves his business card; it reads, "Jefferson Boone, Handyman."

During his time travelling the globe, Boone made many friends who frequently call on his help. Boone is called when a fascist plot attempts to stop an old friend from signing her land to the United States government; fights terrorist groups, rescues kidnapped diplomats, finds missing geologists, retrieves stolen money and stops revolutions.

Behind the Scenes

Jon Messmann (1920–2004) initially worked as a writer for Fawcett Comics, working on Captain Marvel Jr. and their western line of comics. Messmann then branched out to crime fiction and westerns. Under the name Jon Sharpe, he wrote several novels in the Trailsman and Canyon O'Grady western series. In the serial vigilante field, he wrote several **Killmasters** under the house name of Nick Carter.

The Books

All books were published by Pyramid Books:

1. *Moneta Papers*, 190 pages, 1973
2. *Game of Terror*, 199 pages, 1973
3. *Murder Today, Money Tomorrow*, 171 pages, 1973
4. *Swiss Secret*, 175 pages, 1974
5. *Ransom*, 160 pages, 1975
6. *Inheritors*, 158 pages, 1975

THE HARD CORPS

Eight books by Chuck Bainbridge

The Hard Corps is a group of five mercenaries, four of whom were a Green Beret team of that name in Vietnam. They are:

• William O'Neal: leader of the group
• James Wentworth III:—second in command, expert martial artist, and comes from a long line of soldiers

- Joe Fanelli: demolitions expert
- Steve Caine: master of the silent kill who went "native" in Vietnam
- John McShayne: Top sergeant, master Mechanic, and coordinator who joined the team after the war.

After leaving Vietnam the team discovered they couldn't readjust to civilian life, so they decided to continue as soldiers for hire, operating out of an old marijuana plantation in the Washington State backwoods. The Hard Corps occasionally do jobs for the CIA, who turns a blind eye to the team's other missions and income. Their contact with the CIA is Joshua "Saintly" St. Laurent.

The team protects freedom fighters, takes out terrorists and drug cartels and protects fledgling African democracies. In the first book, *Hard Corps*, the background of each member is given in great detail as they protect their compound against attack, such as that Wentworth was raised in Japan by his Uncle Harmon after the death of his father, and that Caine had lived on the street and had deserted the army to join a Montagnard tribe. While these asides add nothing to the action of the story, they give us a better sense of these men and the reasons why they have embarked on this life.

Behind the Scenes

Chuck Bainbridge is a house name used by William Fieldhouse and Chris Lowder. William Fieldhouse has written a number of books in the **Executioner** franchise, including **Phoenix Force** and **Stony Man**. Under his own name, Fieldhouse has written several westerns including *Klaw* and *Gun Lust*.

Chris Lowder was a British author and comic book writer. Under the name Jack Adrian, he scripted several adventures of Judge Dredd for 2000AD and as Jack Hamilton Teed he contributed to the Gunships series set in the Vietnam war.

The Books

All books were published by Jove:

1. *Hard Corps*, 325 pages, 1986 (Fieldhouse)
2. *Beirut Contract*, 179 pages, 1987 (Fieldhouse)
3. *White Heat*, 185 pages, 1987 (Fieldhouse)
4. *Slave Trade*, 185 pages, 1987 (Fieldhouse)
5. *Mercenary Justice*, 186 pages, 1988
6. *An American Nightmare*, 170 pages, 1988
7. *Scorched Earth*, 202 pages, 1989
8. *Devil's Plunder*, 188 pages, 1989 (Lowder)

HARDBALL (RANDALL DANE)

Three books by William Sanders

Randall Dane is a Special Forces veteran, having served in Vietnam, and former CIA sharpshooter, who retired at age forty to a little island off the coast of Texas. The island had been the base of a drug dealer and confiscated by the DEA, who handed it to the CIA. Dane had lived on the island as caretaker and security man and eventually to undertake several highly classified actions; Dane became the owner of the island. His only friend in this retirement is Billy Jumper, an eighty-year-old Seminole Baptist preacher who retired to run a boat and bait shop in Bayport, Texas.

However, the retirement quickly becomes a semi-retirement when Dane discovers how much repairs to his island hideaway cost, especially after a hurricane. Randall becomes a freelance operative, taking missions to fund the repairs to his hideaway. Due his past as a sharpshooter, Dane is frequently called to kill people but he no longer undertakes these missions. Instead he tackles white supremacist militias, and prison breaks for American citizens held as political prisoners, wiping out drug operations and rescuing kidnapped engineers.

Behind the Scenes

William Sanders is a science fiction and mystery author who lives in Oklahoma. Sanders was approached by Berkley Books to write a series for them that would be "the next Travis McGee." The series was marketed as action adventure and, after three books, was cancelled. Sanders was also responsible for several mystery and science fiction novels, including *Pockets of Resistance* and *J.*

The Books

All books were published by Diamond Books:

1. *Hardball*, 214 pages, 1992
2. *Aryan Legion*, 199 pages, 1992
3. *Skorpion*, 200 pages, 1992

HAWK (MICHAEL HAWK)
Fourteen books by Dan Streib

Michael Hawk is a freelance reporter, specializing in covering and exposing human rights violations. This specialty has not endeared him to dictators and communist regimes around the world. After being released from a Soviet gulag, Hawk's next investigation is to uncover the identity of a recluse living on a Greek island. The recluse is the daughter of a dictator deposed by the Soviet Union. The daughter has been hiding from Soviet assassins.

Hawk's investigation has led the assassins to her and with her dying breath she left Hawk the access codes to the secret account that holds all of the money that her father had stashed. Suddenly Hawk is in control of a vast fortune and now instead of just reporting events, he is able to influence them and establishes Crusader, Inc., to that end. Hawk uses his money to fight against people who exploit the weak, such as cult leaders, saboteurs, assassins, neo-Nazis, con artists, mobsters, terrorists, white slavers and mad scientists. During all of his investigations, Hawk is hunted by the KGB, who seeks to get his money and gain revenge for his reporting its human rights violations.

Behind the Scenes

Dan Streib, born in 1928, served in the U.S. Army during the Korean War (1950–53) and died in 1996 of a heart attack. An extensive traveler for both work and pleasure, San Diego–based Streib used the locales he visited in his works, which include the **Counter Force** series under his own name, **Death Squad** series as Frank Colter, romances under the names of Louise Grandville and Lee Davis Whilloughby, and westerns under the names Jonathan Schofield and J. Faragut Jones.

The Books

All books were published by Sphere:

1. *Deadly Crusader*, 192 pages, 1980
2. *Mind Twisters*, 203 pages, 1980
3. *Power Barons*, 185 pages, 1980
4. *Predators*, 192 pages, 1980
5. *California Shakedown*, 183 pages, 1981
6. *Seeds of Evil*, 215 pages, 1981
7. *Death Riders*, 208 pages, 1981
8. *Enemy Within*, 187 pages, 1981
9. *Down Under and Dirty*, 183 pages, 1981
10. *Cargo Gods*, 188 pages, 1981
11. *Terror Merchants*, 188 pages, 1981
12. *Virgin Stealers*, 188 pages, 1981
13. *Hawaiian Takeover*, 188 pages, 1981
14. *Treasure Divers*, 188 pages, 1981

Hawk Macrae

Six books by Albert Barker

Hawk Macrae is the son of a Scottish oil speculator father and a Chiricahua Apache mother. Little is known about his early life but Macrae was raised by his mother on a reservation in the Southwest.

Macrae broke into the movies and became a major star in westerns.

But what his fans don't know is that Macrae is also a fully trained agent of the DIA and also freelances for Interpol. Macrae's Hollywood career gives him the perfect cover to travel anywhere in the world either filming a movie, scouting and preparing for a movie, or living the jet-setting lifestyle of a Hollywood star.

Hawk investigates the kidnapping of the widow of a former president, and investigates a drug ring for his uncle, who works for Interpol, which leaves him addicted to drugs under the cover of the USO. A trip to China to film a documentary to improve relations between the two countries serves as a cover to meet anti-communists rebels. Hawk also stops a conspiracy to destabilize America while filming in Alaska. Traveling with his Interpol agent uncle in Portugal, Hawk discovers a counterfeiting ring and finally Hawk investigates stolen art when his body double is released from jail.

Behind the Scenes

Albert Barker, born 1900, has written several reference books for young readers on topics such as the history of printing, the spice trade and town planning. Barker is also the author of the **Reefe King** series for Award Books. Given the similarity of the two series, it is possible that some of Macrae books were unused books from the King series.

The Books

All books were published by Curtis Books:

1. *If Anything Should Happen to Me*, 1973
2. *Big Fix*, 1973
3. *Dragon in Spring*, 1973
4. *Blood of Angels*, 192 pages, 1974
5. *Diamond Hitch*, 1974
6. *The Straw Virgin*, 1975

HAWKER (JAMES HAWKER)

Eleven books by Carl Ramm

James Hawker is an ex-Chicago cop, founder of Chicago SWAT, and decorated detective. He retired for personal reasons and went into partnership with Jacob Montgomery Hayes, one of the wealthiest men in the world. Together, they have worked together in a vigilante partnership, with Hawker as the man of action and Hayes financing the operation. Hawker has copper-colored hair and grew up in the Irish section of Chicago.

Hawker tackles the threats the police are unable to handle, such as helping people combat the gangs and eliminating the leaders, or stopping a South American organization from destabilizing America and even avenging the death of a friend. Like many serial vigilantes, Hawker leaves a calling card, usually a chalk drawing of a hawk's head.

Behind the Scenes

Carl Ramm is the pseudonym of Randy Wayne White. White, under his own name, writes the "Doc" Ford Eco–Adventure Mysteries, which have been often been compared to Travis McGee. White is a former boat captain and tour guide operating out of southwest Florida. He has also written several nonfiction works on his fishing adventures. Under the pen name Randy Striker, White also writes the Dusky MacMorgan series.

The Books

All books were published by Dell Books:

1. *Florida Firefight*, 191 pages, 1984
2. *L.A. Wars*, 188 pages, 1984
3. *Chicago Assault*, 190 pages, 1984
4. *Deadly in New York*, 176 pages, 1984
5. *Houston Attack*, 173 pages, 1985
6. *Vegas Vengeance*, 172 pages, 1985
7. *Detroit Combat*, 173 pages, 1985
8. *Terror in D.C.*, 175 pages, 1986
9. *Atlanta Extreme*, 170 pages, 1986
10. *Denver Strike*, 173 pages, 1986
11. *Operation Norfolk*, 174 pages, 1987

HELL RIDER (JESSE HELLER)

Two books by Dan Killerman

Jesse Heller is a Vietnam veteran who on his return to America became a bounty hunter. When his family and fiancée are killed by the Satan's Avengers Biker gang, he conducts his own investigation and collects evidence to put these men away. When the law does not convict them, Heller takes matters in to his own hands, taking violent revenge on the bikers. The public applaud Heller's war on the bikers, but the police, somewhat embarrassed by how effective his war is, try to arrest him and point out that while just, his actions are illegal. Heller is hunted by Detective Garrett, who also investigated his family's murder.

Garrett and Heller have many discussions on justice and the law. While Garrett points out that society does not allow killing, Heller points that society had no problems giving him a gun and sending him to Vietnam to kill. This is the same society that shunned him and his fellow veterans when they returned from Vietnam and helped create biker gangs like the Satan's Avengers, comprised of disaffected Vietnam veterans unable to return to society. Heller gains his revenge on the people who killed his family but is on the run from their fellow bikers and the police. No longer fighting for revenge, Heller is fighting for his survival against the various rednecks and backwoods sheriffs he encounters on the run.

Behind the Scenes

Dan Killerman is the pen name of Dan Schmidt. Schmidt is the author of a number of horror novels as well as writing several **Executioners** as Don Pendleton and, as Frank Garrett, he wrote the **Killsquad** series.

The Books
Both books were published by Pinnacle:

1. *Hellrider*, 1985
2. *Blood Run*, 168 pages, 1985

HIT MAN (MIKE ROSS)
Eight books by Kirby Carr

By day Mike Ross is a private eye based in Los Angeles but by night he dons his skintight black costume and a hockey mask to eliminate those the system wouldn't allow him to deal with during the day. The Hitman is somewhat unique in the serial vigilante field in that he maintains a secret identity and wears a mask. In many ways, Ross more closely resembles his pulp ancestors, the Shadow and the Whisperer, and comic book cousins Batman and the Adrian Chase version of the Vigilante than other serial vigilantes. The Hitman is a legendary figure only hinted at by the media. The Hitman wages war on crime from his artillery-laden van. Ross in the guise of the Hitman fights murders, cop killers and religious cults with seeming supernatural abilities, cop killers and religious cults

Behind the Scenes
Kirby Carr is the pen name of Kin Platt. Platt, born in 1911, made his break into writing working on the radio shows for George Burns and Jack Benny. He then moved into screenwriting, working for Disney. Platt then moved into comic book both as an artist and writer. His series the Mask, written and drawn for Exciting Comics in the '40s, featured district attorney-turned-vigilante Tony Colby, a character blinded by gangsters who secretly regained his sight and fought crime as the Mask.

After the war Platt moved into humor writing both in comics and animation working on *The Flintstones*, *Yogi Bear* and *The Jetsons* as well as creating Supermouse. Platt also wrote a number of young adult mystery novels, including contributions to the Three Investigator series.

The Books
Books 1–4 were published by Canyon Books. Books 5–8 were published by Major Books:

1. *Who Killed You, Candy Castle?*, 190 pages, 1974
2. *Let Me Kill You, Sweetheart*, 1974
3. *Girls Who Came to Murder*, 1974
4. *You Die Next, Jill Baby*, 191 pages, 1975
5. *They're Coming to Kill You, Jane*, 1975
6. *Don't Bet on Living, Alice*, 1975
7. *You're Hired, You're Dead*, 1975
8. *The Impossible Spy*, 176 pages, 1976

THE HITMAN (DIRK SPENCER)
Three books by Norman Winski

In many ways, this series harks back to the pulp heroes that inspired the serial vigilante genre. While serial vigilantes tend to be ordinary blue-collar types, the pulp heroes were typically rich playboys (**the Spider**, the Shadow, the Phantom Detective, etc.). Dirk, like those pulp heroes, is a wealthy playboy. An electronic genius, he runs a multimillion-dollar company with his father.

Dirk, Cherokee on his father's side, studied at West Point, as well as serving in Vietnam and now crusades against those who escape justice. Like many of the other serial vigilantes, he leaves a calling card (**the Executioner** originally left a marksman medal and **the Penetrator** left a flint arrowhead). In the Hitman's case, it's a glass eye and false teeth signifying an eye for an eye and a tooth for a tooth.

The Hitman tackles neo-Nazis, child pornographers, drugged-out sex cults, drug dealers and others who escape the law. The Hitman is one of the few serial vigilantes to wear a mask; his balaclava forms part of his Hitman outfit. The Hitman also has his red Lamborghini Contach riddled with secret compartments and various devices he finds useful in his fight against crime.

Behind the Scenes

Norman Winski was also the author of the novelization of *The Sword and the Sorcerer* and several works on astrology. Winski was also a member of the Chicago Beat scene and Charles Bukowski (*Barfly*) was godfather to his son.

The Books

All three books were published by Pinnacle Books:

1. *Chicago Deathwinds*, 192 pages, 1984
2. *LA Massacre*, 184 pages, 1984
3. *Nevada Nightmare*, 169 pages, 1984

HOME TEAM
Three books by Dennis Chalker, USN (Ret.), and Kevin Dockery

Serving in Bosnia, Navy SEAL chief Ted "Grim" Reaper disobeyed a direct order from a corrupt superior, Captain Cary Paxtun, and was forced to leave the military or face court martial. After settling into civilian life as a gunsmith with Keith Deckert, a former army sergeant confined to a wheelchair after a racing accident, the pair developed the Jackhammer, an automatic shotgun. Paxtun, now a trusted member of al Qaueda, kidnapped Reaper's wife and son to force him to make a batch of Jackhammers for a terrorist attack. Reaper, not being one to surrender to terrorist demands, formed a small strike force of former special operations personnel consisting of:

• Titus "Bear" Parnell: former SEAL

• Max Warrick: former Marine and sharpshooter

• Ben MacKenzie: Former para-rescue jumper and paramedic

• Enzo Caronti: Special Boat commander

The team rescues Reaper's family and prevents the terrorist attack but with the loss of Bear. The team is about to be arrested when Reaper's old admiral, Alan Straker, intervenes and makes the team a deal. Straker now works for Homeland Security and offers to make the team unofficial consultants and troubleshooters for the department. As part of Homeland Security, the team has since prevented a Mexican drug cartel and terrorists from smuggling a "dirty" nuclear warhead into America and biological weapons from being used in America.

Behind the Scenes

Dennis Chalker rose to the rank of Command Master Chief serving with the SEALs. He was a founding member of SEAL Team Six under Richard Marcinko and later joined Marcinko in Red Cell, the unit that tested the security of naval bases. Chalker gives a brief autobiography in Marcinko's *The Real Team*. Born in Ohio in 1954, Chalker was a three-and-a-half-year veteran in the Army before joining the SEALs. Since his retirement Chalker has joined GSGI, a training and advisory firm. It was this work that landed him a role as a SEAL in the Nicholas Cage–Sean Connery film *The Rock*.

Kevin Dockery is a military historian who co-authored two special-warfare books with Dennis Chalker: *Hell Week: SEALS in Training* and *One Perfect Op: Navy SEAL Special Warfare Teams* as well as writing a documentary on the SEALs which aired on the History Channel.

The Books

All books were published by Avon Books:

1. *Undeclared War*, 392 pages, 2004

2. *Hostile Borders*, 362 pages, 2005

3. *Weapons Grade*, 373 pages, 2006

THE HUNTER (JOHN YARD)

Five books by Ralph Hayes

John Yard is a Vietnam veteran who was able to set himself up as a big-game hunter in Africa, thanks to an inheritance from a rich uncle. He and his friend Moses Ngala, a private investigator, become hunters of men when Maurice Lavelle, owner of Maurice Pharmaceuticals, sells drugs to a friend of Yard's that cause chromosome damage to infants.

After that hunt, Yard and Ngala decide to hunt down men, predators who operate outside the law and cannot be handled by the system, including a former Nazi turned mercenary and a scientist using homeless subjects to test a new supervirus designed for biological warfare. In *A Taste for Blood*, Yard and Ngala are stranded in an African swamp after a plane crash and one of their fellow passengers is a communist assassin wiping out the party one by one. While Yard uncovered the first of their targets, Maurice Lavelle, it is Ngala who uncovers most of their target through his investigations. The pair rationalizes their hunts as a similar service to killing rogue elephants or man-eating lions.

Behind the Scenes

Ralph Hayes was born in 1927 and served in the Air Force 1945–47. After leaving the Air Force, he studied and became a lawyer, specializing in insurance. In 1969, Hayes became a freelance writer, writing a number of travel guides and individual novels as well as the Buffalo Hunter western series and **Stoner, Agent for COMISEC** and **Checkforce** series. Under the Nick Carter house name, he wrote eight **Killmaster** books. Hayes travelled extensively and utilized that experience for his travel guides and the settings for his books (Contemporary Authors Online, 2002).

The Books

All books were published by Leisure Books:

1. *Scavenger Hunt,* 183 pages, 1975
2. *Night of the Jackal,* 179 pages, 1975
3. *A Taste for Blood,* 186 pages, 1975
4. *Track of the Beast,* 1975
5. *Deadly Prey,* 174 pages, 1975

ICEMAN (HENRY HIGHLAND WEST)

Seven books by Joseph Nazel

Henry Highland West grew up in Harlem and through a combination of brains and brawn was able to get out of the ghetto and become a very wealthy man. In the Nevada Desert, West runs the Oasis, a casino resort for the very wealthy. West keeps informed about his guests and their habits with a supercomputer. The man only known as XXL Christmas Tree is the Oasis' head of security and Tree is assisted by West's security force/harem of kung fu explosives experts. These women serve as both West's bodyguards and his lovers. West has the money for the finest equipment so we see him riding in caddys, helicopters, dune buggies and a private jet.

While West is now a successful man, he has not forgotten where he came from and he is always ready to help an old friend. This ranges from stopping the government from selling bad gas in his old neighborhood to travelling to Africa to fight a slavery ring and helping a beautiful singer when she discovers that her record company is controlled by the Syndicate. West's extensive business holdings also offer opportunity as the Mafia attempt to takeover the Oasis and crooked bookies try to ruin West's NFL Gridiron team.

Behind the Scenes

Joseph Nazel is an African-American writer, who served in Vietnam with the Air Force and studied to be a priest. The latter training was put to use in *Black Exorcist,* which is a blaxploitation novel about demon possession. Nazel's output of sixty novels ranged from horror to soft-core porn to biographies of Thurgood Marshall and Ida B. Wells. Later in his career, he served as an editor for *Players Magazine*, an African American version of *Playboy*.

He died at age sixty-two of a brain cancer.

The Books

All books were published by Holloway House Publishing:

1. *Billion Dollar Death*, 192 pages, 1973
2. *Golden Shaft*, 217 pages, 1973
3. *Slick Revenge*, 218 pages, 1973
4. *Sunday Fix*, 221 pages, 1974
5. *Spinning Target*, 224 pages, 1974
6. *Canadian Kill*, 224 pages, 1974
7. *Shakedown*, 221 pages, 1975

THE INQUISITOR (FRANCIS XAVIER KILLEY)

Six books by Simon Quinn

The Catholic Church has a secret order known as Militia Christi. The order conducts inquisitions and intelligence work for the church investigating terrorist threats, satanic cults and other threats to world security. The top operative for Militia Christi is Francis Xavier Killey, a Vietnam veteran and former CIA agent. Killey travels the globe fighting the threats that the Militia Christi assigns him, but Killey is equally likely to encounter threats from his earlier careers and to operate on his own, hunting down rogue soldiers and hunting for Soviet gold. At the end of each exploit Killey must attend confession and recount his adventures and for each life Killey takes he must do ten-day penance in the catacombs with only bread and water.

Behind the Scenes

Simon Quinn is a pen name used by Martin Cruz Smith. Born Martin William Smith in 1942, he legally changed his name to Martin Cruz Smith when he discovered that another Martin Smith was already publishing books. Smith is the author of *Nightwing* (1977) and *Gorky Park* (1981). Prior to the publication of those works, Smith published a number of books under pseudonyms, including the Inquisitor series and contributed to the **Killmaster** series as Nick Carter and the Slocum western series as Jake Logan.

The Books

All books were published by Dell:

1. *His Eminence, Death*, 160 pages, 1974
2. *Nuplex Red*, 192 pages, 1974
3. *Devil in Kansas*, 192 pages, 1974

4. *Last Time I Saw Hell*, 192 pages, 1974
5. *Midas Coffin*, 188 pages, 1975
6. *Last Rites for the Vulture*, 191 pages, 1975

INTERSECT FILES
Two books by John Cannon

International Security Systems, Inc., better known as INTERSECT, was founded in the 1960s by Ronald Vicker, a former World War II Army Ranger and OSS operative with the single goal of the frustration and eradication of terrorism. The men and women of INTERSECT will go anywhere, do anything, at anytime to that end, for a price. As a private organization, INTERSECT is not bound by the same rules and regulations that often frustrate conventional anti-terrorist groups.

Vicker's most potent weapon in the war on terrorism is his elite team consisting of:
- Thomas Drake: former member of Britain's Special Air Service
- Brad Hunter: ex-United States Army Ranger and Black Beret
- Aaron Gold: retired member of Israel' Saiyet Commando Force
- Hans Schroeder: former member of West Germany's GSG 9
- Carlo Galante: trained by Italy's Squadra Anti-commando
- Paul Bouchard: veteran of France's elite Gigene.

These six men, drawn from six of the best anti-terrorist groups in the world, are the team sent in for the most dangerous missions, such as tackling a terrorist alliance striking all over the world or the liberation of a hijacked ocean liner.

Behind the Scenes

John Cannon is the pseudonym used by Mike Newton for this series. Newton trained with Don Pendleton co-writing several **Executioners** with Pendleton for Pinnacle Books and writing numerous books for that series for Gold Eagle, making him the most prolific writer of Executioner novels. Newton has also written several western series under the pen name Lyle Brandt as well as four entries in the **Destroyer** series. Newton is also the author or several nonfiction works, including *How to Write Action-Adventure Fiction*, and several reference works on serial killers and cryptozoology.

The Books

Both books were published by Carousel Adventure Books:

1. *Web of Terror*, 160 pages, 1980
2. *Death Cruise*, 160 pages, 1980

INVASION USA (TOM BRANNON)

Two books by William Johnstone

Tom Brannon had served his country in Vietnam and returned to his hometown Little Tucson, Arizona, and raised his family and opened a small auto parts store. Then the Mexican gang Mara Salvatruca, more commonly known as M-15, decided that Little Tucson would be an ideal location to cross the border and ferry their contraband. Tom couldn't stand by and do nothing so he formed the Patriot Project to stop this corruption of his town after several murders. The Patriot Project patrolled the border with no support from any government department, especially the Border Patrol. This led to a final devastating battle for the town of Little Tucson. After the defeat of M-15, Tom returned to his regular life.

Months after the battle for Little Tucson, Tom's niece Laura from Laredo, Texas, is on a field trip when her class is kidnapped by Los Lobos de la Noche, the Night Wolves, to sell as sexual slaves. But this was merely a diversion by Night Wolves leader Col. Guerrero to cover the kidnapping of his daughter, Angelina. When the American authorities discover that the girls have been taken into Mexico, they abandon them in the interest of good international relations and so Tom forms a small team of the combat veteran parents of the students to rescue the girls. These veterans of the Gulf and Iraq wars are joined by various law enforcement officer and mercenaries.

Behind the Scenes

The series was created by William W. Johnstone, author of numerous horror, adventure and western novels. Johnstone was discharged from the French Foreign Legion for being underage, then worked in a carnival, became a deputy sheriff and did a stint in the Army. He started writing in 1970 but did not make his first sale until 1979 with *The Devil's Kiss*. Johnstone died in 2004 in Shreveport, Louisiana.

The Books

Both books were published by Kensington Pinnacle Books:

1. *Invasion USA* (with Fred Austin), 302 pages, 2006
2. *Invasion USA: Border War* (with J. A. Johnstone), 319 pages, 2006

JASON STRIKER: MASTER OF MARTIAL ARTS

Five books by Piers Anthony and Roberto Fuentes

Jason Striker is a martial arts master who operates his own dojo. Striker leads a quiet life, training his students and preparing them for tournaments, until the day that he is challenged to a match by a renegade Judoka, wanted for murder. The match ends with a draw and Striker is drawn into the seamy side of the martial arts. Striker investigates the murders that Judoka is accused of and discovers that a rival instructor is killing the competition with a death touch.

The murders are being committed so that the killer can win the tournament organized by a Nicaraguan millionaire to find the best martial artist in the world. Striker's star pupil is to attend this tournament but when he is injured in training, Striker takes his place and wins the contest. In winning, Striker discovers that the killer is ninja master Fu Antos and is struck by a death touch. Striker then travels to the island of Hokkaido to find a Ki master who may be able to save him. Attacked by waves of ninja, Striker is able to find the master and be saved. Striker then begins a quest to find and destroy Fu Antos. He travels the world hunting Antos and his minions and fighting to earn money.

Behind the Scenes

Piers Anthony was born in England in 1934 and his family moved to America in 1940, where he became an American citizen. Being British made Anthony something of an outsider, bullied and picked on by bigger children. Anthony's escape was in books and reading, a love that his parents had instilled in him from young age.

After a two-year stint in the Army (1957–59), Anthony went to college, decided to become a writer and started writing and selling short stories. Working primarily in science fiction and fantasy, Anthony is the author several series such as Bio of a Space Tyrant, Xanth, Geodyssey, Cython, Mode and Apprentice Adept.

Roberto Fuentes is a judo instructor and has collaborated with Piers Anthony on several books, including *Dead Morn* and the Jason Striker series.

The Books

All books were published by Berkley Books:

1. *Kia!*, 191 pages, 1974
2. *Mistress of Death*, 192 pages, 1974
3. *Bamboo Bloodbath*, 188 pages, 1974
4. *Ninja's Revenge*, 188 pages, 1975
5. *Amazon Slaughter*, 204 pages, 1976

KILLMASTER (NICK CARTER)

261 books by Nick Carter (Pseudonym)

There have been three incarnations of Nick Carter over the years (for an examination of the earlier two, see Jess Nevin's site http://www.geocities.com/jessnevins/carter.html). The third incarnation is the super spy Nick Carter, the Killmaster. Nicholas J. Huntington Carter served as a soldier in World War II before joining the OSS and then moving to AXE, the super-secret agency that reports only to the National Security Council, Secretary of Defense and the President. Nick Carter gets his missions from David Hawk. Carter is codenamed the Killmaster and is classified N3, AXE's equivalent to James Bond's license to kill, and Carter used that license quite frequently in his missions.

Carter undertakes everything: engaging in counter-espionage, helping defectors to the West, foiling Neo-Nazi plots, foiling Communist agents, killing traitors and stopping assassins. The Killmaster also exterminates religious cults, the Mafia and other threats to America. Carter is as attractive to the ladies as he is deadly and falls into bed with his female companions on his missions. Carter is the master of several martial arts and smokes custom-made cigarettes with his initials embossed on the tube and we discover that his parents were killed by a bomb.

Behind the Scenes

This reinvention of Nick Carter was the brain child of Lyle Kenyon Engel. Engel was behind the creation of a number of series, including **The Baroness**, Blade, **The Butcher**, as well as packaging a number of historical family sagas such as those of Pearl S. Buck and John Jakes. Engel also wrote a number of nonfiction works many of which were about cars and car racing.

Engel founded the fiction factory Book Creations, Inc. (BCI), in 1973. This company conceived books and series, then hired writers to write the books and then sold the publication rights to paperback publishers. Engel passed away in 1986. Control of BCI went to Engel's brother George who ran the company until 1991, when it ceased business.

Prominent authors include:

- Valerie Moolman, the first female writer of serial vigilantes, working with Michael Avallone on the first book in this series and contributing to another ten books. Moolman's other writings have been nonfiction and have included self-help books on sleeping, buying and selling cars and preventing burglary. She is also the author of a Time-Life series, the Epic of Flight.

- Michael Avallone, most famous as author of the private eye Ed Noon as well as writing tie-in novels for the *Man from U.N.C.L.E.*, *I-Spy* and the *Partridge Family* television series. Avallone also wrote several books in **the Butcher** series under the name Stuart Jason.

- Joseph Rosenberger, who became a professional writer at the age of twenty-one after selling an article. After working a series of jobs including Korean karate instructor, circus pitchman and private eye, he became a full-time writer in 1961. Rosenberger was the author of **the Death Merchant, the Murder Master, the Shadow Warrior** and **C.O.B.R.A.** series and, under the pseudonym Lee Chang, created and wrote the first martial arts series **Kung Fu (Mace)**.

- Chet Cunningham, who lives in San Diego. Cunningham has also written numerous western novels both under his own name and under pseudonyms. A veteran of the Korean War, Cunningham has also written several volumes of military history. Cunningham is also the author of **the Avenger** and **the Specialists** series; under the pen name of Lionel Derrick, he wrote The Penetrator. He has also written several **Executioner** and SuperBolan (see Executioner) novels.

- Jon Messmann (1920–2004) initially worked as a writer for Fawcett Comics and worked on Captain Marvel Jr. and Fawcett's western comics as Eric Jon Messmann. Messmann then branched out to crime fiction and westerns. Under the name Jon Sharpe he wrote several novels in the Trailsman and Canyon O'Grady western series. In the serial vigilante field, under his own name, he wrote **the Revenger** (Ben Martin).

- Dan Streib, born in 1928, served in the U.S. Army during the Korean War (1950–53) and died in 1996 of a heart attack. An extensive traveler for both work and pleasure, San Diego based Streib used the locales he visited in his works which include the **Counter Force** series under his own name, **Death Squad** series as Frank Colter, romances under the names of Louise Grandville and Lee Davis Whilloughby, and westerns under the names Jonathan Schofield and J. Faragut Jones.

- Jerry Ahern is the author of the Survivalist and the Defender post apocalyptic series as well as **the Takers** and **Surgical Strike** and under the name Alex Kilgore **(They Call Me) The Mercenary** series. Ahern has also written more than 600 articles for various magazines and is the former president of Deutronics Firearms.

- Ralph Hayes, who was born in 1927 and served in the Air Force 1945–47. After leaving the Air Force he studied and became a lawyer specializing in insurance. In 1969, Hayes became a freelance writer, writing a number of travel guides and individual novels as well as the Buffalo Hunter western series and **Stoner, Agent for COMISEC** and **Checkforce** series. Under the Nick Carter house name he wrote eight **Killmaster** books. Hayes travelled extensively and utilized that experience for his travel guides and the settings for his books.

- Martin Cruz Smith, born Martin William Smith in 1942, legally changed his name to Martin Cruz Smith when he discovered that another Martin Smith was already publishing books. Smith is the author of *Nightwing* (1977) and *Gorky Park* (1981). Prior to the publication of those works Smith published a number of books under pseudonyms, including **the Inquisitor** series, and contributed to the Killmaster series as Nick Carter and the Slocum western series as Jake Logan.

The Books

Award Books published books 1 to 112; Charter books published books 113 to 227; Jove books, 228 to 261:

1. *Run, Spy, Run*, 158 pages, 1964 (Michael Avallone, Val Moolman)
2. *The China Doll*, 158 pages, 1964 (Avallone, Moolman)
3. *Checkmate in Rio*, 158 pages, 1964 (Moolman)
4. *Safari for Spies*, 158 pages, 1964 (Moolman)
5. *Fraulein Spy*, 157 pages, 1964 (Moolman)
6. *Saigon*, 157 pages, 1964 (Avallone, Moolman)
7. *A Bullet for Fidel*, 159 pages, 1965 (Moolman)
8. *The Thirteenth Spy*, 159 pages, 1965 (Moolman)
9. *The Eyes of the Tiger*, 156 pages, 1965 (Manning Lee Stokes)
10. *Istanbul*, 155 pages, 1965 (Stokes)
11. *Web of Spies*, 156 pages, 1966 (Stokes)
12. *Spy Castle*, 156 pages, 1966 (Stokes)
13. *The Terrible Ones*, 157 pages, 1966 (Stokes)
14. *Dragon Flame*, 156 pages, 1966 (Stokes)

15. *Hanoi*, 156 pages, 1966 (Moolman)
16. *Danger Key*, 156 pages, 1966 (Lew Louderback)
17. *Operation Starvation*, 158 pages, 1966 (Nicholas Browne)
18. *The Mind Poisoners*, 157 pages, 1966 (Lionel White, Moolman)
19. *The Weapon of Night*, 160 pages, 1967 (Moolman)
20. *The Golden Serpent*, 158 pages, 1967 (Stokes)
21. *The Red Guard*, 156 pages, 1967 (Stokes)
22. *Double Identity*, 159 pages, 1967 (Stokes)
23. *Devil's Cockpit*, 158 pages, 1967 (Stokes)
24. *Chinese Paymaster*, 157 pages, 1967 (Browne)
25. *Seven Against Greece*, 158 pages, 1967 (Browne)
26. *Korean Tiger*, 160 pages, 1967 (Stokes)
27. *Assignment Israel*, 159 pages, 1967 (Stokes)
28. *Mission to Venice*, 156 pages, 1967 (Stokes)
29. *Filthy Five*, 160 pages, 1967 (Stokes)
30. *Bright Blue Death*, 160 pages, 1967 (Browne)
31. *Macao*, 157 pages, 1968 (Stokes)
32. *Operation Moon Rocket*, 160 pages, 1968 (Louderback)
33. *Judas Spy*, 155 pages, 1968 (Lawrence Rohde)
34. *Hood of Death*, 155 pages, 1968 (Rohde)
35. *Amsterdam*, 156 pages, 1968 (Rohde)
36. *Temple of Fear*, 186 pages, 1968 (Stokes)
37. *Fourteen Seconds to Death*, 154 pages, 1968 (Jon Messmann)
38. *The Defector*, 156 pages, 1968 (George Snyder)
39. *Carnival for Killing*, 154 pages, 1968 (Messmann)
40. *Rhodesia*, 156 pages, 1968 (Rohde)
41. *Red Rays*, 153 pages, 1969 (Stokes)
42. *Peking/The Tulip Affair*, 154 pages, 1969 (Arnold Marmor)
43. *The Amazon*, 156 pages, 1969 (Messmann)
44. *The Sea Trap*, 156 pages, 1969 (Messmann)
45. *Berlin*, 155 pages, 1969 (Messmann)
46. *The Human Time Bomb*, 154 pages, 1969 (Rohde)
47. *The Cobra Kill*, 154 pages, 1969 (Stokes)
48. *Living Death*, 153 pages, 1969 (Messmann)
49. *Operation Che Guevara*, 154 pages, 1969 (Messmann)
50. *Black Death*, 154 pages, 1969 (Stokes)
51. *Doomsday Formula*, 150 pages, 1969 (Messmann)
52. *Operation Snake*, 187 pages, 1969 (Messmann)

53. *Casbah Killers*, 155 pages, 1969 (Messmann)
54. *Arab Plague/Slavemaster*, 156 pages, 1970 (Messmann)
55. *Red Rebellion*, 155 pages, 1970 (Messmann)
56. *Executioners*, 155 pages, 1970 (Messmann)
57. *Mind Killers*, 151 pages, 1970 (Messmann)
58. *Time Clock of Death*, 157 pages, 1970 (Snyder)
59. *Cambodia*, 154 pages, 1970 (Snyder)
60. *The Death Strain*, 156 pages, 1970 (Messmann)
61. *Moscow*, 155 pages, 1970 (Snydern)
62. *Jewel of Doom*, 156 pages, 1970 (Snyder)
63. *Ice Bomb Zero*, 156 pages, 1971 (Snyder)
64. *Mark of the Cosa Nostra*, 154 pages, 1971 (Snyder)
65. *Cairo Mafia*, 154 pages, 1972 (Ralph Hayes)
66. *Inca Death Squad*, 169 pages, 1972 (Smith)
67. *Assault on England*, 156 pages, 1972 (Hayes)
68. *Omega Terror*, 156 pages, 1972 (Hayes)
69. *Code Name: Werewolf*, 167 pages, 1973 (Smith)
70. *Strike Force Terror*, 186 pages, 1972 (Hayes)
71. *Target Doomsday Island*, 187 pages, 1973 (Richard Hubbard)
72. *Night of the Avenger*, 186 pages, 1973 (Chet Cunningham, Dan Streib)
73. *Butcher of Belgrade*, 186 pages, 1973 (Hayes, Larry Powell)
74. *Assassination Brigade*, 154 pages, 1973 (Thomas Chastain)
75. *Liquidator*, 186 pages, 1973 (Hubbard)
76. *The Devil's Dozen*, 184 pages, 1973 (Martin Cruz Smith)
77. *Code*, 183 pages, 1973 (Powell)
78. *Agent Counter Agent*, 184 pages, 1973 (Hayes)
79. *Hour of the Wolf*, 189 pages, 1973 (Jeffrey Miner Wallman)
80. *Our Agent in Rome Is Missing*, 187 pages, 1973 (Al Hine)
81. *Kremlin File*, 184 pages, 1973 (Willis Todhunter Ballard)
82. *Spanish Connection*, 200 pages, 1973 (Bruce Cassiday)
83. *The Death's Head Conspiracy*, 187 pages, 1973 (Colby)
84. *Peking Dossier*, 186 pages, 1973 (Stewart)
85. *Ice Trap Terror*, 172 pages, 1974 (Wallmann)
86. *Assassin Code Name Vulture*, 170 pages, 1974 (Hayes)
87. *Massacre in Milan*, 188 pages, 1974 (Hine)
88. *Vatican Vendetta*, 150 pages, 1974 (Hayes)
89. *Sign of the Cobra*, 171 pages, 1974 (James Fritzhand)
90. *The Man Who Sold Death*, 203 pages, 1974 (Lawrence Van Gelder)

91. *N Three Conspiracy*, 188 pages, 1974 (Dennis Lynds)

92. *Death of the Falcon*, 187 pages, 1974 (Jim Bowser)

93. *Beirut Incident*, 185 pages, 1974 (Forrest Perrin)

94. *Aztec Avenger*, 204 pages, 1974 (Saul Wernick)

95. *Jerusalem File*, 191 pages, 1975 (Linda Stewart)

96. *Counterfeit Agent*, 203 pages, 1975 (Douglas Marland)

97. *Six Bloody Summer Days*, 170 pages, 1975 (De Witt Copp)

98. *Z Document*, 169 pages, 1975 (Homer Morris)

99. *Kathmandu Document*, 171 pages, 1975 (Fritzhand)

100. *Dr. Death*, 365 pages, 1975 (Craig Nova) (reprints: *Run, Spy, Run* and *The Preposterous Theft* (one of the Victorian-era Nick Carter novels)

101. *Ultimate Code*, 172 pages, 1975 (William Odell)

102. *Assignment Intercept*, 170 pages, 1976 (Marilyn Henderson)

103. *Green Wolf Connection*, 171 pages, 1976 (Dennis Lynds)

104. *Death Message/Oil Seventy Four Two*, 171 pages, 1976 (Dee Stuart, Ansel Chapin)

105. *The List*, 170 pages, 1976 (Fritzhand)

106. *Fanatics of Al Asad*, 170 pages, 1976 (Wernick)

107. *Snake Flag Conspiracy*, 175 pages, 1976 (Wernick)

108. *Turncoat*, 170 pages, 1976 (Leon Lazarus)

109. *Sign of the Prayer Shawl*, 170 pages, 1976 (Hasberg)

110. *Vulcan Disaster*, 187 pages, 1976 (Warren)

111. *High Yield in Death*, 171 pages, 1976 (Bowser)

112. *The Nichochev Plot*, 206 pages, 1976 (Nova)

113. *Triple Cross*, 202 pages, 1976 (Lynds)

114. *Gallagher Plot*, 200 pages, 1976 (Wernick)

115. *Plot for the Fourth Reich*, 200 pages, 1977 (Bob Latona)

116. *Revenge of the Generals*, 194 pages, 1978 (Wernick)

117. *Under the Wall*, 186 pages, 1978 (Copp)

118. *Ebony Cross*, 191 pages, 1978 (Jack Canon)

119. *Deadly Doubles*, 184 pages, 1978 (Van Gelder)

120. *Race of Death*, 218 pages, 1978 (Hagberg)

121. *Trouble in Paradise*, 178 pages, 1978 (Steeley)

122. *The Pamplona Affair*, 212 pages, 1978 (Stuart, Chapin)

123. *Doomsday Spore*, 242 pages, 1979 (Warren)

124. *Asian Mantrap*, 252 pages, 1979 (Odell)

125. *Thunderstrike in Syria*, 184 pages, 1979 (Joseph Rosenberger)

126. *Redolmo Affair*, 184 pages, 1979 (Canon)

127. *Jamaican Exchange*, 183 pages, 1979 (Lazarus)

128. *Tropical Death Pact*, 242 pages, 1979 (Stokesberry)
129. *Pemex Chart*, 175 pages, 1979 (Dwight Vreeland Swain)
130. *Hawaii*, 207 pages, 1979 (Daniel Prince)
131. *The Satan Trap*, 216 pages, 1979 (Jack Canon)
132. *Reich Four*, 202 pages, 1979 (Frederick Vincent Huber)
133. *The Nowhere Weapon*, 238 pages, 1979 (Odell)
134. *Strike of the Hawk*, 276 pages, 1980 (Gilmore)
135. *Day of the Dingo*, 248 pages, 1980 (John Stevenson)
136. *And Next the King*, 248 pages, 1980 (Steve Simmons)
137. *Tarantula Strike*, 171 pages, 1980 (Dan Reardon)
138. *Ten Times Dynamite*, 212 pages, 1980 (Frank Adduci)
139. *Eight Card Stud*, 142 pages, 1980 (Robert Edward Vardeman)
140. *Suicide Seat*, 217 pages, 1980 (George Warren)
141. *Death Mission Havana*, 184 pages, 1980 (Ron Felber)
142. *War from the Clouds*, 217 pages, 1980 (Gilmore)
143. *Turkish Bloodbath*, 215 pages, 1980 (Jerry Ahern)
144. *Coyote Connection*, 194 pages, 1981 (Bill Crider, Jack Davis)
145. *Q Man*, 217 pages, 1981 (Stevenson)
146. *Society of Nine*, 218 pages, 1981 (Canon)
147. *Ouster Conspiracy*, 213 pages, 1981 (Hagberg)
148. *Golden Bull*, 195 pages, 1981 (Stevenson)
149. *Dubrovnick Massacre*, 247 pages, 1981 (Rasof, Williamson)
150. *Solar Menace*, 215 pages, 1981 (Vardeman)
151. *Strontium Code*, 214 pages, 1981 (Hagberg)
152. *Pleasure Island*, 242 pages, 1981 (Robert Randisi)
153. *Cauldron of Hell*, 203 pages, 1981 (Mike Jahn)
154. *Parisian Affair*, 199 pages, 1981 (Ed Hunsberger)
155. *Chessmaster*, 209 pages, 1982 (Randisi)
156. *The Last Samurai*, 200 pages, 1982 (Algozini)
157. *The Puppet Master*, 222 pages, 1982 (Hagberg)
158. *Norwegian Typhoon*, 212 pages, 1982 (Vardeman)
159. *Damocles Threat*, 226 pages, 1982 (Hagberg)
160. *Dominican Affair*, 210 pages, 1982 (Algozin)
161. *Deathlight*, 212 pages, 1982 (Ahern)
162. *Israeli Connection*, 180 pages, 1982 (Steeley)
163. *Treason Game*, 209 pages, 1982 (Gilmore)
164. *Earth Shaker*, 198 pages, 1982 (Vardeman)
165. *Hunter*, 198 pages, 1982 (Hagberg)

166. *Operation McMurdo Sound*, 208 pages, 1982 (Hagberg)
167. *Appointment in Haiphong*, 209 pages, 1982 (Hagberg)
168. *Retreat for Death*, 216 pages, 1982 (Hagberg)
169. *Mendoza Manuscript*, 209 pages, 1982 (Randisi)
170. *Death Star Affair*, 226 pages, 1982 (Canon)
171. *Doctor DNA*, 196 pages, 1982 (Vardeman)
172. *Christmas Kill*, 213 pages, 1983 (Gilmore)
173. *Greek Summit*, 196 pages, 1983 (Randisi)
174. *Outback Ghosts*, 181 pages, 1983 (Vardeman)
175. *Hide and Go Die*, 196 pages, 1983 (Canon)
176. *Kali Death Cult*, 177 pages, 1983 (Vardeman)
177. *Operation Vendetta*, 198 pages, 1983 (Gilmore)
178. *Yukon Target*, 198 pages, 1983 (Vardeman)
179. *Death Dealer*, 195 pages, 1983 (Canon)
180. *Istanbul Decision*, 191 pages, 1983 (Hagberg)
181. *Decoy Hit*, 200 pages, 1983 (Randisi)
182. *Earthfire North*, 194 pages, 1983 (Hagberg)
183. *Budapest Run*, 193 pages, 1983 (Canon)
184. *Caribbean Coup*, 195 pages, 1983 (Randisi)
185. *Algarve Affair*, 195 pages, 1984 (Canon)
186. *Zero Hour Strike Force*, 195 pages, 1984 (Hagberg)
187. *Operation Sharkbite*, 195 pages, 1984 (Canon)
188. *Death Island*, 194 pages, 1984 (Hargberg)
189. *Night of the Warheads*, 194 pages, 1984 (Canon)
190. *Day of the Mahdi*, 198 pages, 1984 (Gayle Lynds)
191. *Assignment Rio*, 195 pages, 1984 (Canon)
192. *Death Hand Play*, 193 pages, 1984 (Hagberg)
193. *The Kremlin Kill*, 194 pages, 1984 (Canon)
194. *The Mayan Connection*, 194 pages, 1984 (Lynds)
195. *San Juan Inferno*, 197 pages, 1984 (Gilmore)
196. *Circle of Scorpions*, 195 pages, 1985 (Canon)
197. *Blue Ice Affair*, 195 pages, 1985 (Felber)
198. *Macao Massacre*, 187 pages, 1985 (Canon)
199. *Pursuit of the Eagle*, 199 pages, 1985 (Lynds)
200. *Vengeance Game*, 157 pages, 1985 (Hagberg)
201. *Last Flight to Moscow*, 193 pages, 1985 (Gilmore)
202. *The Normandy Code*, 189 pages, 1985 (Canon)
203. *White Death*, 197 pages, 1985 (Lynds)

204. *Assassin Convention*, 192 pages, 1985 (Gilmore)
205. *Blood of the Scimitar*, 196 pages, 1985 (Canon)
206. *Execution Exchange*, 198 pages, 1985 (Lynds)
207. *Tarlov Cipher*, 181 pages, 1985 (Canon)
208. *Target Red Star*, 192 pages, 1986 (Canon)
209. *Killing Ground*, 189 pages, 1986 (Hagberg)
210. *Berlin Target*, 177 pages, 1986 (Canon)
211. *Mercenary Mountain*, 193 pages, 1986 (Lynds)
212. *Blood Ultimatum*, 165 pages, 1986 (Felber)
213. *Cyclops Conspiracy*, 195 pages, 1986 (Canon)
214. *Tunnel for Traitors*, 190 pages, 1986 (Canon)
215. *Samurai Kill*, 200 pages, 1986 (Lynds)
216. *Terror Times Two*, 196 pages, 1986 (Canon)
217. *Death Orbit*, 195 pages, 1986 (Hagberg)
218. *Slaughter Day*, 192 pages, 1986 (Canon)
219. *The Master Assassin*, 194 pages, 1986 (Lynds)
220. *Operation Petrograd*, 195 pages, 1986 (Hagberg)
221. *Crossfire Red*, 194 pages, 1987 (Canon)
222. *Blood of the Falcon*, 193 pages, 1987 (Lynds)
223. *The Death Squad*, 200 pages, 1987 (Canon)
224. *The Terror Code*, 191 pages, 1987 (Canon)
225. *Holy War*, 189 pages, 1987
226. *Blood Raid*, 1987 (Canon)
227. *East of Hell*, 195 pages, 1987 (Garside)
228. *Killing Games*, 198 pages, 1987 (Canon)
229. *Terms of Vengeance*, 199 pages, 1987 (Canon)
230. *Pressure Point*, 190 pages, 1987 (Garside)
231. *Night of the Condor*, 200 pages, 1987
232. *The Poseidon Target*, 192 pages, 1987 (Canon)
233. *The Andropov File*, 190 pages, 1988 (Garside)
234. *Dragonfire*, 195 pages, 1988
235. *Blood Trail to Mecca*, 200 pages, 1988 (Canon)
236. *Deathstrike*, 191 pages, 1988
237. *Lethal Prey*, 195 pages, 1988 (Garside)
238. *Spykiller*, 195 pages, 1988 (Canon)
239. *Bolivian Hunt*, 153 pages, 1988 (Canon)
240. *Rangoon Man*, 192 pages, 1988 (Canon)
241. *Code Name Cobra*, 194 pages, 1988 (Canon)

242. *Afghan Intercept*, 198 pages, 1988 (Garside)
243. *Countdown to Armageddon*, 197 pages, 1988 (Canon)
244. *Black Sea Bloodbath*, 198 pages, 1988 (Garside)
245. *Deadly Diva*, 198 pages, 1988 (Canon)
246. *Invitation to Death*, 197 pages, 1989 (Canon)
247. *Day of the Assassin*, 196 pages, 1989 (Canon)
248. *Korean Kill*, 197 pages, 1989 (Canon)
249. *Middle East Massacre*, 197 pages, 1989 (Canon)
250. *Sanction to Slaughter*, 194 pages, 1989 (Garside)
251. *Holiday in Hell*, 198 pages, 1989 (Canon)
252. *Law of the Lion*, 194 pages, 1989
253. *Hong Kong Hit*, 189 pages, 1989 (Canon)
254. *Deep Sea Death*, 198 pages, 1989 (Garside)
255. *Arms of Vengeance*, 191 pages, 1989
256. *Hell Bound Express*, 199 pages, 1989 (Canon)
257. *Isle of Blood*, 198 pages, 1990 (Canon)
258. *Singapore Sling*, 194 pages, 1990 (Garside)
259. *Ruby Red Death*, 198 pages, 1990 (Garside)
260. *Arctic Abduction*, 197 pages, 1990 (Garside)
261. *Dragon Slay*, 195 pages, 1990 (Canon)
    The books began numbering with book 181.

The Movies

Since the launching of the Killmaster series in 1964, there have been three Nick Carter movies. The first two were made in France and starred Eddie Constantine as Nick Carter in *Nick Carter va tout casser* (*License to Kill*) (1964) and *Nick Carter et le Trefle Rougue* (*Nick Carter and the Red Gang*) (1965) and were based on the French Nick Carter pulp novels based on the pulp incarnation of Nick Carter. The 1972 television movie *The Adventures of Nick Carter* starred Robert Conrad as Nick Carter and was based on the original dime novel incarnation of Nick Carter. There have been no movies based on the Killmaster novels.

KILLSQUAD

Ten books by Frank Garrett

CIA agent John Smith, code-named Hangman, envisioned a super-secret anti-terrorist strike team of expendable soldiers code-named Killsquad. This six-man assault force was drawn not from the military but rather from death row. Hangman Smith reviewed many hundreds of dossiers and criminal records before he decided on his team:

- Leroy "Lightning Bomber" Walker: This heavyweight boxer was on the path to the championship when he discovered that his manager and promoter had ripped him off. Fuelled by cocaine, his rage was such that he killed three people. An all-white jury sentenced the black boxer to the electric chair.

- Rollo "Ice Pick" Barnes: A Harlem hit man, Barnes eliminated any competition with an ice pick. This was so effective that Barnes' Black Murder, Inc., had successfully kept La Cosa Nostra out of his territory and Barnes had eliminated fifty rivals. Eventually, one of Barnes' cronies turned him over to the law in revenge for Barnes' sleeping with his wife. Barnes was sentenced to death row.

- Tommy Williams: A career criminal, Williams' scar-faced, one-eyed visage made him famous as "the One-Eyed Pirate" during his four-year robbery and murder spree. Each robbery was conducted with military precision. When the law caught up with him, the resulting stand-off had Williams riddled with bullets. The wounds had only just healed enough for Williams to be executed before the Hangman snatched him from death row.

- Mac White: The mountain-sized former Klansman, White left the Klan after six months as he also hated his fellow Klansmen. Eventually, White fought against the Klan when they took a black family hostage. White, the perfect killing machine, wiped out his former colleagues.

- James Jackson: the odd man out in this crew, this father of ten found that commercial fishing didn't pay enough and he turned to drug smuggling. After ditching a load of cocaine to rescue a shipwrecked fishing crew, the drug lords framed Jackson for the murder of three agents and sent him to the electric chair.

- Lucien Schnell: This German-born soldier of fortune took his love of killing to any part of the world that allowed him free reign: South Africa, Southeast Asia, Central America. This crewcut, blonde-haired and blue-eyed mercenary's father and uncle served in the Gestapo, responsible for the slaughter of Jewish and Polish prisoners in Nazi Germany. Schnell's hunt for his family led him to kill several West German Nazi hunters and to a rape and murder spree across ten states in America.

This dirty half-dozen confront the hardest and dirtiest missions that the CIA can throw at them, tackling jihadist terrorists, religious zealots, and other threats to national security.

Behind the Scenes

Frank Garrett is the pseudonym of Dan Schmidt, the author of a number of horror novels and the **Eagle Force** series as well as several **Executioners** as Don Pendleton.

The Books

All books were published by Avon Books:

1. *Counter Attack*, 180 pages, 1986
2. *Mission Revenge*, 167 pages, 1986
3. *Lethal Assault*, 165 pages, 1986
4. *Judas Soldiers*, 169 pages, 1987

5. *Blood Beach*, 164 pages, 1987
6. *Body Count*, 154 pages, 1987
7. *Polar Assault*, 169 pages, 1987
8. *Slaughter Zone*, 154 pages, 1987
9. *Devil's Island*, 153 pages, 1987
10. *Mob War*, 152 pages, 1988

K'ING KUNG FU (CHONG FEI K'ING)

Seven books by Marshall Macao

Prior to Pearl Harbor, a number of American volunteers went and joined the war, know officially as the American Volunteer Group and unofficially as the Flying Tigers. These aviators fought the Japanese. It was in 1941 that a hawk-nosed member of the Flying Tigers met Lin Fong, who at the age of sixty was the world's greatest master of kung fu.

The pair became friends and Chong Fei K'ing, the Flying Tiger's son, eventually came to be raised by Lin Fong and trained in kung fu. Later, Lin Fong took another student, Kak Nan Tang. The pair trained in the martial arts with their master but Kak became seduced by the Red Circle, the dark and evil cult of martial artists bent on taking over the world. Kak killed Lin Fong and fought K'ing to a standstill. The pair chased each other around the world with K'ing vowing to slay his master's murderer.

K'ing's hunt brought him allies such as the beautiful Sun Lee Fong, who later becomes his wife, and the Moor, another martial arts master who continues K'ing's training inducting him into the Blue Circle.

K'ing battles Red Circle plots such as drug running, slavery, war mongering and fermenting racial violence.

Behind the Scenes

Marshall Macao is a pen name used by Thaddeus Tuleja (born 1941). Tuleja is a freelance author who has penned books on language, song lyrics and self-help, gaining a reputation as a quick and efficient writer able to meet deadlines.

The Books

All books were published by Freeway Press:

1. *Son of the Flying Tiger*, 188 pages, 1973
2. *Return of the Opium Wars*, 189 pages, 1973
3. *Rape of Sun Lee Fong*, 187 pages, 1974
4. *Kak-Abdullah Conspiracy*, 197 pages, 1974
5. *Red Plague in Bolivia*, 178 pages, 1975
6. *New York Necromancy*, 180 pages, 1975
7. *Mark of the Vulture*, 186 pages, 1975

KUNG FU (MACE)

Eight books by Lee Chang (1–6) and C. K. Fong (7–8)

Victor George Mace Sr., an American who served in Communist China during the Korean War and married a Chinese girl, Su Li Nai, died at the hands of the Communist Chinese government while aiding refugees from a giant concentration camp in China to Hong Kong. Victor Jr. was less that a year old when his father died. Two years later, Su Li Nai married Po Wa Hong, who sent his stepson to the Shao Lin temple to be trained in the martial arts.

At age twenty-five and completely trained in kung fu, aikido, karate, savate, tai chi, ninjitsu and other martial arts, the slender 6'2" martial artist travelled to visit his uncle in New York City. Discovering the crime and corruption in Chinatown, the young man cleaned up the vicious elements. He was then offered the chance to work with the CIA to help them with their problems. These missions took him all over the world, using his martial arts skill to follow Pi Tuh-t'l-tu, the kung fu principal of justice. In doing so Mace tracks down moles, stops viral attacks, avenges the death of friends and foils the spread of communism.

Behind the Scenes

This series was one of the first kung fu series. Lee Chang was the pseudonym of Joseph Rosenberger, who also wrote **The Death Merchant, Murder Master** and **C.O.B.R.A.** series.

Leonard Levinson also used the Lee Chang pen name for this series. Levinson born in 1935 served the US Army from 1954 to 1957. Under a number of pseudonyms and house names, he has contributed to a number of series, including **Bronson, Butler, the Sharpshooter** and **the Sexecutioner.**

C. K. Fong was the pseudonym of Bruce Cassidy. Cassidy, who was born in 1920, started writing for the pulp magazines and wrote many stories that appeared in the pulps; he contributed *The Spanish Connection* to **the Killmaster** series and, under the pen name of Carson Bingham, wrote several of the Phantom novels that appeared in the 1970s based on the newspaper strip.

The Books

All books were published by Manor Books

1. *The Year of the Tiger*, 219 pages, 1973 (Rosenberger)
2. *The Year of the Snake*, 189 pages, 1974 (Rosenberger)
3. *The Year of the Rat*, 192 pages, 1974 (Rosenberger)
4. *The Year of the Dragon*, 192 pages, 1974 (Rosenberger)
5. *The Year of the Horse*, 192 pages, 1974 (Rosenberger)
6. *The Year of the Boar*, 190 pages, 1975 (Levinson)
7. *The Year of the Cock*, 222 pages, 1975 (Cassidy)
8. *The Year of the Ape*, 186 pages, 1975 (Cassidy)

LINCOLN BLACKTHORNE
Four books by Geoffrey Marsh

Lincoln Blackthorne is the tailor for the sleepy town of Iverness, New Jersey. The tailor business made enough to keep afloat and keep Blackthorne busy. But what his clients never knew or suspected was that Lincoln Blackthorne was more than a tailor. Blackthorne's secret is known only to three people: Macon and Palmer Crowley and Old Alice. All three are over fifty and live vicariously through their adventurer friend, but they also serve the purpose of an early warning system, keeping Blackthorne informed of any suspicious activity in town. Blackthorne, or "Blackie" to his friends, travels through the secret door in his shop and begins his true vocation of treasure hunter and international soldier of fortune.

Blackthorne is one of the best in the business and is frequently hired to locate rare artifacts such as cursed jeweled playing cards, relics believed to have curative powers and other mystical items. These quests take Blackthorne all over the world and Blackthorne is in competition to retrieve these items.

Behind the Scenes

Geoffrey Marsh was born in England and served in the Black Watch during World War II. After a family tragedy prevented him from completing his religious studies at Trinity College (Cambridge), he emigrated to the United States and taught literature at a New Jersey private school.

Or so the author biography would have us believe. In truth, Geoffrey Marsh is the pen name of Charles L. Grant. Grant was born in New Jersey in 1942. He studied at Trinity College (Hartford) and started a career as a teacher of English, drama and history in the New Jersey public school system in 1964. After serving in Vietnam as an Army military police officer (1968–70) and receiving a bronze star, he returned to teaching but left in 1974 to pursue writing. Grant is considered the master of quiet horror and, under his own name, wrote the Greystone Bay series and several original tie-in novels for the X Files. Under several pseudonyms, Grant has written Gothic romances and horror parodies. Under the Marsh pen name, Grant also wrote the novelization for Hudson Hawk.

The Books

All books were published by Tor Books:

1. *The King of Satan's Eyes*, 281 pages, 1984
2. *The Tail of the Arabian Knight*, 278 pages, 1986
3. *Patch of the Odin Soldier*, 182 pages, 1987
4. *Fangs of the Hooded Demon*, 281 pages, 1988

THE LIQUIDATOR (JAKE BRAND)
Five books by R. L. Brent

Jake Brand was a tough Miami cop until his investigations into the Mafia got too close. The Mafia then killed his father and brother and framed Brand for murders he didn't commit. On the run from the police he used to work with and his name disgraced, Brand swore revenge against the Mafia. Unfettered by the rules and outside the system, Brand is taking down the Mafia one mobster at a time.

This war on the Mafia makes Brand the target of hit men and he has to not only elude the police but these vicious killers out to collect the price on his head. Brand also disrupts any Mafia activity he uncovers, from smashing major narcotics rings by invading their headquarters to attacking prostitution and pornography rings. In his final adventure, Brand is approached by the man due to become the next United States Attorney General who is being pressured by the Mafia to drop a pending case as they have kidnapped the future AG's estranged daughter. Brand is offered a deal—find the missing daughter and Brand will be given amnesty and a new identity.

Behind the Scenes

R. L. Brent is a pseudonym used by Larry Powell. Under the Nick Carter house name he wrote two books for the **Killmaster** series and co-wrote one of the **Able Team** novels as Dick Stivers. Under the pen name Lee Parker he wrote the Donovan's Devils series. Powell was also the author a number of western short stories that appeared in *Zane Grey's Western Magazine*.

The Books

All books were published by Award Books:

1. *Liquidator*, 186 pages, 1974
2. *Contract for a Killing*, 185 pages, 1974
3. *Cocaine Connection*, 188 pages, 1974
4. *Invitation to a Strangling*, 186 pages, 1975
5. *The Exchange*, 188 pages, 1978

LONE WOLF (BURTON WULFF)

Fourteen books by Mike Barry (Barry N. Malzberg)

Burton Wulff was a decorated Vietnam veteran who, after his return to America, became a New York narcotics police officer. The same skills that he employed in the Vietnam War he brought to the war on drugs.

Wulff's no-nonsense and incorruptible policing did not sit well with the politically minded members of the police force and Wulff was demoted back to patrolling the streets in a patrol car with a rookie partner, a young black officer, David Williams.

It was during Wulff's first ride with his new partner that he received an anonymous tip about the location of the body of a drug overdose. Upon arrival Wulff discovers that the overdose isn't an ordinary junkie but the body of his fiancée, Marie Calvante. Convinced that she was killed by corrupt cops and the drug barons, Wulff quit the police then and there and started the personal war on drug.

Beginning with two low-level drug dealers, Wulff works his way through the drug supply chain. His only ally in this new war is his new partner Williams. After cleaning up New York, Wulff travelled America, bringing his drug war to the drug barons following the clues that he discovered in earlier battles; in one case he follows a corrupt New York narcotics officer to Las Vegas. In Wulff's final exploit, Mike Barry brings the series to conclusion with Wulff descending into a full psychosis, travelling from bar to bar, shoot patrons because they might be involved in the drug trade, forcing David Williams to shoot and kill him.

Behind the Scenes

Mike Barry is the pseudonym of science fiction author Barry Malzberg. Malzberg was initially a writer of literary short stories before the discovery that the shrinking market for these stories were not lucrative enough to support him. The expanding science fiction market could, on the other hand, support a productive writer and Malzberg turned his energies to that market. Malzberg has several themes that run through his work such as the state of the science fiction and how it has failed to fulfill the task of telling us how to save ourselves from perdition. For Malzberg, bureaucracy and corruption are virtually synonyms, with his novels *Beyond Apollo* and *Revelations* (both 1972) being damning indictments of the American government's handling of the space program.

The Lone Wolf novels can be seen as an example of this theme. In the collection of essays *Breakfast in the Ruins* (2007), Malzberg discusses the Lone Wolf series in the essay "Some Notes on The Lone Wolf" (pp. 295–298). Malzberg reveals the original name of the Lone Wolf was to be Wulff Conlan but it was too close to the name of a publisher and had to be changed. Since the 1990s, Malzberg has stopped writing novels and has turned to the short story. He has over 300 to his credit.

The Books

All books were published by Berkley:

1. *Night Raider*, 192 pages, 1973
2. *Bay Prowler*, 192 pages, 1973
3. *Boston Avenger*, 192 pages, 1973
4. *Desert Stalker*, 192 pages, 1974
5. *Havana Hit*, 192 pages, 1974
6. *Chicago Slaughter*, 192 pages, 1974
7. *Peruvian Nightmare*, 189 pages, 1974
8. *Los Angeles Holocaust*, 192 pages, 1974
9. *Miami Marauder*, 186 pages, 1974
10. *Harlem Showdown*, 186 pages, 1975
11. *Detroit Massacre*, 186 pages, 1975
12. *Phoenix Inferno*, 186 pages, 1975
13. *Killing Run*, 186 pages, 1975
14. *Philadelphia Blowup*, 185 pages, 1975

MALKO /SAS (PRINCE MALKO LINGE)

171 books by Gerard De Villiers

Son altesse serenissime (His Serene Highness) Malko Linge is an Austrian prince who is a freelance operative for the CIA. Initially reluctant to work for any intelligence agency, his need for money to restore his castle in Austria eventually overcame this and the fees from the high-risk freelance operations allow Malko to pay for the restoration. Initially residing in America, Malko moved permanently into his castle after the repairs had reached a certain stage.

The prince is an Olympic athlete, having represented Austria in several games competing in combat shooting events, preferring his personal Luger or the latest model Beretta 9mm. At 6'1", with blonde hair and golden brown eyes, Malko has no trouble attracting female attention, a trait that he frequently exploits in his missions.

As an Austrian prince, Malko is a member of the jet set and has friends in the diplomatic and journalistic circles. This playboy image allows Malko to travel around the world unsuspected and his European heritage allows him access to places and people that an American agent might not be able to access. These factors allow Malko to be a highly successful operative.

Malko's code name with the CIA is SAS, play on both his title and the British Special Air Service. Malko has been involved in nearly two hundred missions and traveled all over the world, troubleshooting for the CIA. His missions have including hunting down rogue agents and assassins, fighting terrorists, investigating sabotage on military assets and preventing the use of biological weapons.

Behind the Scenes

Gerard De Villiers was born in 1929 and studied journalism. He established himself as a journalist covering the Vietnam War. After the death of Ian Fleming in 1964, De Villiers decided to attempt the fill the void with his own series. De Villiers brings his journalist training to his writing and travels the world visiting the settings of his books. In several cases, the Malko novels have predicted major espionage news events.

Due to his right-wing views, De Villiers books are not carried in many bookstores but rather sold in airports and train stations. The French translations and editions of **the Executioner** and **the Destroyer** are published under the banner "Gerard De Villiers presents."

The Books

All books were published by Plon:

1. *SAS à Istanbul*, 188 pages, 1965
2. *SAS contre CIA*, 176 pages, 1965
3. *Opération Apocalypse*, 127 pages, 1965
4. *Samba pour SAS*, 175 pages, 1966
5. *Rendez-vous à San Francisco*, 252 pages, 1966
6. *Le Dossier Kennedy*, 253 pages, 1967

7. *Broie du noir*, 334 pages, 1967

8. *SAS aux Caraïbes*, 253 pages, 1967

9. *SAS à l'ouest de Jeruzalem*, 160 pages, 1968

10. *L'or de la rivière Kwaï*, 179 pages, 1968

11. *Magie noire à New York*, 191 pages, 1968

12. *Les trois veuves de Hong Kong*, 254 pages, 1968

13. *L'Abominable sirene*, 255 pages, 1969

14. *Les pendus de Bagdad*, 254 pages, 1969

15. *La panthère d' Hollywood*, 206 pages, 1969

16. *Escale à Pago-Pago*, 254 pages, 1969

17. *Amok à Bali*, 253 pages, 1970

18. *Que viva Guevara*, 180 pages, 1970

19. *Cyclone à ONU*, 157 pages, 1970

20. *Mission à Saigon*, 254 pages, 1970

21. *Le bal de la comtesse Adler*, 251 pages, 1971

22. *Les parias de Ceylon*, 254 pages, 1971

23. *Massacre à Amman*, 256 pages, 1971

24. *Requiem pour Tontons Macoutes*, 252 pages, 1971

25. *L'homme de Kabul*, 252 pages, 1972

26. *Mort à Beyrouth*, 251 pages, 1972

27. *Safari à La Paz*, 253 pages, 1972

28. *L'héroïne de Vientiane*, 252 pages, 1972

29. *Berlin, Check-Point Charlie*, 252 pages, 1973

30. *Mourir pour Zanzibar*, 249 pages, 1973

31. *L'ange de Montevideo*, 252 pages, 1973

32. *Murder, Inc., Las Vegas*, 253 pages, 1973

33. *Rendez-vous à Boris Gleb*, 251 pages, 1974

34. *Kill Henry Kissinger*, 253 pages, 1974

35. *Roulette Cambodgienne*, 251 pages, 1974

36. *Furie à Belfast*, 255 pages, 1974

37. *Guêpier en Angola*, 254 pages, 1975

38. *Les otages de Tokio*, 252 pages, 1975

39. *L'ordte regne a Santiago*, 251 pages, 1975

40. *Les sorciers du Tage*, 253 pages, 1975

41. *Embargo*, 255 pages, 1976

42. *Le disparu de Singapore*, 254 pages, 1976

43. *Compte à rebours en Rhodesie*, 249 pages, 1976

44. *Meurtre à Athènes*, 250 pages, 1976

45. *Le trésor du Négus*, 254 pages, 1977

46. *Protection pour Teddy Bear*, 251 pages, 1977

47. *Mission impossible en Somalie*, 253 pages, 1977

48. *Marathon à Spanish Harlem*, 248 pages, 1977

49. *Nauffrage aux Seychelles*, 245 pages, 1978

50. *La printemps de Varsovie*, 247 pages, 1978

51. *Le gardien d'Israël*, 249 pages, 1978

52. *Panique au Zaïre*, 249 pages, 1978

53. *Croisade à Managua*, 252 pages, 1979

54. *Voir Malte et mourir*, 245 pages, 1979

55. *Shanghai Express*, 250 pages, 1979

56. *Opération Matador*, 243 pages, 1979

57. *Duel à Barranquilla*, 249 pages, 1980

58. *Piège à Budapest*, 245 pages, 1980

59. *Carnage à Abu Dhabi*, 245 pages, 1980

60. *Terreur à San Salvador*, 245 pages, 1980

61. *Le complot du Caire*, 245 pages, 1981

62. *Vengeance romaine*, 251 pages, 1981

63. *Des armes pour Khartoum*, 250 pages, 1981

64. *Tornade sur Manille*, 248 pages, 1981

65. *Le fugitif de Hambourg*, 251 pages, 1982

66. *Objectif Reagan*, 242 pages, 1982

67. *Rouge Grenade*, 275 pages, 1982

68. *Commando sur Tunis*, 251 pages, 1982

69. *Le tueur de Miami*, 250 pages, 1983

70. *La filière bulgare*, 246 pages, 1983

71. *Aventure au Surinam*, 253 pages, 1983

72. *Embuscade à la Khyber Pass*, 251 pages, 1983

73. *Le vol 007 ne répond plus*, 251 pages, 1984

74. *Les fous de Baalbek*, 254 pages, 1984

75. *Les enragés d'Amsterdam*, 248 pages, 1984

76. *Putsch à Ouagadougou*, 250 pages, 1984

77. *La blonde de Pretoria*, 247 pages, 1985

78. *La veuve de l'ayatollah*, 254 pages, 1985

79. *Chasse à l'homme au Pérou*, 249 pages, 1985

80. *L'affaire Kirsanov*, 254 pages, 1985

81. *Mort à Gandhi*, 256 pages, 1986

82. *Danse macabre à Belgrade*, 248 pages, 1986

121. *La résolution 687*, 255 pages, 1996
122. *Opération Lucifer*, 255 pages, 1996
123. *Vengeance tchétchène*, 252 pages, 1996
124. *Tu tueras ton prochain*, 253 pages, 1996
125. *Vengez le vol 800*, 254 pages, 1997
126. *Une lettre pour La Maison-Blanche*, 255 pages, 1997
127. *Hong Kong Express*, 252 pages, 1997
128. *Zaïre adieu*, 255 pages, 1997
129. *La manipulation Yggdrasil*, 251 pages, 1998
130. *Mortelle Jamaïque*, 255 pages, 1998
131. *La peste noire de Bagdad*, 253 pages, 1998
132. *L'espion du Vatican*, 248 pages, 1998
133. *Albanie mission impossible*, 252 pages, 1999
134. *La source Yahalom*, 250 pages, 1999
135. *SAS Contre P.K.K.*, 286 pages, 1999
136. *Bombes sur Belgrade*, 246 pages, 1999
137. *La piste du Kremlin*, 255 pages, 2000
138. *L'amour fou du Colonel Chang*, 251 pages, 2000
139. *Djihad*, 255 pages, 2000
140. *Enquête sur un genocide*, 254 pages, 2000
141. *L'otage de Jolo*, 254 pages, 2001
142. *Tuez le Pape*, 250 pages, 2001
143. *Armageddon*, 253 pages, 2001
144. *Li Sha-Tin doit mourir*, 245 pages, 2001
145. *Le Roi fou du Népal*, 250 pages, 2002
146. *Le Sabre de Bin Laden*, 249 pages, 2002
147. *La manip du Karin A*, 250 pages, 2002
148. *Bin Laden: La Traque*, 249 pages, 2002
149. *Le Parrain Du '17 Novembre*, 247 pages, 2003
150. *Bagdad-Express*, 247 pages, 2003
151. *L'or D'Al-Qaida*, 253 pages, 2003
152. *Pacte avec le diable*, 252 pages, 2003
153. *Ramenez-les vivants*, 248 pages, 2004
154. *Le Réseau Istanbul*, 244 pages, 2004
155. *Le Jour de la Tcheka*, 244 pages, 2004
156. *La Connexion Saoudienne*, 248 pages, 2004
157. *Otages en Irak*, 249 pages, 2005
158. *Tuez Iouchtchenko!*, 252 pages, 2005

159. *Mission: Cuba*, 318 pages, 2005

160. *Aurore Noire*, 303 pages, 2005

161. *Le programme III*, 301 pages, 2006

162. *Que la bête meure*, 300 pages, 2006

163. *Le trésor de Saddam: Tome 1*, 314 pages, 2006

164. *Le trésor de Saddam: Tome 2*, 315 pages, 2006

165. *Le Dossier K.*, 304 pages, 2006

166. *Rouge Liban*, 304 pages, 2006

167. *Polonium 210*, 302 pages, 2007

168. *Le defecteur de Pyongyang: Tome 1*, 304 pages, 2007

169. *Le defecteur de Pyongyang: Tome 2 — Cruel Soleil Levant!*, 318 pages, 2007

170. *Otage des Taliban*, 300 pages, 2007

171. *L'Agenda Kosova*, 281 pages, 2008

The British Editions

All books were published by New English Library:

1. *SAS vs CIA*, 124 pages, 1969 (French #2: SAS contre CIA)

2. *SAS: West of Jerusalem*, 126 pages, 1969 (French #9: SAS à l'Ouest de Jeruzalem)

3. *SAS: Operation Apocalypse*, 127 pages, 1970 (French #3: Opération Apocalypse)

4. *SAS: Black Magic in New York*, 124 pages, 1970 (French #11: Magie Noire à New York)

The American Editions

All books were published by Pinnacle Books:

1. *West of Jerusalem*, 217 pages, 1973 (French 9: SAS à l'Ouest de Jeruzalem)

2. *Operation New York*, 191 pages, 1973 (French 11: Magie noire à New York)

3. *Man from Kabul*, 218 pages, 1973 (French 25: L'homme de Kabul)

4. *Versus the CIA*, 187 pages, 1974 (French 2: SAS contre CIA)

5. *Angel of Vengeance*, 210 pages, 1974 (French 31: L'ange de Montevideo)

6. *Kill Kissinger*, 180 pages, 1974 (French 34: Kill Henry Kissinger)

7. *The Countess and the Spy*, 250 pages, 1974 (French 21: Le bal de la comtesse Adler)

8. *Death on the River Kwai*, 179 pages, 1975 (French 10: L'or de la rivière Kwaï)

9. *Checkpoint Charlie*, 180 pages, 1975 (French 29: Berlijn: Checkpoint Charlie)

10. *Que Viva Guevara*, 180 pages, 1975 (French 18: Que viva Guevara)

11. *Hostage in Tokyo*, 182 pages, 1976 (French 38: Les otages de Tokio)

12. *The Belfast Connection*, 178 pages, 1976 (French 36: Furie à Belfast)

13. *Death in Santiago*, 180 pages, 1976 (French 39: l'Ordre regne a Santiago)

14. *The Portuguese Defection*, 166 pages, 1977 (French 40: Les sorciers du Tage)

15. *Embargo*, 208 pages, 1977 (French 41: Embargo)

One book was published by Medallion Books:
1. *A Game of Eyes Only*, 293 pages, 1986 (French 60: Terreur au San Salvador)
The Malko novels have also been translated into Dutch, Italian, German and Romanian.

The Movies

In 1982, *SAS: San Salvador* was released, starring former Tarzan actor Miles O'Keefe as Prince Malko Linge. The film was based on the sixtieth book, *Terreur an San Salvador*. In 1989, *The Eye of the Widow* was released, starring Richard Young. This movie was based on *Vengeance romaine* (1981) and *La veuve de l'ayatollah* (1985).

The Comics

In 2006, Glénat Benelux published four issues of a comic series adapting the SAS series.
1. *Pacte avec le Diable*, 2006
2. *Le sabre de Bin-Laden*, 2006
3. *Mission Cuba*, 2007
4. *Bin-Laden: la traque*, 2007

MARC DEAN: MERCENARY
Nine books by Peter Buck

Marcus Matthew Dean was born June 6, 1944, to a country doctor who had lied about his age to become a World War I aviator. Marc spent his life in the military in one capacity or another. Highly decorated in Vietnam, he later joined the Peace Corps in Central Africa. After several years, Dean became an international arms salesman and eventually hired out his skills as a mercenary in 1975. Successful on missions throughout Africa and the Middle East, Dean and his team of mercenaries became one of the top mercenary teams in the world. On occasion the CIA has been known to hire Dean and his men through his contact Quinnell. Due to the illegal nature of his work, Dean no longer resides in America but rather in Paris. The team is taken on a case-by-case basis subject to the needs of the mission and availability. These men include:
• Edmond Mazzari: Formerly of the Congolese Army, a large and tough African who speaks with a British accent thanks to his English education.
• Sean Hammer: Irish American whose Protestant family left Ireland for America when the Catholic South gained independence in 1920. Short and wiry, he is one of the toughest and calmest fighters Dean has ever met.

Dean and his men tackle a variety of threats, ranging from preventing Neo-Nazis from building a nuclear reactor in Brazil, to thwarting revolutions, preventing assassinations, and protecting business interests and important people.

Behind the Scenes

Peter Buck is the pen name of Peter Leslie. Leslie contributed to the Man from U.N.C.L.E. novels as well as several books in **The Executioner** series.

The Books

All books were published by Signet Books:

1. *Thirteen Is for the Kill*, 231 pages, 1981
2. *The Secret of San Felipe*, 224 pages, 1981
3. *The Deadly Birdman*, 214 pages, 1981
4. *Operation Icicle*, 233 pages, 1982
5. *School for Slaughter*, 214 pages, 1982
6. *Ready, Aim Die*, 219 pages, 1982
7. *Black Gold Briefing*, 220 pages, 1983
8. *Megadeath Option*, 217 pages, 1983
9. *Passport to Peril*, 239 pages, 1983

THE MARKSMAN (PHILLIP MAGELLAN)

Twenty-three books by Frank Scarpetta

Phillip Magellan's family was murdered by the Mafia. Magellan was in the car with his wife and son when the Mafia hit men opened fire on the car. He saw his wife torn apart by a sawn off shotgun and felt his son's brains splatter on him as the dum-dum bullet hit him in the head. Somehow, Magellan, a former Green Beret, survived the assault and with a white-hot rage vowed to stop the Mafia.

Magellan's philosophy is that the current system recycles criminals, releasing them after short terms of imprisonment to commit crimes again and again. He believes that his system is a better way. The verdict is final and the criminals he kills never commit another crime. Magellan is unique in that he will kill law enforcement officers if they get in his way. This means that Magellan doesn't get the level of unofficial understanding that other serial vigilantes get from law enforcement agencies. Magellan's proficiency at disguise allows him to avoid road blocks and surveillance at airports and bus terminals. Magellan travels in and out of America, gathering information in Puerto Rico, France and Mexico and other sources of illicit drugs and contraband smuggled into America. He returns to America and wreaks vengeance against the Mafia operations that he uncovered in his travels.

Behind the Scenes

Frank Scarpetta is a house name used by Peter McCurtin and Aaron Fletcher. Peter McCurtin was an editor for Belmont Towers books before becoming an author. McCurtin, under his own name, was the author of several western series such as Carmody and Sundance as well as the **Soldier of Fortune/Death Dealer** series; under various pen names he contributed to the **Sexecutioner** and **Sharpshooter** series. McCurtin also novelized the movie *The Exterminator* as well as several exposés on organized crime, such as *Mafioso, The Syndicate* and *Omerta*.

Aaron Fletcher is the author of several western novels and thrillers as well as the Outback series, covering the settling of the Australian outback.

The Books

All books were published by Belmont Tower:

1. *Vendetta*, 1973
2. *Death Hunt*, 1973
3. *Kill Them All*, 181 pages, 1973
4. *Mafia Wipeout*, 171 pages, 1973
5. *Head Hunter*, 159 pages, 1973
6. *Death to the Mafia*, 153 pages, 1973
7. *Slaughterhouse*, 1973
8. *Stone Killer*, 174 pages, 1974
9. *Body Count*, 182 pages, 1974
10. *Open Contract*, 166 pages, 1974
11. *Counter Attack*, 182 pages, 1974
12. *Mafia Massacre*, 168 pages, 1974
13. *Kiss of Death*, 163 pages, 1974
14. *Kill*, 165 pages, 1974
15. *Die, Killer Die*, 1975
16. *The Animal Must Die*, 1975
17. *Killer on the Prowl*, 170 pages, 1975
18. *Torture Contract*, 179 pages, 1975
19. *Icepick in the Spine*, 204 pages, 1975
20. *Murder Machine*, 1975
21. *Bloody Sunday*, 192 pages, 1976
22. *Times Square Connection*, 183 pages, 1976
23. *Reckoning*, 192 pages, 1981

THE MERCENARIES

Five books by Jon Hart

During the 1960s there was much political unrest in Africa and, in the Congo, mercenaries were hired to help the army (ANC) to quell the unrest. Mike Hoare was hired to lead the mercenary forces in a group he called Five Commando.

From that real-world situation, Jon Hart wrote the Mercenaries, which follows the adventures of Major Robert Kane's team from Five Commando, which are referred to as Killer Commando. In the first book, *Black Blood*, we see the team fighting the Simba rebel forces in the Congo. Due to political machinations from a general opposed to the use of mercenaries, the team is expelled from the Congo after shooting down an ANC plane that was attacking the mercenaries.

Throughout this all-action, adult adventure series, many of the team are killed and replaced, but there is always the core team:
• Robert Kane: British commander of the unit
• Otto Hassell: German fighting man and son of Nazi Iron Cross winner
• Jack O'Neal: Former CIA observer
• Davey Tatum: American who left his studies in search of adventure

The men of Killer Commando decide to stay together after being expelled from the Congo and tackle missions such as destroying drug dealers in the Golden Triangle between Laos, Thailand and Burma; rescuing hostages from guerrillas in Ethiopia; and providing security in Mexico.

Behind the Scenes

Jon Hart is the pseudonym of James Barton. Barton, born in 1938, wrote many western series under several pseudonyms, including Hart the Regulator as John B. Harvey, Apache as William M. James, Herne the Hunter as John J. McLaglen and Lawman as J. B. Dancer. Barton, under his own name, has written the Charlie Resnick crime novels as well as several movie novelizations and even scripts for several British television productions.

The Books

All books were published by Mayflower Publishers:
1. *Black Blood*, 128 pages, 1977
2. *High Slaughter*, 128 pages, 1977
3. *Triangle of Death*, 128 pages, 1977
4. *Guerrilla Attack*, 128 pages, 1977
5. *Death Raid*, 128 pages, 1978

(THEY CALL ME) THE MERCENARY (HANK FROST)

Eighteen books by Axel Kilgore

Henry "Hank" Frost is a mercenary captain who lost his left eye in an attack by a renegade mercenary commander and was left for dead. He recovered and gained revenge, killing the man who took his eye.

Frost was one of the many Americans to serve in Vietnam, where he saw his commanding officer killed by a mercenary hired by the Viet Cong. After the war Frost was unable to settle back into civilian life and became a mercenary.

The one-eyed merc travels the globe with his reporter girlfriend Beth Stallman, fighting in trouble spots. Frost fights Neo-Nazi groups, battles drug kingpins and prevents assassinations. He also been hired as a bodyguard for a genius, and in the course of his travels has fought against numerous terrorist organizations and renegade arms dealers. Due to these battles, Frost is also frequently targeted by enemies and he has been poisoned, suffered amnesia, and drugged and imprisoned in Siberia. On other occasions, Beth stumbles into trouble while reporting for the International News Bureau and Frost becomes involved to help her.

Behind the Scenes

Axel Kilgore is the pen name of Jerry Ahern. Jerry Ahern is the author of the Survivalist and the Defender post-apocalyptic series as well as **Track, The Takers** and **Surgical Strike.** He has also written several books for the **Killmaster** series under the house name of Nick Carter. Ahern has also written more than 600 articles for various magazines and is the former president of Deutronics Firearms.

The Books

All books were published by Zebra Books:

1. *The Killer Genesis*, 238 pages, 1980
2. *The Slaughter Run*, 240 pages, 1980
3. *Fourth Reich Death Squad*, 238 pages, 1980
4. *The Opium Hunter*, 240 pages, 1981
5. *Canadian Killing Ground*, 224 pages, 1981
6. *Vengeance Army*, 224 pages, 1981
7. *Slave of the Warmonger*, 206 pages, 1981
8. *Assassin's Express*, 214 pages, 1981
9. *The Terror Contract*, 223 pages, 1982
10. *Bush Warfare*, 207 pages, 1982
11. *Death Lust*, 191 pages, 1982
12. *Headshot*, 223 pages, 1982
13. *Naked Blade, Naked Gun*, 201 pages, 1983
14. *Siberian Alternative*, 188 pages, 1983
15. *Afghanistan Penetrator*, 206 pages, 1983
16. *China Bloodbath*, 193 pages, 1983
17. *Buckingham Blowout*, 190 pages, 1984
18. *Eye for an Eye*, 203 pages, 1984

MIA HUNTER (MARK STONE)

Seventeen books by Jack Buchanan

Mark Stone is a former POW, Green Beret and a MIA hunter; that is, he looks for soldiers who were listed as "Missing in Action" in Vietnam, although later in the series he expands his operation to all conflicts. To aid in this, he owns and operates Stone Investigative Consultants as a private eye, which is basically run by his sidekick, Ben Zedicher. Stone's real work, however, is done with Hog Wiley, a giant redheaded Texan, and Terrance Lloughlin, a British demolition expert.

Initially, Stone's work is totally unsanctioned but eventually, after embarrassing the CIA on several occasions, Stone is asked to work for the CIA and help track down their MIA agents. Stone does this although he often acts on his own agenda. In #10 *Miami Massacre*, Stone acts on his own to rescue an old army buddy now working for the DEA who has gone MIA.

Behind the Scenes

Jack Buchanan hides the identity of Steve Mertz (who outlined and plotted all of the stories) and his collaborators Bill Crider and Joe R. Lansdale. Steve Mertz, along with Mike Newton, got his start working with Don Pendleton on **the Executioner** for Pinnacle Books, later ghostwriting a number of Executioner and **Able Team** novels for Gold Eagle books. Bill Crider, born in 1941, is the author of the Tru Smith and Sheriff Dan Rhodes mystery series and co-wrote *The Coyote Connection* under the house name Nick Carter for **the Killmaster** series.

Joe R. Lansdale, born 1951, is a Texan writer of horror, fantasy and mystery novels, including the Hap Collins and Leonard Pines series. He has also written for comics, including Batman, Lone Ranger and Jonah Hex. Lansdale also completed Edgar Rice Burrough's uncompleted Tarzan manuscript, *Tarzan, the Lost Adventure*, and his short story "Bubba Ho Tep" was filmed, starring Bruce Campbell and Ossie Davis.

The Books

All books were published by Jove:

(One book of the series is not part of the numbering sequence and has been placed in publication sequence unnumbered.)

1. *MIA Hunter*, 197 pages, 1985
2. *Cambodian Hellhole*, 181 pages, 1985
3. *Hanoi Deathgrip*, 197 pages, 1985
4. *Mountain Massacre*, 196 pages, 1985
5. *Exodus from Hell*, 197 pages, 1986
6. *Blood Storm*, 182 pages, 1986
   Stone: MIA Hunter, 261 pages, 1987
7. *Saigon Slaughter*, 199 pages, 1987
8. *Escape from Nicaragua*, 198 pages, 1987
9. *Invasion USSR*, 185 pages, 1988
10. *Miami Warzone*, 184 pages, 1988
11. *Crossfire Kill*, 170 pages, 1989
12. *Desert Deathraid*, 168 pages, 1989

13. *LA Gang War*, 165 pages, 1990
14. *Back to 'Nam*, 186 pages, 1990
15. *Heavy Fire*, 200 pages, 1991
16. *China Strike*, 193 pages, 1991

MIND MASTER (BRITTE ST. VINCENT)

Five books by John F. Rossman and Ian Ross

Britte St. Vincent served in Vietnam and the horrors of that conflict activated his latent psychic abilities. When the military discovered his abilities, he was recruited into a top-secret psychic research project.

It was at this research project that St. Vincent met the love of his life, another test subject in the project. The pair decided to leave the project and get married, but during their escape attempt, she died. St. Vincent was sent away and warned to stay out of psychic matters and not mention anything about his experiences or he would suffer an even worse fate. Britte lived by those conditions, becoming an international race car driver. The adrenalin rush was like a drug that kept his mind from his past.

One night, driving down a lonely highway, St. Vincent is passed by a ghost car driven by his former lover. Following the car, he discovers that it was a projection from the Mero Institute, a civilian agency determined to keep psychic research benign and for non-military applications. The group is formed by a number of former military researchers, many of whom had faked their deaths.

Britte agrees to become their field agent; his reputation as a playboy/race car driver is the ideal cover for this. Britte must track down the agents of the other psychic research and to maintain his cover he has to kill those other agents. Britte travels the world, hunting crazy Nazi researchers, a resurrected Jack the Ripper, all-female psychic Amazon tribes, hermaphrodite Korean agents, resurrected dead soldiers, psychic cyborgs and lesbian scientists.

The series ends with both Britte St. Vincent and the Mero Institute exposed.

Behind the Scenes

John F. Rossman, born 1942, served in the Missouri National Guard from 1965 to 1967 as well as working in a number of public relations/communications roles. While the first three books in the Mind Masters series appear under his own name, the final two books in the series were published under the pseudonym of Ian Ross. This move may have come from the publisher in an attempt to create a house name to continue the series as Rossman left the series to concentrate on children's books and writing about Christian meditation.

Rossman has this to say about why he left the series: "Even though the 'Mind Masters' series is viable for continuation, my market research data show conclusively that, due to working women dropping out of the work force at the moment because of economic slowdown and other factors, there will be a 'baby boom' which will result in approximately three and a half million new births per year through the early 1980's. Children's books for three- to five-year-olds will be in great demand within two years, and I already have underway two series of children's books for this age group." (Contemporary Authors Online).

The Books
All books were published by Signet Books:
1. *Mind Masters*, 232 pages, 1974 (John Rossman)
2. *Shamballah*, 220 pages, 1975 (John Rossman)
3. *Door*, 168 pages, 1975 (John Rossman)
4. *Amazons*, 172 pages, 1976 (Ian Ross)
5. *Recycled Souls*, 170 pages, 1976 (Ian Ross)

MISSIONS OF ALEX KANE
Six books by John Preston

Alex Kane is unique in the world of serial vigilantes. This tall, green-eyed, muscular freelance operative only takes the missions that interest him. Just as the **Executioner** declared war on the Mafia and later terrorism, Alex Kane has become the defender of the gay community, declaring war on bigotry and intolerance.

Primarily operating in the United States, Kane travels from city to city to protect the gay community from threats such as trashy tabloids inciting violence against gay men or foreign intelligence agencies blackmailing prominent government officials with their secret gay liaisons. Kane is not limited to operating in America; in *Secret Danger*, he travels to Bosnia to rescue a gay travel group when hijackers take over their flight to Europe. Throughout the series Kane develops a romantic relationship with his sidekick Danny but has encounters with other men.

Behind the Scenes
John Preston was an openly gay author. Many of his works were about the gay experience and gay erotica. Under the name Preston Mac Adam, he wrote the **Shield** series and, under the Jack Hild house name, Preston contributed several books to the **Soldiers of Barrabas** series. With the creation of Alex Kane, Preston was able to combine his two genres and created a gay action hero. During the early days of AIDS awareness, Preston became an advocate of safe sex and in 1994 he passed away due to complications from AIDS.

The Books
All books were published by Alyson Publications
1. *Sweet Dreams*, 122 pages, 1984
2. *Golden Years*, 126 pages, 1984

3. *Deadly Liars*, 126 pages, 1985
4. *Stolen Moments*, 125 pages, 1986
5. *Secret Dangers*, 124 pages, 1986
6. *Lethal Silence*, 118 pages, 1987

MONDO: MAN OF VIOLENCE

Three books by Anthony DeStefano

The man known as Mondo was a master thief working for the Mob until they killed his wife and son but failed to kill him. Mondo, knowing that his life was in danger, fell off the radar. When the Mob discovered that they had failed to kill Mondo, they realized that his inside knowledge was a danger. Mondo had to be killed. Eventually Mondo was tracked down to a hobo camp and a hobo thought to be Mondo was killed. But the mob was dead wrong. The man they killed was Mondo's best friend and now Mondo was coming after them.

Mondo is violent in his quest for revenge, often killing his victims with swords. His methods lead his enemies to declare that if Mondo kills you quick he's doing you a favor. After killing the men who killed his family, Mondo continues his fight against drug dealers and other criminals.

Behind the Scenes

Anthony De Stefano also writes under the name Anthony John. Under the John name, De Stefano wrote the thrillers *Predator* and *Judas Voice*.

The Books

All books were published by Manor Books:

1. *Mondo*, 192 pages, 1975
2. *Cocaine Kill*, 234 pages, 1977
3. *Minute to Pray, Second to Die*, 188 pages, 1977

MURDER MASTER (LOUIS LUTHER KING)

Three books by Joseph Rosenberger

Louis Luther King is a hard man and — unlike his near namesake, Martin Luther King — is a violent man, so much so that he is called the Murder Master. A government agent and master of disguise, this African American travels the world tackling the problems that are too difficult to be handled by conventional law enforcement. King's mastery of disguise allows him to impersonate an elderly man and a white man, making him an expert infiltrator, able to destroy an organization from the inside. King is highly educated and to establish his superiority frequently uses words like "pygmalionist."

King fights the Italian Mafia, outwitting their death traps to wipe out one of the many Mafia families. Then he travels to the Caribbean to destroy a Neo-Nazi heroin smuggling ring. In his final adventure, King poses as a Mack Man in Harlem to bring down the Boss Pimp, who is behind a plot blackmailing United Nations diplomats.

Behind the Scenes

Joseph Rosenberger became a professional writer at the age of twenty-one after selling an article. After working a series of jobs including Korean karate instructor, circus pitchman and private eye, he became a full-time writer in 1961. Rosenberger was the author of the **Death Merchant** and **C.O.B.R.A.** series and, under the pseudonym Lee Chang, created and wrote the first martial arts series **Kung Fu (Mace)**. Rosenberger had an interest in the occult and paranormal and wrote a number of articles for *Fate* magazine. It is believed that Rosenberg passed away in the early 1990s and his final series, Geneva Force, has only one book.

The Books

All books were published by Manor Books:

1. *Death Trap*, 191 pages, 1973
2. *Caribbean Caper*, 191 pages, 1973
3. *Operation Hooker*, 192 pages, 1974

NIGHT HUNTER (DAN BRADY)

Six books by Robert Faulcon (Robert Holdstock)

Dan Brady was a British military researcher of paranormal phenomenon with a very limited understanding of what he was researching. That all changed just before Christmas when his family was abducted. As the abductors left, Brady was left alive, as he was considered be unimportant and no threat to them. That was their first mistake.

The second mistake was revealing that the name of the organization that stole his family, Arachne. Contacting a fellow researcher, Ellen Bancroft of the Ennean Institute of Paranormal Research, Brady began to hunt for his family. Ellen taught Brady about the psychic world and how to protect himself against psychic and magical attacks.

Ellen was an early victim of the psychic and spiritual attacks against Brady and her ghost acts as an advisor, often warning him of impending threats. Brady tracks down various plots orchestrated by Arachne, such as the collection of various demons and spirits of shamans and wizards by powerful psychics called accumulators and the abductions of other people like his family. Brady gains allies in his fight against Arachne, such as Police Superintendent Andrew Sutherland, who investigated the Bradys' kidnapping and feeds Brady information, and Professor Sheila Roache and her team of psychic researchers.

Arachne's goal is the resurrection of total magic in the world and Brady's daughter Marianna has special powers and abilities that will allow Arachne to breach the mystical barriers that constrain magic. Brady tracks his family to Arachne's stronghold, a labyrinth constructed underground along the Ley lines in the North of England. Brady rescues his family and foils Arachne's plot.

Behind the Scenes

Robert Faulcon is the pen name of Robert Holdstock. Later books in the series reveal the secret to capitalize on the World Fantasy Award Holdstock won for his novel *Mythago Wood*. Holdstock in the author of many science fiction and fantasy novels published under his own name. Under a variety of pen names he also wrote a number of "hasty commercial efforts," as one critic referred to them (Dictionary of Literary Biography Online) these included the Raven sword and sorcery series written as Robert Kirk (with **Revenger** author Angus Wells) and a number of novelizations for the Professionals television series under the name Ken Blake.

The Books

All books were published by Arrow Books:
1. *The Stalking aka Night Hunter*, 199 pages, 1983
2. *The Talisman*, 200 pages, 1983
3. *The Ghost Dance*, 192 pages, 1983
4. *The Shrine*, 219 pages, 1984
5. *The Hexing*, 207 pages, 1984
6. *The Labyrinth*, 283 pages, 1987

NINJA MASTER (BRETT WALLACE)

Sixteen books by Wade Barker

The path of the ninja master to get that rank was long and arduous. His real name wasn't Brett Wallace but Brian "Tiger" Williams and he was the child of parents made wealthy from a lawsuit against the summer camp where his younger brother Bart drowned. Brian spent a decade studying martial arts and moved to Japan. While there he met and married his wife, Kyoko. The couple returned to America and started a family, but Kyoko and the baby were murdered by a gang of drug-addled murders. Brian Williams returned to Japan and began training as a ninja. After a decade he returned to America under his new identity of Brett Wallace.

Brett was determined to prevent anyone else from suffering the same fate as him and the ninja master began to kill the victimizers, those who preyed on society.

Brett worked with his ninja clan:
- Shiban Kan Hama; the next highest ninja sent by Wallace's ninja trainers to watch Brett
- Rhea Tagashi: studied ninjitsu with Wallace and fell in love with him, following him to America
- Jeff Archer: Brett's American student of ninjitsu

The clan fought pimps, muggers, child abusers and mobsters. The initial series ended with the ninja clan fighting an out-of-control gang of vigilantes known as the Revenge House based out of the Cannon Crossing Gun Club. The psychological effects of that battle and Brett's war on crime were played out in the Year of the Ninja Master series. In War of the Ninja Master, Brett discovered that the Japanese ninja clan who trained him was in fact exploiting him and he went to war against them.

Behind the Scenes

Wade Barker is the pseudonym for Ric Meyers. Meyers has also ghosted for Dirty Harry and **the Destroyer**. Under his own name, he has written Jackie Chan comics and several nonfiction works on martial arts films.

The Books

All books were published by Warner Books:

1. *Vengeance Is His*, 187 pages, 1981
2. *Mountain of Fear*, 158 pages, 1981
3. *Borderland of Fear*, 175 pages, 1982
4. *Million-Dollar Massacre*, 173 pages, 1982
5. *Black Magician*, 159 pages, 1982
6. *Death's Door*, 174 pages, 1982
7. *Skin Swindle*, 173 pages, 1983
8. *Only the Good Die*, 174 pages, 1983

Year of the Ninja Master

1. *Dragon Rising* (Spring), 280 pages, 1985
2. *Lion's Fire* (Summer), 276 pages, 1985
3. *Serpent's Eye* (Autumn), 243 pages, 1985
4. *Phoenix Sword* (Winter), 246 pages, 1986

War of the Ninja Master

1. *Kohga Ritual*, 276 pages, 1988
2. *Shimbo Discipline*, 279 pages, 1988
3. *Himitsu Attack*, 215 pages, 1988
4. *Zakka Slaughter*, 246 pages, 1988

ORION (SEBASTIAN CORD)

Three books by Aaron Allston, Warren Spector, and David Cook

In the beginning, there was the Web. Web was a vast conspiracy, so big that every time the authorities stumbled on one of their divisions it was thought that a whole new group was discovered. The Web is known by many different names which are sadly never revealed in this series but it is tempting to suggest that many different criminal organizations seen in other series might be divisions of the Web.

Conventional law enforcement agencies could be effective against the various arms of the Web within their own jurisdictions but given the global nature of the Web syndicate, there was little they could do to bring down this conspiracy. What was needed was an organization similar in scope to the Web, equally unfettered by the rules and boundaries of society. Ironically, the source of this organization was Web itself. In the wake of their criminal operations, a number of victims decided to fight back against the Web. These victims found each other and began to start pooling resources and information. The Orion Foundation was born.

The top team of the Orion Foundation is the M-Squad, a three-person, highly mobile team consisting of:

- Sebastian Cord: code-named Mercury; team leader who came to the attention of Web when he won at blackjack against a Web operative. The money wasn't the operative's to gamble and he tried to kill Cord. Cord was rescued by Orion operatives and decided to join.
- Gilda Ginsel: code-named the Mechanic; this blonde German bombshell is a mechanical genius and a lethal shot.
- Rodrigo the Great: code-named the Magician; a stage magician, Rodrigo is a part-time operative of Orion and uses his stagecraft to distract his adversaries.
- Scott Beattie: the Runner; joins the team when he is framed by the Web for one of their assassinations which formed the basis for their first adventure.

Being mobile, the team is able to track and fight the Web around the world, including missions such as assisting Web defectors who are kidnapped by UFO.

Behind the Scenes

The series was developed by TSR as scenario for their TOP SECRET role playing game and was published in their Double Agent format as a double novel, initially paired with Flint Dille and David Marconi's Agent 13 pulp series, then with the Agents of Fortune series. Aaron Allston is also the author of the Doc Savage–inspired fantasy series Doc Sidhe.

The Books

All books were published by TSR Books:

1. *Web of Danger*, 210 pages, 1988 (Aaron Allston)
2. *The Hollow Earth Affair*, 314 pages, 1988 (Warren Spector)
3. *Glitch*, 318 pages, 1988 (David Cook)

The Comic

In 1990, TSR Comics published a four-issue mini-series, 13 Assassin, which featured the modern-day adventures of their Agent 13 novel series, set in the 1930s. The exploits of Orion formed the basis of the backup feature, *The Final Weapon*. This story follows Roger Mason and his disillusionment with the Orion Foundation and the discovery of

Web double agents in Orion. Issue 3 provides character information and statistics for Mason and his ally Twyla Nash. *The Final Weapon* was written by Scott Haring with art by Frank Springer and Brian Garvey.

OVERLOAD
Twelve books by Bob Ham

Mark Lee and Carl Browne are ex-Delta Force anti-terrorist commandos who, after retiring, formed the Leeco Trucking Company. These highly trained warriors wanted a simple life in their retirement but found that the trucking business was nearly as dangerous and deadly as their time in Delta Force. With old enemies seeking revenge, Lee and Browne find that they cannot lay down their guns when they are attacked by Middle Eastern terrorists. But their new life also exposes them to new threats, such as attempted Mafia takeovers, drug cartels seeking to use their trucks to ferry drugs and motorcycle gangs attacking the Leeco Trucking Company.

The pair operates as disciplined soldiers facing these threats, understanding that force is not always the answer but when necessary they do not hold back, relying on their training to protect both themselves and their employees. This is in direct contrast to their enemies, such as the biker Wraith. Wraith is also a veteran but he uses his skills to lead his biker gang to inflict punishment and pain on the 99 percent of society he hates. We see this especially with the biker known as Shark who bites hunks of flesh off his live victims and spits the chunks back in their faces.

Behind the Scenes

Bob Ham's only credit is for the Overload series. The 2002 audio book of Christopher Newman' *Knock-Off* is credited to Bob Ham, suggesting that Ham may be the pseudonym of Newman. Christopher Newman is the author of the Lt. Joe Dante mystery series.

The Books

All books were published by Bantam Books:
1. *Personal War*, 159 pages, 1989
2. *Wrath*, 180 pages, 1989
3. *Highway Warriors*, 179 pages, 1989
4. *Tennessee Terror*, 260 pages, 1989
5. *Atlanta Burn*, 165 pages, 1989
6. *Nebraska Nightmare*, 168 pages, 1990
7. *Rolling Vengeance*, 1990
8. *Ozark Payback*, 193 pages, 1990
9. *Huntsville Horror*, 216 pages, 1991
10. *Michigan Madness*, 197 pages, 1991

11. *Alabama Bloodbath*, 196 pages, 1991
12. *Vegas Gamble*, 168 pages, 1991

THE PEACEMAKER (BARRINGTON HEWES-BRADFORD)

Four books by Adam Hamilton

The Peacemaker Foundation is a nonprofit organization dedicated to world peace and bringing justice to the world. It has a staff of troubleshooters ready to go into action at a moment's notice and an intelligence collection service that put many official intelligence agencies to shame. The Peacemaker Foundation was founded by Barrington Hewes-Bradford. Hewes-Bradford is one of the richest men in the world, chairman of the board for HB Enterprises, HB Shipping, Zeus Airlines and Interco Oil. Not only is Hewes-Bradford incredible wealthy, he is in great physical condition and has a love of adventure and a sense of fair play. It was the latter two qualities that lead him to form the Peacemaker Foundation and to serve as the foundation's top troubleshooter.

Hewes-Bradford travels to the world's trouble spots, seeking to nip problems in the bud before they can escalate into wars. The Peacemaker hunts down international crime figures such as Zaharan, who kills his enemies with impunity, carving a Z to taunt his pursuers, and terrorists from the nation Kuska who have come into possession of a deadly nerve agent and threaten to release it into a major city unless a number of their fellow terrorists are set free. The Peacemaker followed this with preventing the politically unstable island nation of Tattago from invasion by neighboring islands and preventing a coup d'etat against the newly crowned King Buri of Balabac by discovering the people behind the sabotage of relief effort organized by the young king.

Behind the Scenes

Adam Hamilton is the pen name of Marilyn Ruth Henderson and Arthur Moore. Henderson was research chemist, but a back injury left her unable to stand for a lengthy periods and she began writing. Henderson is a keen traveler and uses her trips as research for her books. Henderson is one of the few female writers in the field and wrote *Assignment Intercept* for **the Killmaster** series under the name Nick Carter. Henderson also wrote a number of young adult books published by Scholastic as M. R. Henderson.

The Books

All books were published by Berkley:

1. *Zaharan Pursuit*, 190 pages, 1974
2. *Yashar Pursuit*, 192 pages, 1974
3. *Xander Pursuit*, 1974
4. *Wyss Pursuit*, 1975

THE PENETRATOR (MARK HARDIN)

Fifty-three books by Lionel Derrick

Mark Hardin is Welsh-Cheyenne born 20 Aug 1945. At age four his parents and three siblings were killed in a car crash. During college, Hardin worked as an insurance investigator, where he was beaten severely after discovering a large-scale insurance fraud. After finishing college, Hardin enlisted in Army and went to Vietnam and spent three years (two tours) in Vietnam. After joining Army Intelligence, he tracked down a ring of black market profiteers who were selling Army supplies. After busting this ring, Hardin was bashed so severely he was sent back to the States and discharged.

After this latest beating Hardin contacts his football coach who puts him in touch with Professor Haskins, who, as it turns out, has been looking for someone like Hardin. It seems Haskins, a former professor of geology, has built a hideaway called the Stronghold and, along with his Cheyenne friend, David Red Eagle, helps Mark come back to health. Red Eagle trains Hardin in the Cheyenne ways, including Sho-tu-ca. Sho-tu-ca is a Cheyenne mental discipline that allows Mark to draw on extra strength and stamina and block pain.

Mark became romantically involved with the professor's niece, Donna Morgan, and they decide to find out more about Mark's parentage. This investigation brings them to the attention of the Mafia, who kill Donna. Haskins, Hardin and Red Eagle then vow to fight crime. Hardin fights the Mafia, terrorists and other criminals, including a vampire who believes he is the descendant of Count **Dracula**. Hardin leaves a calling card of a flint arrowhead. Hardin also uses a series of pseudonyms such as John Savage and Mack Colan. Hardin changes hairstyles and facial hair through the series so the police don't capture him. Hardin does have a love interest and occasional assistant, Joanna Tambler, who is a Justice Department agent working at a front agency, Diogenes Investigations. Hardin is aided unofficially by Dan Griggs of the Justice department, who is Joanna's supervisor and head of the Penetrator Task Force, which is to capture the Penetrator.

Behind the Scenes

This series was conceived by Pinnacle Books, who gave the name the Penetrator and Mark Hardin to writers Mark Kelly Roberts and Chet Cunningham. Together, the two writers created all of the other details about the series, including the description of the hero as well as his allies. The pair shared the writing duties and the pen name of Lionel Derrick.

All of the odd-numbered books were written by Mark Kelly Roberts. Roberts is also the author of the Liberty Corps series, and co-authored the **Soldier for Hire** series. All of the even-numbered were by Chet Cunningham, who lives in San Diego. Cunningham has also written numerous western novels both under his own name and pseudonyms. A veteran of the Korean War, Cunningham has written several volumes of military history. Cunningham is also the author of **the Avenger** and **the Specialists** series. Cunningham has also written several **Executioner** and SuperBolan (see Executioner) novels.

The Books

All books were published by Pinnacle Books:

1. *The Target Is H*, 156 pages, 1973

2. *Blood on the Strip*, 184 pages, 1973
3. *Capitol Hell*, 188 pages, 1974
4. *Hijacking Manhattan*, 179 pages, 1974
5. *Mardi Gras Massacre*, 178 pages, 1974
6. *Tokyo Purple*, 184 pages, 1974
7. *Baja Banditos*, 179 pages, 1974
8. *Northwest Contract*, 175 pages, 1975
9. *Dodge City Bombers*, 184 pages, 1975
10. *Hellbomb Flight*, 182 pages, 1975
11. *Terror in Taos*, 181 pages, 1975
12. *Bloody Boston*, 183 pages, 1976
13. *Dixie Death Squad*, 177 pages, 1976
14. *Mankill Sport*, 184 pages, 1976
15. *Quebec Connection*, 180 pages, 1976
16. *Deepsea Shootout*, 184 pages, 1976
17. *Demented Empire*, 176 pages, 1976
18. *Countdown to Terror*, 179 pages, 1977
19. *Panama Power Play*, 178 pages, 1977
20. *Radiation Hit*, 181 pages, 1977
21. *Supergun Mission*, 147 pages, 1977
22. *High Disaster*, 177 pages, 1977
23. *Divine Death*, 149 pages, 1977
24. *Cryogenic Nightmare*, 180 pages, 1978
25. *Floating Death*, 176 pages, 1978
26. *Mexican Brown Death*, 184 pages, 1978
27. *Animal Game*, 182 pages, 1978
28. *Skyhigh Betrayers*, 184 pages, 1978
29. *Aryan Onslaught*, 182 pages, 1979
30. *Computer Kill*, 184 pages, 1979
31. *Oklahoma Firefight*, 170 pages, 1979
32. *Showbiz Wipeout*, 174 pages, 1979
33. *Satellite Slaughter*, 174 pages, 1979
34. *Death Ray Terror*, 178 pages, 1979
35. *Black Massacre*, 182 pages, 1979
36. *Deadly Silence*, 176 pages, 1980
37. *Candidate's Blood*, 177 pages, 1980
38. *Hawaiian Trackdown*, 183 pages, 1980
39. *Cruise into Chaos*, 182 pages, 1980

40. *Assassination Factor*, 177 pages, 1981
41. *Hell's Hostages*, 181 pages, 1981
42. *Inca Gold Hijack*, 182 pages, 1981
43. *Rampage in Rio*, 195 pages, 1981
44. *Deep Cover Blastoff*, 186 pages, 1981
45. *Quaking Terror*, 200 pages, 1982
46. *Terrorist Torment*, 186 pages, 1982
47. *Orphan Army*, 196 pages, 1982
48. *Jungle Blitz*, 195 pages, 1982
49. *Satan's Swarm*, 184 pages, 1983
50. *Brotherhood of Blood*, 201 pages, 1983
51. *Neutron Nightmare*, 198 pages, 1983
52. *Plundered Paradise*, 196 pages, 1983
53. *City of the Dead*, 200 pages, 1983

Lionel Derrick is a pseudonym: the odd-numbered books were by Mark Kelly Roberts and the even-numbered by Chet Cunningham. In 1991 the first eight of Cunningham's books were reissued as double books under his own name by Leisure Books.

The Movies

There are two pornographic parodies of the Terminator movies called *The Penetrator* and *The Penetrator 2: Grudge Day* but neither has any connection to these books. However, the 1991 film *The Firing Line* appears to be an unauthorized movie based on the Penetrator. It stars Reb Brown (*Yor* and the Captain America TV movies) as an American Military advisor, Mark Hardin. Hardin helps the government forces capture Communist rebel leader Rodriguez only to discover that they have executed Rodriguez before he can be brought to trial and the same forces have raped and killed the female rebels that were also captured. When Hardin starts asking questions, he is imprisoned and tortured. Hardin is able to escape and rescues American exercise-equipment saleswoman Sandra Spencer, who is also suspected of being a spy. The pair escapes and joins the rebel forces where Hardin quickly assumes a leadership role and leads the rebels to several victories, as he explains that this is his way of making up for the actions he caused in the past. There is no reference to Hardin being the Penetrator or to any of his friends or allies, but Reb Brown does bear a marked resemblance to the cover illustrations of the Pinnacle novels and especially those of the 1991 Leisure books reprints.

Cameos and References

In book #11 *Terror in Taos*, the Penetrator is asked to translate from a paperback about "a white dude and a gook snuffing people for the government" and makes reference to television and soap operas; implicitly, this is a **Destroyer** novel.

Phoenix Force

Fifty-one books by Gar Wilson

This was the second of Gold Eagle's spinoffs of **the Executioner**. Unlike **Able Team**, none of the characters had appeared previously in the Executioner series. While Able Team was formed to battle American terrorism, Phoenix Force was assembled to combat overseas threats and was selected by Mack Bolan while he was using the name John Phoenix, hence the name.

Initially this five man team consisted of:

• Col. Yakov "Katz" Katzenbelenbogen: a French Israeli who is the veteran of many wars and lost his right arm from the elbow down in fighting in the Middle East

• David McCarter: British former SAS officer, involved in the Iran Embassy hostage situation

• Gary Manning: Canadian demolitions expert, special forces in Vietnam

• Rafael Encizo: Cuban survivor of the Bay of Pigs and Castro's re-education prisons

• Keio Ohara: Japanese martial artist and electronics expert

Ohara died in action in #12: *The Black Alchemists* and was replaced by Calvin James, an American SWAT team member.

After the series finished, the adventures of Phoenix Force were recorded in the **Stony Man** series. In these adventures, Katz retired, McCarter became new team leader and T. J. Hawkins joined the team.

Behind the Scenes

Gar Wilson is reportedly the pseudonym used by an anti-terrorism expert who served with the Special Operations Group in Vietnam, Delta Unit, and had a seat on the Coordinating Committee on Terrorism with the National Security Council and had worked with the special forces of many countries. The truth is that Gar Wilson is a house name used by William Fieldhouse, Michael Linaker, Robert Hoskins, Dan Marlowe, Thomas P. Ramirez, Sgt. Rex Swanson, Paul Glen Neuman, and Dan Streib.

Streib, born in 1928, served in the U.S. Army during the Korean War (1950–53) and died in 1996 of a heart attack. An extensive traveler for both work and pleasure, San Diego–based Streib used the locales he visited in his works, which include the **Hawk** and **Counter Force** series under his own name, romances under the names of Louise Grandville and Lee Davis Whilloughby, and westerns under the names Jonathan Schofield and J. Faragut Jones.

William Fieldhouse has written a number of books in the Executioner franchise including Phoenix Force and Stony Man. Under his own name, Fieldhouse has written several westerns, including *Klaw* and *Gun Lust*. As Chuck Bainbridge, he wrote several books for **the Hard Corps** series.

The Books

All books were published by Gold Eagle Books:

(Books 1–3 attributed to Don Pendleton and Gar Wilson; all other books attributed to Gar Wilson alone.)

1. *Argentine Deadline,* 188 pages, 1982 (Robert Hoskins)
2. *Guerrilla Games,* 186 pages, 1982 (Dan Marlowe)
3. *Atlantic Scramble,* 184 pages, 1982 (Thomas Ramerez)
4. *Tigers of Justice,* 188 pages, 1983 (William Fieldhouse)
5. *The Fury Bombs,* 188 pages, 1983 (Robert Hoskins)
6. *White Hell,* 188 pages, 1983 (Ramerez)
7. *Dragon's Kill,* 189 pages, 1983 (Fieldhouse)
8. *Aswan Hellbox,* 186 pages, 1983 (Ramerez & Sgt. Rex Swenson)
9. *Ultimate Terror,* 188 pages, 1984 (Fieldhouse)
10. *Korean Killground,* 184 pages, 1984 (Ramerez)
11. *Return to Armageddon,* 184 pages, 1984 (Fieldhouse)
12. *The Black Alchemists,* 186 pages, 1984 (Fieldhouse)
13. *Harvest Hell,* 185 pages, 1984 (Fieldhouse)
14. *Phoenix in Flames,* 185 pages, 1984 (Fieldhouse)
15. *The Viper Factor,* 186 pages, 1985 (Fieldhouse)
16. *No Rules, No Referee,* 186 pages, 1985 (Fieldhouse)
17. *Welcome to the Feast,* 187 pages, 1985 (Fieldhouse)
18. *Night of the Thugee,* 188 pages, 1985 (Fieldhouse)
19. *Sea of Savages,* 187 pages, 1985 (Neuman & Fieldhouse)
20. *Tooth and Claw,* 188 pages, 1985 (Fieldhouse)
21. *The Twisted Cross,* 187 pages, 1986 (Paul Glen Neuman & Fieldhouse)
22. *Time Bomb,* 187 pages, 1986 (Fieldhouse)
23. *Chip Off the Bloc,* 187 pages, 1986 (Neuman)
24. *The Doomsday Syndrome,* 218 pages, 1986 (Fieldhouse)
25. *Down Under Thunder,* 218 pages, 1986 (Neuman)
26. *Hostaged Vatican,* 219 pages, 1986 (Fieldhouse)
27. *Weep, Moscow, Weep,* 221 pages, 1987 (Fieldhouse)
28. *Slow Death,* 218 pages, 1987 (Neuman)
29. *The Nightmare Merchants,* 221 pages, 1987 (Fieldhouse)
30. *The Bonn Blitz,* 221 pages, 1987 (Neuman)
31. *Terror in the Dark,* 221 pages, 1987 (Fieldhouse)
32. *Fair Game,* 220 pages, 1987 (Neuman)
33. *Ninja Blood,* 221 pages, 1987 (Fieldhouse)
34. *Power Gambit,* 219 pages, 1988 (Fieldhouse)
35. *Kingston Carnage,* 219 pages, 1988 (Fieldhouse)
36. *Belgrade Deception,* 221 pages, 1988 (Fieldhouse)
37. *Show of Force,* 219 pages, 1988 (Dan Streib)
38. *Missile Menace,* 221 pages, 1988 (Mike Linaker)

39. *Jungle Sweep*, 220 pages, 1989 (Fieldhouse)
40. *Rim of Fire*, 219 pages, 1989 (Streib)
41. *Amazon Strike*, 221 pages, 1989 (Linaker)
42. *China Command*, 219 pages, 1989 (Fieldhouse)
43. *Gulf of Fire*, 221 pages, 1989 (Fieldhouse)
44. *Main Offensive*, 219 pages, 1989 (Fieldhouse)
45. *African Burn*, 220 pages, 1990 (Fieldhouse)
46. *Iron Claymore*, 221 pages, 1990 (Fieldhouse)
47. *Terror in Guyana*, 221 pages, 1990 (Fieldhouse)
48. *Barracuda Run*, 220 pages, 1990 (Linaker)
49. *Salvador Assault*, 219 pages, 1990 (Fieldhouse)
50. *Extreme Prejudice*, 219 pages, 1990 (Linaker)
51. *Savage World*, 219 pages, 1991 (Fieldhouse)

Gold Eagle also used their longer format with Super Phoenix Force:
1. *Fire Storm*, 348 pages, 1988 (Fieldhouse)
2. *Search and Destroy*, 347 pages, 1989 (Linaker)
3. *Cold Dead*, 349 pages, 1990 (Fieldhouse)
4. *Wall of Flame*, 346 pages, 1991 (Fieldhouse)

And Phoenix Force featured in the Heroes Anthology series:
1. *Heroes I*, 588 pages, 1992 (contains *Survival Run* by Gar Wilson [Michael Linaker])
2. *Heroes II*, 586 pages, 1992 (contains *Hell Quest* by Gar Wilson [William Fieldhouse] and *Dirty Mission* by Gar Wilson [Linaker])
3. *Heroes III*, 445 pages, 1992 *(Contains Terror in Warsaw by Gar Wilson [Fieldhouse])*

Members of Phoenix Force have also appeared in various Executioner, Super Bolan (see Executioner) and Able Team novels as well as appearing in the Stony Man series.

PRINCE ZARKON
Five books by Lin Carter

Prince Zarkon was sent back from the far future to prevent the events that led to his future. Zarkon was the last of a line of experimental supermen. His physique was so symmetrical that many failed to notice how well built he was. Zarkon generally dressed completely in gray, which matched his gray hair and reminded many of ancient Roman statues.

On his arrival in the 1970s, Zarkon, dubbed the Lord of the Unknown, formed the crime-fighting organization Omega. He recruited five men, all at the end of their tether ready to die, or descend into drugs, alcohol or crime. The Omega team consisted of:
• Theophilus "Doc" Jenkins: memory master with a completely photographic memory
• Aloysius Murphy "Scorchy" Muldoon: red-headed Irish ex-boxer with a thirst for adventure.

• Nick Naldini: former Vaudeville magician and escape artist who worked with Houdini
• Mendel Lowell "Menlo" Parker: famous scientist and inventor
• "Ace" Harrigan: expert pilot, the son of famed World War II pilot "Hop" Harrigan

Together, the Prince Zarkon and his Omega crew tackle villains that hark back to the pulp era with names like the Grim Reaper and Lucifer, with weapons that kill instantly. The pulp-era connection is even stronger as Zarkon is a member of the Cobalt Club and frequently interacts with pulp characters and locations from Doc Savage, the Shadow, Batman, the Avenger, the Saint and other pulp series.

Behind the Scenes

Linwood Carter (1930–1988) was a fantasy editor for Ballentine Books and was responsible for bringing writers such as Robert E. Howard, H. P. Lovecraft and J. R. R. Tolkein back into print. A prolific author, he wrote new adventures of Robert E. Howard's Conan the Barbarian as well as the Edgar Rice Burroughs–inspired Callisto and Zanthodon series. The Zarkon series was inspired by the Doc Savage and Avenger pulp series.

The Books

All books were published by Doubleday:

1. *Nemesis of Evil*, 172 pages, 1975
2. *Invisible Death*, 173 pages, 1975
3. *Volcano Ogre*, 177 pages, 1976
4. *Earth-shaker*, 175 pages, 1982
5. *Horror Wears Blue*, 174 pages, 1987

THE PROTECTOR (ALEX DARTANIAN)

Six books by Rich Rainey

Alex Dartanian is the owner and operator of Dartanian Security Service (DSS), which is a nationwide security outfit based out of Manhattan. The DSS works with and liaises with the CIA, DIA, FBI, DEA, and the various other American agencies. The DSS is just a cover for Dartanian's true work as the Protector. The inner workings of DSS are actually known as ICE (Inner Court Executions). Dartanian believed that America was in danger of descending into total lawlessness and the missions that ICE undertook, called ICE storms, were to rekindle the nation's conscience and take America away from the brink of anarchy and back to civilization.

ICE is run by Dartanian along with Mick Porter, a former Special Forces operative, and Sim Simara, a Japanese martial arts instructor who came up through the ranks of Japanese secret societies. These three form the ICE core and take other operatives as needed to take down the various criminal elements. They encounter including cults, assassins, body snatchers (for illegal organ transplants), and pornographers.

Behind the Scenes

Rich Rainey, under his full name Richard Rainey, has written several nonfiction works on the occult and the horror genre. Rainey has also produced several books in the **Executioner** franchise; he contributed to the **SOB (Soldiers of Barrabas)** series as Jack Hild and the final book in the post-apocalyptic Warlord series as Jason Frost.

The Books

All books were published by Pinnacle Books:

1. *Venus Underground*, 198 pages, 1982
2. *Porn Tapes*, 155 pages, 1982
3. *Hit Parade*, 202 pages, 1983
4. *Cult .45*, 186 pages, 1984
5. *Nightmare Network*, 186 pages, 1984
6. *Dragon Slaying*, 181 pages, 1985

PULSAR INTERNATIONAL (TIM KYLE)

Two books by Robin Moore and Al Dempsey

Tim Kyle is the founder and owner of Pulsar International, an international security company, with clients including governments, multinational companies and various intelligence agencies. Kyle is a hands-on leader and frequently becomes embroiled in the problems that Pulsar encounters. With his computer-like brain, the forty-two-year-old Kyle is able to quickly and accurately assess any situation, but Kyle is not just a brain, he is capable of rapid violent action when his analysis calls for it. Through his clients and contacts, Kyle is able to go anywhere and get in anywhere. Such is Pulsar's clout that Kyle has diplomatic status. Kyle also has access to various weapons, such as the Beretta Gatling–type 12-shot shotgun. Kyle tackles crimes such as kidnapping, gold smuggling, thefts, stock swindles and impersonations.

Behind the Scenes

Robin Moore is the pen name of Robert L. Moore, Jr., born 1925. Moore served in the US Army Air Force from 1944 to 1946. Moore also served as a civilian and trained with the Green Berets in Vietnam. His experiences formed the basis of the novel *The Green Berets*, which was filmed starring John Wayne. Moore also wrote *The French Connection*, the film version starring Gene Hackman.

Moore also frequently collaborated with other writers. His most frequent collaborator is Al Dempsey. Aside from the Pulsar series, the pair also wrote *The Red Falcons* and *Phase of Darkness*. Alone, Dempsey also wrote several western novels.

The Books

Both books were published by Pinnacle Books:

1. *The London Switch*, 204 pages, 1974 (reprinted as *The London Connection* 1980)
2. *The Italian Connection*, 180 pages, 1975

RAKER
Two books by Don Scott

Raker — he's never given a first name — was working undercover gathering information on the peace movement for the company (implicitly the CIA), when he received the telegram informing him of the death of his younger brother, Corporal Timothy Raker, in Kua Ling, Vietnam. It was then that Raker was invited to become freelance, unofficially working for the company as their troubleshooter. His first mission was no longer to monitor the peace movement but to take action. From then on, Raker tackled the problems the company declared too tough for conventional channels.

As far as Raker's superiors are aware, he works alone, but Raker has built up several agents such as Flame Wiley, a female agent, and Lawson Phipps, a Harvard-educated African American, both of whom have abilities and talents that Raker doesn't possess and can go places he can't.

Based out of New York, Raker tackles problems across America. Raker doesn't kill indiscriminately, only when necessary, but he has killed many times and doesn't keep track.

In his first recorded adventure, he tackles the Black Liberation Army (BLA) and its cop-killing spree across America. Then in his second adventure, he tackles smuggling across the Mexican border.

Behind the Scenes

Don Scott is the author of sleaze or erotic novels such as *Naughty Neighborhood*, *Suck Loving Schoolgirl*, *Hot Mouth Librarian* and *Loving the Neighbors*.

The Books

Both books were published by Pinnacle Books:

1. *Raker*, 185 pages, 1982
2. *Tijuana Traffic*, 197 pages, 1982

RAPTOR FORCE
Three books by Bill Yenne

The United States has become signatory to a United Nations treaty which allows only the world body the authority for any nation to operate militarily outside its own borders, issuing International Validation certificates. Hailed as a measure that will ensure peace, it is quickly discovered that terrorist organizations were not bound by this treaty and could act with impunity. In the wake of a terrorist attack reminiscent of the September 11 attacks, with terrorists flying a plane into the Nothal Corp tower, the tallest building in Denver, information was obtained that the terrorist training camp was located across the Mexican border. While the United Nations expressed public sympathy for the attacks, it refused to allow American troops to retaliate against terrorists.

In frustration, President Thomas Livingstone contacted an old friend, Ret. General

Buckley Peighton, and asked him to form a rapid response team modeled on the American Volunteer Group, better known as the Flying Tigers from World War II. The Flying Tigers were retired American military aviators who, as civilians, were able to fight the Japanese in China, not bound by the neutrality of the American government. Livingstone's new American Volunteer Group operated in a similar fashion. Comprised of retired American servicemen, this group could act against terrorist threats without needing international validation.

General Peighton recruited a seven-man Special Forces team. The team had last seen duty in 1997, during an aborted mission code-named Operation Raptor. Taking the name Raptor Force, this unit consisted of

- Dave Brannon: team leader
- Jack Rodgers: second-in-command and interrogation expert
- Brad Townsend: communications expert
- Jason Houn: Arabic-American soldier, translator and covert infiltrator
- Ray Couper : explosives expert
- Will Casey: master sniper
- Greg Boyinson: expert chopper pilot, considered the best in Special Operations Command

While on their first mission, the team rescues Professor Anne McCaine, an archaeologist whose husband died in the Nothal Corp terrorist attack. The professor becomes an unofficial member of the team. She is able to track the relics that the terrorists had been selling to the buyers and, in later missions, her academic credentials give the team the cover identity of a dig team, allowing them access to the leader of a terrorist plot.

Behind the Scenes

Bill Yenne is the author of numerous nonfiction works on military history as well as *The Legend of Zorro* (1991) which examines the history of Zorro in print, film and television.

The Books

All books were published by Berkeley Books:

1. *Raptor Force*, 297 pages, 2006
2. *Holy Fire*, 296 pages, 2007
3. *Corkscrew*, 304 pages, 2007

REEFE KING

Two books by Albert Barker

Jimmie Sainsbury, the son of a doctor, attended Chicago University intending to study chemistry and go on to a long career in that field. As a hobby, he joined an acting group and while he possessed limited acting skills, he had the "look." He was been spotted by an agent named Manny who offered him a career in the movies. Changing his name to Reefe King, Sainsbury made a career in film and on television as an action movie star. Naturally athletic, King had experience with guns, women and fighting. He also knew some karate and often performed his own stunts. His style of acting with barely moving lips and a self-effacing grin proved very popular.

One summer, while visiting his Uncle Neal in Paris, King was asked to keep an eye on the Cannes film festival. Neal was a high-ranking member of Interpol and needed a man who could go places a regular agent couldn't go. Thinking it would be a fun lark, King agreed. At Cannes, strange things did happen, with a young actress known as "cinema's virgin" suddenly performing a strip tease on a crowded beach and a western actor appearing in drag and attempting to seduce a male police officer. King investigates and brings down a drug trail that runs from Cannes to East Berlin. King is next called to action when the CIA discovers an affair between an Apollo astronaut and a reporter. Not only are the Soviets interested in embarrassing the American space program, but the reporter is pregnant and the child might be infected with a space virus that could destroy the world.

Behind the Scenes

Albert Barker, born 1900, has written several reference books for young readers on topics such as the history of printing, the spice trade and town planning. Barker is also the author of the **Hawk Macrae** series for Curtis Books.

The Books

Both books were published by Award Books:

1. *The Gift from Berlin*, 156 pages, 1969
2. *The Apollo Legacy*, 156 pages, 1970

REVENGER (BEN MARTIN)

Six books by Jon Messmann

Ben Martin lived a normal and peaceful life in New York until mobsters killed his family. Martin vowed revenge and began hunting the Mafia across America. Aided by his girlfriend, Martin blasted mobsters in New York and Chicago.

After his first two battles with the Mafia, Martin retreated to a small town outside of Indianapolis before Corbett, a hired killer, tracked him down and tried to eliminate him. Realizing that he could never return to a normal life, Martin returned to Mafia-hunting with a vengeance, wiping out the mob in Indianapolis and Pennsylvania.

Martin also foils the plot by gangster Johnny Lupo to kidnap the beautiful daughter of Judge Salvatore Cozzi. Judge Cozzi's hard-line stand against organized crime has been causing problems and it was hoped that his daughter would be the leverage to eliminate this problem. Martin eliminates Lupo after a fight on the Statue of Liberty. Martin, while capable of violent action, is more introspective than many of his fellow Mafia busters.

Behind the Scenes

Jon Messmann (1920–2004) initially worked as a writer for Fawcett Comics and worked on Captain Marvel Jr. and their western line of comics. Messmann then branched out to crime fiction and westerns. Under the name Jon Sharpe, he wrote several novels in the Trailsman and Canyon O'Grady western series. In the serial vigilante field, he wrote several **Killmasters** under the house name of Nick Carter and, under his own name, the Handyman series. This series should not be confused with the British Revenger series by Joseph Hedges, which was renamed Stark (see **Revenger II/Stark**) for American reprints.

The Books

All books were published by Signet Books:

1. *Revenger*, 136 pages, 1973
2. *Fire in the Streets*, 135 pages, 1974
3. *Vendetta Contract*, 158 pages, 1974
4. *Stiletto Signature*, 1974
5. *City for Sale*, 144 pages, 1975
6. *Promise for Death*, 176 pages, 1975

REVENGER II/STARK (JOHN STARK)

Twelve books by Joseph Hedges

John Stark was a low-level criminal working for the criminal organization known as the Company. He agreed to help with the payroll robbery of Danton Electronics but the robbery went bad and Stark was sent to jail. While he was in jail, the Company murdered the only woman that John Stark had ever loved.

On hearing the news, Stark escaped from jail and gained bloody retribution on the people who killed the only person who mattered to him and in the process disrupted a number of Company operations. Stark then became a man on the run with a price on his head, a thousand-pound reward from Danton Electronics for Stark's recapture and a twenty-thousand-pound open contract from the Company to kill him. Stark realized that he would be marked for life and his only action was to destroy as much of the Company and its operations before they eventually killed him. Stark began traveling the world, smashing the Company's operations where ever he found them. Stark is often assisted by people wronged by the Company.

Behind the Scenes

In Great Britain, Corgi Books was printing British editions of Don Pendleton's **Executioner** with great success and, as was the case in America, other publishers began to create their own characters in the same vein. The Sphere Books entry into this market was the Revenger. The silver covers even mimicked those of the Corgi Executioners.

The task of creating the series fell to Terry Harknett. Harknett, born in 1936, had served in the Royal Air Force (1955–57) before working a variety of newspaper jobs. During his newspaper career, Harknett wrote several novels. His first success was the novelization of the Clint Eastwood film *A Fist Full of Dollars* (1972) as Frank Chandler. Harknett created a series of spaghetti western novels with the Edge series, which told the exploits of Josiah Hedges (a likely source of the Joseph Hedges pen name) under the pseudonym of George G. Gilman. Under that same pen name, he created the Steele and Undertaker western series and wrote three books where Edge and Steele worked together.

Angus Wells took over the pen name Joseph Hedges for the final two Revenger adventures when Harknett became too busy. Wells, along with Robert Holdstock, wrote the fantasy series Raven. Wells, born in 1943, also wrote a number of western series under a variety of pen names.

When Pyramid Books reprinted the books in America, they changed the series name to Stark to avoid confusion with Jon Messmann's **the Revenger** series, published by New American Library.

The Books

All books were published by Sphere Books:

(Books 1–10 were written by Terry Harknett; books 11–12 were written by Angus Wells.)

1. *Funeral Rites*, 173 pages, 1973
2. *Arms for Oblivion*, 189 pages, 1973
3. *Chinese Coffin*, 206 pages, 1974
4. *Gold Plated Hearse*, 188 pages, 1974
5. *Rainbow Colored Shroud*, 186 pages, 1974
6. *Corpse on Ice*, 188 pages, 1974
7. *Mile Deep Grave*, 158 pages, 1975
8. *Mexican Mourning*, 188 pages, 1975
9. *Stainless Steel Wreath*, 190 pages, 1976
10. *Chauffeur Driven Pyre*, 160 pages, 1976
11. *Gates of Death*, 143 pages, 1976
12. *Angel of Destruction*, 141 pages, 1977

RIG WARRIOR (BARRY RIVERS/RIVERA)

Three books by William Johnstone

Barry Rivers was raised in the cabin of a truck in New Orleans. When he grew up, he joined the Army and was an A-Team commander in Vietnam. Later, in civilian life, he became a military consultant and arms dealer. Then, in 1987, Barry discovered that his father, Big Joe Rivers, was apparently being muscled by the Mafia. So he took a leave of absence from his company and uncovered a much larger scheme; Barry's partner in his company and his brother were involved in illicit scientific experiments on homeless veterans and illegal aliens and the pair had decided to eliminate him. Barry foiled their scheme and closed down their operation, but his new wife Kate was killed by a bomb blast meant for him. Barry was caught in the blast and left in a coma.

After much plastic surgery, Barry Rivers was given a new face and a new name Barry Rivera. Barry was then given a big, blue, armor-plated Kenworth truck and adopts the code name Dog, inspired by **the Dog Team**. Given the mandate to fight crime by the unnamed president (implicitly Ronald Reagan), Barry Rivera and his husky named Dog travel the highways of America fighting injustice and crime. In the mountains of Virginia, Rivera helps break the power of the degenerate Anson family over Dade County. Later after an unsuccessful hijacking of his rig, Rivera discovers and blows open a terrorist alliance.

Behind the Scenes

The series was created by William W. Johnstone, author of numerous horror, adventure and western novels. Johnstone was discharged from the French Foreign Legion for being underage, then worked in a carnival, became a deputy sheriff and did a stint in the army. He started writing in 1970 but did not make his first sale until 1979 with *The Devil's Kiss*. Johnstone is the author of **Codename, Dog Team**, and **Invasion USA** series. Johnstone died in 2004 in Shreveport, Louisiana.

The Books

All books were published by Kensington Books' Zebra Imprint and reprinted in 2000 under Kensington's Pinnacle Books imprint:

1. *Rig Warrior*, 285 pages, 1987
2. *Wheels of Death*, 252 pages, 1988
3. *Eighteen Wheel Avenger*, 252 pages, 1988

ROGUE ANGEL (ANNJA CREED)

Ongoing series by Alex Archer

Annja Creed was an orphan raised in New Orleans. She studied archaeology and eventually became a presenter for the cable show *Chasing History's Monsters*. The show investigates various monsters throughout history and seeks to explain them. Annja frequently battles her producer Doug Morell over his constant desire to sensationalize her stories, fighting to keep the history accurate.

While researching the Beast of Gevaudan, Annja made an incredible discovery, a medallion that leads her to a secret order of monks and fighting for her life. Even more remarkable was the old man she met when she found the medallion. The old man was named Roux and he was over 500 years old. He eventually revealed that he and his apprentice Garin were present when Joan of Arc was burned at the stake and that the medallion was the final piece of her shattered sword.

When Annja came into the presence of the sword, the blade reformed and now Annja uses the sword to fight evil around the world. Sometimes she is helped by Roux. Garin, fearing that Annja's restoration of Joan's sword means the end to his immortality, has found himself working with and against Annja at various times. Annja struggles with the implications of her new role; is she merely to punish the guilty or defend the weak as well?

Since finding the sword, Annja has found that she has increased speed, strength and stamina. The sword is stored in another dimension, which Annja can mentally summon at any time. Annja has battled demons, renegade monks, spider gods, and otherworldly creatures as well as racing for various treasures and relics.

Behind the Scenes

This series has been described as Tomb Raider meets Witchblade and is an attempt to create a modern version of Joan of Arc. The series has been written by Mel Odom, Victor Milan and John Merz. Mel Odom is the author of a number of children's books, including the junior novelization of the first Tomb Raider movie as well as a number of books for **the Executioner** and its spinoff series. Victor Milan has co-written the War of Powers series with Robert R. Vardeman, as well as several Star Trek and Battletech novels.

The Books

All books were published by Gold Eagle Books:

1. *Destiny*, 346 pages, 2006 (Mel Odom)
2. *Solomon's Jar*, 346 pages, 2006 (Victor Milan)
3. *The Spider Stone*, 346 pages, 2006 (Odom)
4. *The Chosen*, 347 pages, 2007 (Milan)
5. *Forbidden City*, 349 pages, 2007 (Odom)
6. *The Lost Scrolls*, 346 pages, 2007 (Milan)
7. *God of Thunder*, 348 pages, 2007 (Odom)
8. *Secret of the Slaves*, 348 pages, 2007 (Milan)
9. *Warrior Spirit*, 346 pages, 2007 (John Merz)
10. *Serpent's Kiss*, 348 pages, 2008 (Odom)
11. *Provenance*, 348 pages, 2008 (Milan)
12. *The Soul Stealer*, 348 pages, 2008 (Merz)
13. *Gabriel's Horn*, 314 pages, 2008 (Odom)
14. *The Golden Elephant*, 320 pages, 2008 (Milan)

The Comic

In 2008, IDW comics produced the five-issue mini-series Rogue Angel: Teller of Tall Tales. Written by Barbara Randall Kesel and illustrated by Renae De Liz, it tells of Annja's hunt for a manuscript that influenced Samuel Clemens (Mark Twain) in his writings.

SABAT (MARK SABAT)

Four books by Guy N. Smith

Mark Sabat, a young man with psychic abilities, trained and became a Catholic priest, but he found that he didn't belong in that role and frequently visited prostitutes. After leaving the priesthood, Sabat joined the SAS where he was trained to kill quickly and efficiently. After being caught in an affair with the dominatrix wife of his commanding officer, Sabat was forced to leave the service.

With that unique skill set, Sabat became an exorcist. In his quest to remove the devil's influence, Sabat discovered the true identity of a man so evil that he was hunted by half the law enforcement agencies of the world and known as "Satan's henchman." It was his own brother, Quentin Sabat, gifted with the same abilities as his brother but taking the left-hand path with evil.

Mark knew that the only way to stop his brother's evil was to kill him. Mark hunted his brother around the world, eventually tracking Quentin to a graveyard. Quentin, trained in voodoo, sought to resurrect all of his deceased followers as an immortal army of followers. Mark was able to kill his brother but was partially possessed by Quentin's evil spirit.

Sabat's quest had only just begun; his inner evil and psychic abilities made him sensitive to the evil in the world around him and Sabat dedicated himself to tackling evil in human form. For Sabat there was only one penalty for those who spread their evil on the world — death. In Sabat's law, the death penalty had never been revoked, allowing him to act swiftly and with finality.

Based in London, Sabat is often unofficially informed of potential threats by a former SAS buddy, Detective Sergeant Clive McKay of the London CIB. Sabat has battled numerous cults, including the Disciples of Lilith, a fascist group run by a man who believed that he was the reincarnation of Adolph Hitler, cannibals, druids and supernatural threats such as vampires.

Behind the Scenes

Guy N. Smith (b. 1939) was first published at age twelve with an article in the local paper. He followed this by numerous short stories before gaining success with horror novels such as the Werewolf and Crabs series.

The Books

All books were published by New English Library:

1. *The Graveyard Vultures*, 160 pages, 1982
2. *The Blood Merchants*, 160 pages, 1982
3. *Cannibal Cult*, 154 pages, 1982
4. *The Druid Connection*, 148 pages, 1983

The four novels were reprinted in an omnibus edition, *Dead Meat: The Complete Books of Sabat* (443 pages, 1996), by Creation Books with two unpublished Sabat adventures, *Vampire Village* and *Hellbeat*, being printed for the first time.

SATAN SLEUTH (PHILIP ST. GEORGE)

Three books by Michael Avallone

Philip St. George was a wealthy man about town and researcher of the paranormal. He had it all — money, the beautiful house and the beautiful wife. During a research trip to investigate the Bermuda Triangle, St. George was called back by the news that his wife had been killed back at their Tudor-style house on the shores of Lake Placid.

Dorothea St. George was a former Miss America and aspiring actress, and her satanic ritual murder was so horrific that it was described as worse than the mutilation of Sharon Tate by Charles Manson and his "family."

Philip mourned his wife for a month and then emerged determined to prevent those who worship Satan from causing any more pain. No longer a dabbler in psychic research, St. George became the Satan Sleuth, hunting down and killing the Satanic forces in the world. After avenging the death of his wife and tackling the cult that murdered her, St. George traveled around America, investigating werewolves, voodoo priests, vampires and witches.

Behind the Scenes

Michael Avallone is most famous as author of the private eye Ed Noon as well as writing tie-in novels for the *Man from U.N.C.L.E.*, *I-Spy* and the *Partridge Family* television series. Avallone also wrote several **Killmaster** novels as Nick Carter and for **the Butcher** as Stuart Jason.

The Books

All books were published by Warner Books:

1. *Fallen Angel*, 175 pages, 1974
2. *Werewolf Walks*, 158 pages, 1974
3. *Devil, Devil*, 174 pages, 1974

Unpublished

1. *Vampires Wild*, 1975
2. *Zombie Depot*, 1976

S-COM

Six books by Steve White

S-Com is short for Strategic Commando, a five-member team formed in 1977 that can be hired for half a million, payable to a bank in Zurich, or in cash, to tackle the threats too big, too tough for anyone else. The team consists of:

• Stone Williams: team leader, mercenary and computer-games designer

• Leah Aviv: former Israeli Secret Service member drummed out for investigating the death of her husband in Lebanon

- Rod Turnbull: Australian outback wild man, brawler and survival expert
- Myles Benet: Haitian-born, Bronx-reared weapons expert and Vietnam veteran
- Gabriel "Lucky" Lopez Guerrero: Cuban explosives expert, his father was injured in the failed Bay of Pigs invasion and Lucky got his start in several anti–Castro groups.

Each member of the team joined because they felt that in S-Com they could achieve more than they could have in their other careers, both military and civilian. The team tackles terrorist groups, quells riots in Ireland, tackles neo-Nazis and fights wars in Africa.

Behind the Scenes

Steve White is the pseudonym used by Robert McGarvey. McGarvey was born on December 13, 1948, in Linden, NJ, son of Robert (a journalist) and Laura McGarvey; and married to Elise Caitlin (an actress, writer, and playwright). He is the author of several guides to e-business and numerous magazine articles for magazines such as *Playboy*, *Boy's Life* and *Oui*.

McGarvey points, out, "Although solidly within the 'men's adventure' genre of blood-and-guts and sex, the White books proceeded with scant editorial interference. Anything could go — and anything did. *The King of Kingston*, for instance, turned into a parable about the decay of Western civilization" (Contemporary Authors Online, 2002). McGarvey views the books as existential, in the truest sense, where the members of S-Com create the meaning and essence of their own lives.

The Books

The series was published by Warner Books under their Men of Action line:

1. *Terror in Turin*, 159 pages, 1981
2. *Stars and Swastikas*, 158 pages, 1981
3. *The Battle in Botswana*, 159 pages, 1982
4. *The Fighting Irish*, 175 pages, 1982
5. *King of Kingston*, 189 pages, 1982
6. *Sierra Death Dealers*, 190 pages, 1982

THE SEXECUTIONER (CHERRY DELIGHT)

Twenty-nine books by Glen Chase

Cherry Delight's real name is Priscilla Dellissio and she works for NYMPHO (New York Mafia Prosecution and Harassment Organization), headed by Avery King. NYMPHO works around the world to stamp out the Mafia. And Cherry, named for her red hair, is the best agent of their Sexecutioner section; she loves sex and hates the Mafia. Cherry's father was a doctor and from studying his medical books, Cherry was able to learn how to cause pleasure and pain.

Cherry narrates all her own adventures and describes her sexual and crime fighting exploits in great detail. Even if she does forget her agency is named NYMPHO and refers to it as SPERM during *The Italian Connection*. Later, Cherry joins DUE (the Department of Unusual Events) and encounters supernatural menaces in the five All New Cherry Delight novels.

The Sexecutioner is a soft-core porn series where Cherry splits her time between sex and Mafia busting. In *The Italian Connection,* her entry to the Mafia is to make one of the dons so sexually dependent on her that he takes her along for his summit in Italy. Unfortunately, the Don's heart gives out during their first session and Cherry has to make alternate arrangements. Similarly, during *Tong in Cheek*, Cherry's plan is to screw an opponent until he is too tired to fight back. Cherry swings both ways and a stakeout can lead to a lesbian encounter. **The Executioner** never had such problems.

Behind the Scenes

The authors for this series include Gardner Fox and Leonard Levinson.

Gardner Fox is a prolific author of both novels and comic books. Born in 1911 and trained as a lawyer, Fox quickly turned to full-time writing; under his own name and pen names he turned out numerous novels of many genres, including historical adventures, fantasy, science fiction, swashbucklers, and romance, writing his own barbarian heroes Kothar and Kyrik as well as working on the soft-core Lady from L.U.S.T. and Sexecutioner series. In the comics field, Fox created and helped further develop many of DC Comics characters, including Superman, Batman, the Flash, the Green Lantern, Zatara, and the Atom as well as writing both the Justice Society of America and the Justice League of America.

Leonard Levinson also used the Glen Chase pen name for this series. Levinson was born in 1935 and served in the US Army from 1954 to 1957. Under a number of pseudonyms and house names he has contributed to a number of series including **Bronson, Butler, the Sharpshooter** and **Kung Fu (Mace)**.

In 1991, Eros Comix published the Sexecutioner by Skylar Owens. This Sexecutioner was Marcia Bolens, who, like the original, fights crime in two three-issue mini-series and teams up with another Eros heroine, Hell Mary from *Bad Habits*, for the three-issue mini-series *Naked Angels*.

The Books

All books were published by Leisure Books:

1. *The Italian Connection*, 165 pages, 1972
2. *Tong in Cheek*, 174 pages, 1972
3. *Silverfinger*, 153 pages, 1972
4. *Up Your Ante*, 186 pages, 1973
5. *Crack Shot*, 151 pages, 1973
6. *I'm Cherry, Fly Me*, 166 pages, 1973
7. *Chuck You Farley*, 187 pages, 1973
8. *Hot Rocks*, 169 pages, 1973
9. *Jersey Bounce*, 184 pages, 1974

10. *Made in Japan*, 179 pages, 1974
11. *Broad Jump*, 202 pages, 1974
12. *Fire in the Hole*, 184 pages, 1974
13. *Over the Hump*, 179 pages, 1974
14. *In a Pinch*, 183 pages, 1974
15. *What a Way to Go*, 178 pages, 1974
16. *Busted*, 173 pages, 1974
17. *Treasure Chest*, 171 pages, 1974
18. *Hang Loose*, 142 pages, 1975
19. *In a Bind*, 173 pages, 1975
20. *Always on Sunday*, 172 pages, 1975
21. *Mexican Standoff*, 173 pages, 1975
22. *Big Bankroll*, 171 pages, 1975
23. *Lights, Action, Murder*, 172 pages, 1975
24. *Roman Candle*, 184 pages, 1975

The All New Cherry Delight:
1. *The Devil to Pay*, 189 pages, 1977
2. *Greek Fire*, 187 pages, 1977
3. *The Moorland Monster*, 176 pages, 1977
4. *Where the Action Is*, 176 pages, 1977 (Levinson)
5. *The Man Who Was God*, 190 pages, 1978

SHADOW WARRIOR (SCOTT WAYLON MCKENNA)

Four books by Joseph Rosenberger

Scott Waylon McKenna is the first non–Japanese to survive the rigorous and dangerous training to become a true ninja. Raised in Hong Kong, McKenna began studying martial arts and eventually mastered ninjitsu.

With his ninja skills, McKenna is a devastating opponent. McKenna is called on by friends to help them in situations, such as being threatened by gangsters, or in need of protection against death squads and protecting treasure hunters. In other cases, the Shadow Warrior is hunted by members of rival ninja clans and other threats from his past. McKenna travels the world from Hong Kong to Cuba, Japan and Burma.

Behind the Scenes

Joseph Rosenberger became a professional writer at the age of twenty-one after selling an article. After working a series of jobs including Korean karate instructor, circus pitchman and private eye, he became a full-time writer in 1961. Rosenberger was the author of the **Death Merchant, Murder Master** and **C.O.B.R.A** series and, under the pseudonym Lee Chang, created and wrote the first martial arts series, **Kung Fu (Mace).**

The Books

All books were published by Dell Books:

1. *Hong Kong Massacre*, 253 pages, 1988
2. *Caribbean Blood Moon*, 191 pages, 1988
3. *Ninja Nightmare*, 184 pages, 1988
4. *Hell Wind in Burma*, 178 pages, 1988

SHARPSHOOTER (JOHNNY ROCK/JOHNNY ROCETTI)

Sixteen books by Bruno Rossi (house name)

Rocetti Designs was a family business run by the Rocetti family until the Mafia tried to take it over. When the family refused to allow the Mafia to use their business, the whole family was killed, except for one son, Johnny Rocetti. Rocetti went to the police for justice for his murdered family but corrupt cops shafted him and the men who killed his parents and brother went free.

At that point Johnny Rocetti ceased to exist and Johnny Rock was born. A Green Beret in Vietnam, Rock had been trained in the use of all types of deadly weapons and even bare handed was dangerous. Rock took the law into his own hands and swore vengeance against the Mafia.

Financed by his family's business, run by a trusted family friend, Rock purchased an arsenal of the finest weapons and travelled the United States fighting his self-appointed war on the Syndicate. Johnny Rock's war on the Syndicate received media coverage, including a feature in one of the true crime magazines complete with photograph taken by telephoto lens. This media coverage allows some of Rock's army buddies to contact him and tip him off to Mafia activities in their area.

Behind the Scenes

Bruno Rossi is a house name used several writers, including Paul Hofrichter, Russell Smith, John Stevenson, Leonard Levinson and Peter McCurtin.

Peter McCurtin was an editor for Belmont Towers books before becoming an author. McCurtin, under his own name, was the author of several western series such as Carmody and Sundance as well as the **Soldier of Fortune/Death Dealer** series; under various pen names he contributed to the **Sexecutioner** and **Marksman** series. McCurtin also novelized the movie *The Exterminator* as well as several exposés on organized crime, such as *Mafioso*, *The Syndicate* and *Omerta*.

Leonard Levinson also used the Bruno Rossi pen name for this series. Levinson, born in 1935, served the US Army from 1954 to 1957. Under a number of pseudonyms and house names, he has contributed to a number of series including **Bronson**, **Butler**, **Kung Fu** and **the Sexecutioner**.

Paul Hofrichter is the author of the post-apocalyptic Roadblaster as well as **Able Team #5:** *Cairo Countdown*.

The Books

All books were published by Leisure Books:

1. *Killing Machine*, 171 pages, 1973
2. *Blood Oath*, 156 pages, 1974
3. *Blood Bath*, 96 pages, 1974
4. *Worst Way to Die*, 95 pages, 1974 (Levinson)
5. *Night of the Assassins*, 185 pages, 1974 (Levinson)
6. *Muzzle Blast*, 147 pages, 1974
7. *Head Crusher*, 182 pages, 1974 (Levinson)
8. *No Quarter Given*, 161 pages, 1974
9. *Stiletto*, 95 pages, 1974
10. *Hitman*, 161 pages, 1974 (Stevenson)
11. *Triggerman*, 161 pages, 1975 (Smith)
12. *Scarfaced Killer*, 181 pages, 1975 (Hofrichter)
13. *Savage Slaughter*, 218 pages, 1975 Hofrichter
14. *Las Vegas Vengeance*, 1975 Stevenson
15. *Dirty Way to Die*, 1975
16. *Mafia Death Watch*, 188 pages, 1975

SHIELD (MICHAEL SHERIFF)

Three books by Preston MacAdam

Management Information Systems (MIS) is in the business of information gathering and has the largest computer system outside of the Pentagon. This information is then sold to the highest bidder approved by the Chairman of the MIS. The Chairman, whose name is never revealed, selects his clients with the aim of world security. MIS is headquartered in a small non-descript building nicknamed the Fort on Route 128 north of Boston.

Michael Sheriff is the main troubleshooter used by the Chairman, who has code-named Sheriff the Shield. Little is known about his history except that he was a CIA agent and that he was married for a short period. At the end of the marriage, Sheriff was estranged from his wife and son Roger.

The series opens with the now adult Roger attempting to reconcile with his father and, as part of that reconciliation, Roger seeks to become an agent of MIS. Michael is opposed to this move but the Chairman accepts Roger's application while Michael in on assignment. As the series progresses Michael and Roger eventually work together. The Shield travels the world, helping to bring stability by undertaking missions such as assisting the pro-democracy Fashanti tribe against the communist-backed Kindu tribe in the African nation of Leikawa, protecting American oil interests in the Arabian nation of Qatar and finally working with his son protecting the holdings of an American conglomerate on the Pacific island nation of Suparta. When not on assignment, Sheriff is renovating and restoring his home, a pre–Revolutionary War house.

Behind the Scenes

Preston MacAdam is the pen name of John Preston, an openly gay author. Many of his works were about the gay experience and gay erotica. Under the Jack Hild house name, Preston contributed several books to the **Soldiers of Barrabas** series. With **the Mission of Alex Kane** series, Preston was able to combine his two genres and created a gay action hero.

The Books

All books were published by Avon:

1. *African Assignment*, 188 pages, 1985
2. *Arabian Assault*, 192 pages, 1985
3. *Island Intrigue*, 204 pages, 1985

SOLDATO (JOHNNY MARONI)

Five books by Al Conroy

Johnny Maroni was a soldato, a soldier or enforcer for the Mafia working for Don Renzo Cappellani. Eventually, Maroni became sickened by his life and turned against his Don, giving evidence against him in court.

The US attorney prosecuting Don Renzi, Riley arranged for Maroni to enter the witness protection program when the Don was acquitted. Maroni, promised that he would be completely safe, set up a new life in Arizona as a storekeeper and eventually married. But after two years, a shady private investigator hired by Don Renzi discovered Maroni in his new life and two hit men were sent to kill Maroni. After a brutal game of cat and mouse in the desert mountains, Maroni dispatches his attackers and takes his wife Mary to New York to eliminate Don Renzi once and for all. After the death of his wife, Maroni vows to redeem his past and uses his skills and knowledge to infiltrate various Mafia families around America and destroy the families from the inside.

Behind the Scenes

Al Conroy is a pen name used by Marvin H. Albert and Gil Brewer. Marvin Albert (1924–1996) wrote a number of private detective series. Under his own name he wrote the Pete Sawyer mysteries about a private eye based in Paris. As Nick Quarry, Albert wrote the Jake Barrow series and as Anthony Rome he wrote the Tony Rome series. As Ian MacAlistair, Albert wrote a number of adventure novels.

Gil Brewer (1922–1983) was a Florida based-writer who wrote a number of sexy crime thrillers as well as novelizations of the espionage television series *It Takes a Thief*. Under the Ellery Queen pen name, he wrote the first novel in the Troubleshooter series.

The Books

All books were published by Lancer Books:

1. *Soldato*, 1972 (Albert)
2. *Death Grip*, 176 pages, 1972 (Albert)
3. *Stranglehold*, 222 pages, 1973 (Brewer)
4. *Murder Mission*, 1973 (Brewer)
5. *Blood Run*, 1973 (Albert)

SOLDIER FOR HIRE (J. C. STONEWALL)

Eight books by Robert Skimin and Mark Kelly Roberts

J. C. Stonewall served in Vietnam but after the war he was unable to return to civilian life. Stonewall decided to sell his soldiering skill becoming a mercenary; if the price is right he will fight and kill.

However, Stonewall will not work for the communists and frequently works with and trains anti-communists forces around the world. This attitude and his violent methods frequently put him at odds with bleeding hearts and left-wing politicians around the world and in America.

Stonewall has served all around the world, including Africa, Laos, Vietnam, Libya, Iran and Indonesia.

Behind the Scenes

Robert Skimin is the author of thirteen historical novels such as *Ulysses* about President Grant, and *Gray Victory*, an alternate history where the South won the Civil War. At age eighteen, Skimin left home and joined the Army, being the first Army pilot to become a Green Beret.

Mark Kelly Roberts is also the author of the Liberty Corps series, and co-authored **the Penetrator** series under the house name of Lionel Derrick with Chet Cunningham. Roberts also co-writes SEALS: Top Secret with Chief James "Patches" Watson.

The Books

All books were published by Zebra Books:

Books 1–4 by Robert Skimin; books 5–8 by Mark K. Roberts

1. *Zulu Blood*, 368 pages 1981
2. *Trojan in Iran*, 335 pages, 1981
3. *UN Sabotage*, 315 pages, 1981
4. *Bloodletting*, 302 pages, 1982
5. *Libyan Warlord*, 224 pages, 1982
6. *Commando Squad*, 235 pages, 1982
7. *Pathet Vengeance*, 224 pages, 1983
8. *Jakarta Coup*, 254 pages, 1983

SOLDIER OF FORTUNE/DEATH DEALER (JIM RAINEY)

Eighteen books by Peter McCurtin

Jim Rainey was born in Beaumont, Texas, during 1939. The son of a third-generation farmer, he had no desire to be a farmer and after two years of college joined the army and was sent to Vietnam. While fighting, Rainey spent six months in the Phoenix Group, discovering and killing subversive elements in the South Vietnamese government and military working with the Viet Cong. After the end of that war, Rainey decided that the only job he was suited for was soldiering and he became a mercenary. He contacted a mercenary contractor known as Mr. Ryan and his first mercenary job was with the Rhodesian Army as the head of an anti-terrorist force.

Rainey then traveled the world, taking missions wherever his skills were needed. Rainey has hunted communists in Argentina, fought Moslems in Beirut, fought Chinese rebels in Hong Kong and attempted to find soldiers listed as missing in action in Vietnam. Rainey also assisted several friends in times of need, such as rescuing fellow mercenaries who have been captured, helping a diplomat friend in Panama and avenging the death of a former lover by a Nicaraguan death squad.

Behind the Scenes

Peter McCurtin was an editor for Belmont Towers books before becoming an author. McCurtin, under his own name, was the author of several western series such as Carmody and Sundance as well as the Assassin series; under various pen names, he contributed to the Sexecutioner and Marksman series. McCurtin also novelized the movie *The Exterminator* as well as several exposés on organized crime such as *Mafioso*, *The Syndicate* and *Omerta*. When New England Library printed British Editions of this series, the name of the series was changed from Soldier of Fortune to Death Dealer.

The Books

Books 1–9 were published by Belmont Towers Books; books 10–18 published by Leisure Books:

1. *Massacre at Umtali*, 191 pages, 1976
2. *The Deadliest Game*, 182 pages, 1976
3. *Spoils of War*, 180 pages, 1976
4. *Guns of Palembang*, 208 pages, 1977
5. *First Blood*, 124 pages, 1977
6. *Ambush at Derati Wells*, 126 pages, 1977
7. *Operation Hong Kong*, 189 pages, 1977
8. *Body Count*, 176 pages, 1977
9. *Battle Pay*, 188 pages, 1978
10. *Yellow Rain*, 224 pages, 1984
11. *Green Hell*, 222 pages, 1984
12. *Moro*, 223 pages, 1984
13. *Kalahari*, 220 pages, 1984

THE SOLDIERS OF BARRABAS (SOB)
Thirty-three books by Jack Hild

The Soldiers of Barrabas are also known as Eagle Squad and are the unofficial force used when conventional armed forces can't be used; as the promotional material says, "they do what the marines wish they could." The team was put together by Walker Jessup, known in Washington as "the Fixer," and he gives the team their assignments. This group of mercenaries is headed by Niles Barrabas, the last man out of Vietnam. The team changes as members die and are replaced by others, but include:

• William Starfoot II (Billy Two): a full-blooded Osage Indian

• Alex Ninos: an expert sailor

• Liam O'Toole: former IRA soldier (a fact that forms the basis of #13: *No Sanctuary*)

• Geoff Bishop: a Canadian pilot

• Lee Hatton: doctor and the only woman on the team

• Nate Beck: electronics wiz

The team takes on missions like rescuing world leaders from kidnapping and assassination, fighting Soviet forces, preventing coups, stopping neo-Nazis and other terrorist groups, and facing enemies from various team members' pasts who seek revenge.

Behind the Scenes

Gold Eagle tells us that they have never met Jack Hild, a US citizen residing outside the United States, contacting him only through a European attorney-agent. Hild has offered to leave money in his will to various brothels around the world to build memorial wings.

In truth, Jack Hild does not exist but is a house name used by Alan Bomack, Robin Hardy, Jack Canon, Alan Philipson, Jack Garside, John Preston, Joe Roberts, Rich Rainey, Roland Green.

Rich Rainey, under his full name Richard Rainey, has written several nonfiction works on the occult and the horror genre. Rainey wrote the **Protector** series and has also produced several books in **the Executioner** franchise and contributed the final book in the post-apocalyptic Warlord series as Jason Frost.

John Preston was an openly gay author. Many of his works were about the gay experience and gay erotica. Under the name Preston McAdams he wrote **the Shield** series. Under his own name, he wrote **the Mission of Alex Kane** about a gay action hero, combining both genres that he worked in.

Alan Bomack (a near anagram of Mack Bolan) is a pseudonym used by the writer of several of **the Executioner** books.

The Books

All books were published by Gold Eagle:

1. *The Barrabas Run*, 221 pages, 1983 (Jack Canon, Robin Hardy & Alan Bomack)
2. *The Plains of Fire*, 221 pages, 1984 (Philipson)
3. *Butchers of Eden*, 219 pages, 1984 (Alan Philipson)
4. *Show No Mercy*, 219 pages, 1985 (Robin Hardy)
5. *Gulag War*, 218 pages, 1985 (Philipson)
6. *Red Hammer Down*, 218 pages, 1985 (Alan Philipson)
7. *River of Flesh*, 222 pages, 1985 (Hardy)
8. *Eye of the Fire*, 222 pages, 1985 (Hardy)
9. *Some Choose Hell*, 220 pages, 1985 (Robin Hardy)
10. *Vultures of the Horn*, 216 pages, 1986 (Alan Philipson)
11. *Agile Retrieval*, 221pages, 1986 (Robin Hardy)
12. *Jihad*, 219 pages, 1986 (Philipson)
13. *No Sanctuary*, 218 pages, 1986 (Hardy)
14. *Red Vengeance*, 220 pages, 1986 (Hardy)
15. *Death Deal*, 219 pages, 1986 (Hardy)
16. *Firestorm USA*, 219 pages, 1987 (Robin Hardy)
17. *Point Blank*, 219 pages, 1987 (Hardy)
18. *Sakhalin Breakout*, 220 pages, 1987 (Jack Garside)
19. *Skyjack*, 218 pages, 1987 (Hardy)
20. *Alaska Deception*, 221 pages, 1987 (Garside)
21. *No Safe Place*, 218 pages, 1987 (Hardy)
22. *Kremlin Devils*, 220 pages, 1988 (Hardy)
23. *Pacific Payload*, 219 pages, 1988 (John Preston)
24. *The Barrabas Creed*, 219 pages, 1988 (Preston)
25. *The Barrabas Raid*, 220 pages, 1988 (Preston)
26. *The Barrabas Edge*, 220 pages, 1988 (Joe Roberts [Robert Randisi])
27. *The Barrabas Fix*, 221 pages, 1988 (William Baetz)
28. *The Barrabas Fallout*, 220 pages, 1989 (Jon Mandeville)
29. *The Barrabas Hit*, 218 pages, 1989 (Roberts)
30. *The Barrabas Heist*, 221pages, 1989 (Roland Green)
31. *The Barrabas Thrust*, 220 pages, 1989 (Rich Rainey)
32. *The Barrabas Fire*, 219 pages, 1989 (Rich Rainey)
33. *The Barrabas Kill*, 219 pages, 1989 (Baetz)

Super Soldiers of Barrabas:

1. *The Barrabas Strike*, 349 pages, 1988 (Philipson)
2. *The Barrabas Sting*, 349 pages, 1988 (Philipson)
3. *The Barrabas Blitz*, 347 pages, 1989 (Rainey)
4. *The Barrabas War*, 346 pages, 1989 (Roland Green)
5. *The Barrabas Sweep*, 347 pages, 1990 (Rich Rainey)

Related Material

Niles Barrabas makes a cameo appearance in the Vietnam War tale "Incident at Hoi Binh" from **the Executioner #63** *The New War Book* (1984). Barrabas is accused of a massacre but Mack Bolan clears his name.

THE SPECIALIST (JACK SULLIVAN)

Eleven books by John Cutter (John Shirley)

Jack Sullivan is a mercenary with a talent for revenge. Prior to his first adventure, he had left the mercenary game for love. His marriage was cut short when his wife was killed violently in an explosion, leaving Sullivan a broken man with grey hair at the temples. At the time of his first adventure, he has been bumming around Europe living on his savings for three and a half years.

Jack Sullivan is no kill-crazy mercenary who will work for anyone; he works for a cause and for the right side, this having been instilled in him by his father. And it is the case of Julia Penn, a woman tortured and traumatized by African dictator Magg Ottoowa, that brings Sullivan out of his retirement. Sullivan is for hire to gain revenge for anyone who has been wronged, tackling dictators, pedophiles, drug lords, and others who prey on the weak.

Behind the Scenes

John Cutter is the pseudonym for John Shirley. Shirley was born in 1953 and is a member of the cyberpunk science fiction writer's movement. He is also a musician and has been in a number of bands.

Under the pseudonym D. B. Drumm, he wrote the post-apocalyptic Traveler series. Under his own name he has written numerous novels, songs and screenplays, including *The Crow.*

The Books

All books were published by Signet Books:

1. *A Talent for Revenge*, 186 pages, 1984
2. *Manhattan, Revenge*189 pages, 1984
3. *Sullivan's Revenge*, 190 pages, 1984
4. *Psycho Soldier*, 190 pages, 1984

The Movie

The 1994 movie *The Specialist* was suggested by the novel series by John Shirley, revealing that John Cutter was a pseudonym. The movie starred Sylvester Stallone, Sharon Stone, Rod Steiger, Eric Roberts and James Woods and was directed by Luis Llosa.

Ray Quick was an explosives expert for the CIA who quits when one of his bombs kills the daughter of a drug dealer. Quick has become a mercenary and eventually is hired by May Munro to help her gain revenge against the Leon crime family, who were responsible for the death of her parents. Quick aids Munro and brings him against an old foe from his CIA days.

THE SPECIALISTS

Three books by Chet Cunningham

When multimillionaire industrialist J. August Marshall retired after a decade as head of the Central Intelligence Agency, he implemented a plan to form his own strike force. Marshall handpicked the best of the best for his covert strike team, free from the restrictions and the political games that marked his time in the CIA.

After a year of screening Marshall formed his team:

- Wade Thorne: team leader, ex-CIA team leader, expert fighter and pilot
- Katherine "Kat" Killinger: this Hawaiian beauty is second in command, a former lawyer, FBI field agent and triathlete
- Ichi Yamagata: Japanese American martial arts master and master gunsmith, the team's weapons master.
- Roger Johnson: former Navy SEAL and demolitions expert.
- Hershel Levine: Mossad agent and computer expert.
- Duncan Bancroft: MI6 agent and intelligence expert, able to procure weapons anywhere in the world, thanks to his contacts.

The team can travel anywhere with access to the resources of Marshall, tackling everything from Nazi conspiracies, hijacked ocean liners, biological weapons threats, stolen nuclear devices and terrorist attacks. The team often splits into smaller teams in the initial investigation of the suspected threat, working capably alone or all together.

Behind the Scenes

The series was written by Chet Cunningham who lives in San Diego. Cunningham has also written numerous western novels both under his own name and pseudonyms. A veteran of the Korean War, Cunningham has written several volumes of military history. Cunningham is also the author of **the Avenger** series and was one of the two men behind the Lionel Derrick pseudonym for **the Penetrator**. Cunningham has also written several **Executioner** and SuperBolan (see **Executioner**) novels

The Books

All books were published by Bantam Books:

1. *Plunder*, 294 pages, 1999
2. *Deadly Strike*, 304 pages, 2001
3. *Nuke Down*, 368 pages, 2001

SPIDER (RICHARD WENTWORTH)

Four books by Grant Stockbridge

Back in 1933, to capitalize on the success of the Shadow, Popular Publications created their own pulp hero, the Spider. The original pulp series ran for 118 issues and featured amateur criminologist, Great War veteran and wealthy man about town, Richard Wentworth, fighting crime under the alias of the Spider in the disguise of hunchback, fangs and fright wig. Wentworth was assisted by his fiancée Nita Van Sloan, his servant Ram Singh and old World War I Army buddy Ronald Jackson. The Spider and his team fought some of the bloodiest and strangest of adversaries and foes in the pulps. The Spider was quite successful, even gaining two movie serials.

Move forward to 1975 and to capitalize on the success of **the Executioner**, Pocket Books reprinted four of the Spider pulps but, unlike other pulp reprints, these updated the character to make him more like the current crop of serial vigilantes. Richard Wentworth was still a wealthy, amateur criminologist but he had served in Korea. The Spider had become Spider; no longer wearing his elaborate fangs and disguise Spider, he wore turtleneck sweaters (white on American covers, black on the British editions) but was still assisted by his loyal followers.

Product and brand names were updated and the World Trade Center, opened in 1973, replaced the Empire State Building in *The City Destroyer*. Much of Ram Singh's flowery speech was also removed.

Spider faced villains who controlled vampire bats, rampaging cavemen, a weapon that weakens steel and a cult that could produce murderous rampages in anyone.

The Books

All four novels were published by Pocket Books of Canada in North America and by Mews Books in the United Kingdom:

1. *Death Reign of the Vampire King*, 128 pages, 1975 (originally the Spider #26 1935)

2. *Hordes of the Red Butcher*, 144 pages, 1975 (originally the Spider #21, 1935)

3. *The City Destroyer*, 143 pages, 1975 (originally the Spider #16, 1935)

4. *Death and the Spider*, 126 pages, 1975 (originally the Spider #100, 1942)

The Comics

In 1990, writer Tim Truman offered a similar updating of the Spider published by Eclipse Comics. Truman re-imagined the character in the '90s — not the 1990s as we knew it, but rather 1990s that a 1930s pulp writer may have imagined, with a 1985 war in India allowing Richard Wentworth to meet Ram Singh. The first three-issue mini-series adapted the pulp *Corpse Cargo* and the second adapted *Death Reign of the Vampire King*.

1. *The Spider*, 1990 (3 issues) (each issue, 42 pages)

2. *Reign of the Vampire King*, 1992 (3 issues) (each issue, 42 pages)

SPRINGBLADE

Nine books by Greg Walker

After three tours of duty in Special Forces, Bo Thornton retired to San Diego to run the Heavy Hook Dive Shop with his old buddy, Frank Hartung, a veteran of both Korea and Vietnam. Thornton converted the shop's loft to an R-and-R center nicknamed "the Locker" where many of the Special Forces, SEALs and other naval personnel in the city came to hang out.

This allowed Thornton to keep up to date with old buddies and with the latest developments in the spec ops world. This put Thornton in an ideal position when an old SEAL buddy turned DEA agent, Calvin Bailey, contacted him with a deal to form and command an elite fighting force to fight the war on drugs, free of the normal rules and regulations. This team would not exist officially and would be assigned their missions by the president and a circle of advisers. All contact for this team would be through Bailey.

During the planning stages, this team was code named Eagle Flight, but Thornton renamed this force Springblade, after the Soviet-made ballistic knife he used. The team consists of:

• Bo Thornton: team leader

• Frank Hartung: mission coordinator and logistics

• Jason Silver: computer and demolition expert, Vietnam veteran who operates an art gallery in San Diego

• David Lee: the team's only active member of the military and a paratrooper

The team is joined after their fourth mission by former Soviet Spetsnaz soldier Peter Chuikov.

Springblade handles the missions that require an immediate response and cannot be handled through any other means. The team has tackled drug dealers, rogue Green Berets, and renegade Russian forces and fought in the first Gulf War.

Behind the Scenes

Greg Walker is a former Special Forces sergeant who operated throughout South and Central America. Currently retired, Walker works with law enforcement in Oregon. Walker is also the author of several books on knife fighting.

The Books

The series was published by Charter Books:

1. *Springblade*, 170 pages, 1989
2. *Machete*, 169 pages, 1990
3. *Stiletto*, 167 pages, 1990
4. *Bowie*, 197 pages, 1990
5. *Border Massacre*, 200 pages, 1990
6. *Battle Zone*, 198 pages, 1990
7. *Sentinel*, 168 pages, 1991
8. *Betrayal*, 199 pages, 1991
9. *Storming Iraq*, 170 pages, 1992

STARK (JOHN HOWARD STARK)

Two books by William W. Johnstone and J. A. Johnstone

John Howard Stark was a former marine who served in Vietnam. After returning to America, Stark became a rancher in the Rio Grande Valley near Del Rio and lived a peaceful life until a Mexican border gang decided that Stark's ranch would make an ideal crossing for bringing drugs into America. Stark refused and in retaliation the gang killed his wife. This caused the Vietnam veteran to reform his old squad and go to war against the gang, taking the battle across the border into Mexico. The fight cost Stark several of his friends but in the end Stark was victorious.

This action made Stark a minor celebrity and saved him from prosecution, forcing the government to back down. Eventually the media lost interest in Stark and he returned to a peaceful life.

That was, until the American government, in a political stunt, decided to allow the Mexican government temporary dominion over the Alamo to commemorate the fall of the Alamo. This move was peacefully protested by veterans from World War II, Korea, Vietnam and the Gulf War with Stark as their leader. A group of Mexican terrorists known as the Reconquistadors took this opportunity to claim the Alamo permanently and Stark and his fellow veterans eventually take a stand in the Alamo as both the American and Mexican governments dither ineffectively in Court.

Behind the Scenes

The series was created by William W. Johnstone, author of numerous horror, adventure and western novels. Johnstone was discharged from the French Foreign Legion for being underage, then worked in a carnival, became a deputy sheriff and did a stint in the army. He started writing in 1970 but did not make his first sale until 1979 with *The Devil's Kiss*. Johnstone died in 2004 in Shreveport, Louisiana.

The Books

Both books were published by Kensington Pinnacle:

1. *Vengeance Is Mine*, 288 pages, 2005
2. *Remember the Alamo*, 320 pages, 2007

Related Works

The unnamed female American president seen in these books has a number of similarities to the unnamed female president seen in Johnstone's **Invasion USA** series, which also deals with the themes of American border security. It is possible that this female president is President Harriet Clayton who appeared in Johnstone's **Codename** and the one-shot **Black Ops**: *American Jihad*.

Remember the Alamo shares a similar plot to **the New Destroyer**: *Guardian Angel*, both were released in 2007 and dealt with a Mexican terrorist group seizing the Alamo.

STONER (MARK STONER)

Four books by Ralph Hayes

Mark Stoner is a treasure hunter and an adventurer travelling the world, hunting valuable items for his salvage and antiquities business in Key West, Florida, which he runs with his partner, ex-shrimp fisherman, Zeb Curry. Mark has done it all: salvage diving, gold prospecting, tomb raiding, and trading in gems and other precious stones. Stoner is tall with brown hair and eyes who in his life of adventuring has made many friends and enemies. Stoner is often called on by his friends to help them to recover treasures that have been stolen or otherwise lost. In other cases, Stoner is contacted by people who are aware of his reputation to help them either recover lost treasures or find missing loved ones who had been hunting treasures.

Behind the Scenes

Ralph Hayes was born in 1927 and served in the Air Force 1945–47. After leaving the Air Force, he studied and became a lawyer specializing in insurance. In 1969, Hayes became a freelance writer, writing a number of travel guides and individual novels as well as the Buffalo Hunter western series and **Agent for COMINSEC, the Hunter** and **Checkforce** series. Under the Nick Carter house name, he wrote eight **Killmaster** books. Hayes travelled extensively and utilized that experience for his travel guides and the settings for his books (Contemporary Authors Online, 2002).

The Books

All books were published by Manor Books:

1. *The Golden God*, 127 pages 1976

2. *The Satan Stone*, 184 pages, 1976
3. *All That Glitters*, 181 pages, 1977
4. *King's Ransom*, 192 pages, 1978

STONY MAN

Ongoing series created by Don Pendleton

When **the Executioner** ended his war on the Mafia (#38), he faked his death and was given the new identity of Col. John Macklin Phoenix. He began his war on terrorism and to conduct this war he was given a base known as Stony Man Farm, which is located in the Blue Ridge Mountains, Virginia. "John Phoenix," **Able Team** and **Phoenix Force** operated out of this base. Eventually, there would be a mission that would require everyone to work together. The first such mission was *Stony Man Doctrine* (which was marketed as the first Super Bolan [see Executioner]) where all three teams worked together. They continue to do so, though Bolan's estrangement leads to only Phoenix Force and Able Team working together. With the demise of Able Team and Phoenix Force as individual series, their continued adventures are recorded in the Stony Man series.

Behind the Scenes

Notable ghosts for the series include Mike Newton, Mel Odom, and Dan Schmidt.

Mike Newton trained with Don Pendleton, co-writing several **Executioners** with Pendleton for Pinnacle Books and writing numerous books for that series for Gold Eagle, making him the most prolific writer of **Executioner** novels. Newton has also written several western series under the pen name Lyle Brandt as well as four entries in the **Destroyer** series. Newton is also the author or several nonfiction works, including *How to Write Action-Adventure Fiction* and several reference works on serial killers and cryptozoology.

Mel Odom is the author of a number of children's books, including the junior novelization of the first Tomb Raider movie as well as a number of books for **the Executioner** and its spinoff series. Under the Alex Archer pen name, he contributes to the **Rogue Angel** series.

Dan Schmidt is the author of a number of horror novels, the **Eagle Force** series under his own name and the **Killsquad** series under the pseudonym Frank Garrett.

The Books

All books were published by Gold Eagle:

1. *Stony Man Doctrine*, 371 pages, 1983 (Dick Stivers)
2. *Stony Man II*, 347 pages, 1991 (Mel Odom)
3. *Stony Man III*, 347 pages, 1991 (Odom)
4. *Stony Man IV*, 346 pages, 1992 (William Fieldhouse)
5. *Stony Man V*, 349 pages, 1992 (Odom)

6. *Stony Man VI*, 346 pages, (Fieldhouse)
7. *Stony Man VII*, 349 pages, 1993 (Mike Newton)
8. *Stony Man VIII*, 346 pages, 1993 (Jerry Van Cook)
9. *Strikepoint*, 349 pages, 1994 (Newton)
10. *Secret Arsenal*, 346 pages, 1994 (Odom)
11. *Target America*, 346 pages, 1994 (Newton)
12. *Blind Eagle*, 347 pages, 1994 (Fieldhouse)
13. *Warhead*, 346 pages, 1994 (Michael Kasner)
14. *Deadly Agent*, 349 pages, 1995 (Van Cook)
15. *Blood Debt*, 349 pages, 1995 (Newton)
16. *Deep Alert*, 346 pages, 1995 (Kasner)
17. *Vortex*, 346 pages, 1995 (Newton)
18. *Stinger*, 346 pages, 1995 (Kasner)
19. *Nuclear Nightmare*, 349 pages, 1995 (Mike Linaker)
20. *Terms of Survival*, 349 pages, 1996 (Odom)
21. *Satan's Thrust*, 346 pages, 1996 (Patrick F. Rogers)
22. *Sunflash*, 348 pages, 1996 (Kasner)
23. *The Perishing Game*, 349 pages, 1996 (Fieldhouse)
24. *Bird of Prey*, 348 pages, 1996 (Kasner)
25. *Skylance*, 349 pages, 1996 (Rogers)
26. *Flashback*, 346 pages, 1997 (Linaker)
27. *Asian Storm*, 347 pages, 1997 (Van Cook)
28. *Blood Star*, 346 pages, 1997 (Newton)
29. *Eye of the Ruby*, 346 pages, 1997 (Kasner)
30. *Virtual Peril*, 349 pages, 1997 (Odom)
31. *Night of the Jaguar*, 346 pages, 1997 (Rogers)
32. *Law of the Last Resort*, 347 pages, 1998 (Odom)
33. *Punitive Measures*, 349 pages, 1998 (Van Cook)
34. *Reprisal*, 346 pages, 1998 (Kasner)
35. *Message to America*, 348 pages, 1998 (Alan Philipson)
36. *Stranglehold*, 346 pages, 1998 (Van Cook)
37. *Triple Strike*, 346 pages, 1998 (Kasner)
38. *Enemy Within*, 349 pages, 1999 (Van Cook)
39. *Breach of Trust*, 348 pages, 1999 (Kasner)
40. *Betrayal*, 347 pages, 1999 (Kasner)
41. *Silent Invader*, 346 pages, 1999 (Tim Somheil)
42. *Edge of Night*, 347 pages, 1999 (Kasner)
43. *Zero Hour*, 347 pages, 1999 (Kasner)

44. *Thirst for Power*, 347 pages, 1999 (Somheil)
45. *Star Venture*, 348 pages, 2000 (Kasner)
46. *Hostile Instinct*, 346 pages, 2000 (Kasner)
47. *Command Force*, 346 pages, 2000 (Linaker)
48. *Conflict Imperative*, 349 pages, 2000 (Kasner)
49. *Dragon Fire*, 347 pages, 2000 (Linaker)
50. *Judgment in Blood*, 348 pages, 2000 (Kasner)
51. *Doomsday Directive*, 346 pages, 2001 (Kasner)
52. *Tactical Response*, 349 pages, 2001 (Dan Schmidt)
53. *Countdown to Terror*, 347 pages, 2001 (Somheil)
54. *Vector Three*, 349 pages, 2001 (Ron Renauld)
55. *Extreme Measures*, 349 pages, 2001 (Linaker)
56. *State of Aggression*, 346 pages, 2001 (Rogers)
57. *Sky Killers*, 348 pages, 2002 (Nick Pollotta)
58. *Condition Hostile*, 346 pages, 2002 (Kasner)
59. *Prelude to War*, 348 pages, 2002 (Somheil)
60. *Defensive Action*, 346 pages, 2002 (Linaker)
61. *Rogue State*, 347 pages, 2002 (Linaker)
62. *Deep Rampage*, 346 pages, 2002 (Pollotta)
63. *Freedom Watch*, 346 pages, 2003 (Kasner)
64. *Roots of Terror*, 346 pages, 2003 (Renauld)
65. *The Third Protocol*, 349 pages, 2003 (Somheil)
66. *Axis of Conflict*, 346 pages, 2003 (Schmidt)
67. *Echoes of War*, 347 pages, 2003 (Schmidt)
68. *Outbreak*, 349 pages, 2003 (Kasner)
69. *Day of Decision*, 348 pages, 2004 (Linaker)
70. *Ramrod Intercept*, 348 pages, 2004 (Schmidt)
71. *Terms of Control*, 349 pages, 2004 (Somheil)
72. *Rolling Thunder*, 349 pages, 2004 (Renauld)
73. *Cold Objective*, 348 pages, 2004 (Schmidt)
74. *The Chameleon Factor*, 348 pages, 2004 (Pollotta)
75. *Silent Arsenal*, 346 pages, 2005 (Schmidt)
76. *Gathering Storm*, 348 pages, 2005 (Linaker)
77. *Full Blast*, 347 pages, 2005 (Linaker)
78. *Maelstrom*, 347 pages, 2005 (Jon Guenther)
79. *Promise to Defend*, 347 pages, 2005 (Tim Tresslar)
80. *Doomsday Conquest*, 349 pages, 2005 (Schmidt)
81. *Sky Hammer*, 349 pages, (Pollotta)

82. *Vanishing Point*, 349 pages, 2006 (Guenther)
83. *Doom Prophecy*, 346 pages, 2006 (Douglas C. Wojtowicz)
84. *Sensor Sweep*, 349 pages, 2006 (Guenther)
85. *Hell Dawn*, 346 pages, 2006 (Tresslar)
86. *Oceans of Fire*, 348 pages, 2006 (Chuck Rogers)
87. *Extreme Arsenal*, 349 pages, 2007 (Wojtowicz)
88. *Starfire*, 346 pages, 2007 (Schmidt)
89. *Neutron Force*, 348 pages, 2007 (Pollotta)
90. *Red Frost*, 348 pages, 2007 (Philipson)
91. *China Crisis*, 349 pages, 2007 (Linaker)
92. *Capital Offensive*, 349 pages, 2007 (Pollotta)
93. *Deadly Payload*, 346 pages, 2008 (Wojtowicz)
94. *Act of War*, 346 pages, 2008 (Pollotta)
95. *Critical Effect*, 346 pages, 2008 (Guenther)
96. *Dark Star*, 317 pages, 2008 (Pollotta)

Related Works

The romance novella collection *Femme Fatale* (375 pages, 2003), featuring "Shaken and Stirred" by Doranna Durgin, "The Getaway" by Meredith Fletcher and "End Game" by Virginia Kantra, all feature heroines who are operatives for Stony Man with references to Stony Man support staff and a reference to Able Team and Phoenix Force. This collection was published by Gold Eagle's sister company, Silhouette Romance, making this a romance serial vigilante hybrid.

SUPERHAWKS

Four books by Mack Maloney

In the wake of the September 11 terror attacks, a mysterious spy known as Bobby Murphy formed a strike force of military personnel who lost family members during those events. This force, called Superhawks and modeled on the post–Munich Israeli hit squads, turned the tables on the al Qaeda terrorists who planned the September 11 attacks, killing them and preventing further terrorist attacks. The Superhawks team consists of over fifty members but focuses on the following members:

• Captain Wayne Bingham: navy officer nicknamed "Bingo"
• Martinez: Army colonel commander of the Delta Force soldiers
• Ron Gallant: Air Force chopper pilot who looks exactly like Clark Kent
• Colonel Ryder Long: USAF reserve officer test pilot for top secret experimental planes in the base nicknamed "war heaven." His wife was returning from a business trip to Boston when her plane crashed into the World Trade Center
• Red Curry: Gallant's fellow special ops chopper pilot

- Gil Bates: National Security Agency (NSA) head spook, electronic counterterrorism expert and super hacker
- Sgt. Dave Hunn: Delta Force infiltration expert

The Superhawks discovered an al Qaeda plot to attack the *USS Abraham Lincoln* in the Gulf of Hormuz. The team is able to stop the attack but several of their members were captured and sent to Guantanamo Bay. The Defense Security Agency (DSA), a new agency formed after September 11 to track missing weapons and missiles and uncover traitors in the armed forces, begins to track the rogue team. This three-person agency consists of:

- Major Carlson Fox: this tall, handsome and rugged former CIA operative was lured out of retirement to head this agency
- Lieutenant Mikael Ozzi: this naval officer is second in command. A third-generation intelligence agent, Ozzi is short and balding, a workaholic who barely leaves his office to sleep
- Mary Li Cho: the daughter of a Marine colonel, Cho discovered just out of college that she had talent for counterterrorism. The Asian American beauty passed on "The Women of the Pentagon" pictorial offered by *Playboy*. Cho's pose as a secretary allows her access to a great deal of intelligence.

The DSA members join forces with the Superhawks to help them prevent terrorist attacks. Their investigations uncover that the terrorist attacks were a cover for a traitorous plot to overthrow the United States government.

Behind the Scenes

Mack Maloney is the author of several series including the Wingman, Starhawks and Chopper Ops series. Maloney's father had served in World War II and read a lot of military books. Mack then started reading them and science fiction. These interests combined the post-apocalyptic Wingman series and the science fiction Starhawks. Maloney is a former sports journalist and publicist for General Electric (mackmaloney.com).

The Books

All books were published by St. Martin's Press:

1. *Strike Force Alpha*, 368 pages, 2004
2. *Strike Force Bravo*, 345 pages, 2004
3. *Strike Force Charlie*, 341 pages, 2004
4. *Strike Force Delta*, 352 pages, 2005

Related Works

Ryder Long had previously appeared in *Thunder Alley* (1988) and *War Heaven* (1991), both written by Maloney and published by Zebra Books. War Heaven is mentioned in Maloney's Chopper Ops series published by Berkeley Books from 1999 to 2000.

SURGICAL STRIKE TEAM
Three books by Jerry Ahern

The Surgical Strike Team was formed by Darwin Hughes, the youngest man to work for the OSS during World War II, after the death of his daughter-in-law on a hijacked airliner and his son's suicide. Hughes recruited three men for this mission:

• Lewis Babcock: African American lawyer and Vietnam veteran
• Abe Cross: former SEAL team commander and the only hostage on the plane to escape
• Feinberg: the youngest member of the team

With the death of Feinberg in the Iranian desert, the three surviving members returned to their civilian lives but their actions had not gone unnoticed and the president authorized that the team be made official with a free hand to operate as they see fit. The three men would be given new identities and operate through their contact, General Argus. The team tackles a variety of missions, including liberating hijacked ships, freeing hostages, preventing terrorist attacks and infiltrating the enemy.

Behind the Scenes

Jerry Ahern is the author of the Survivalist and the Defender post-apocalyptic series as well as **Track** and, under the name Alex Kilgore, **(They Call Me) the Mercenary** series. Ahern has also written more than 600 articles for various magazines and is the former president of Deutronics Firearms. Sharon Ahern is Jerry's high school sweetheart and wife. She has provided all the photos to Jerry's articles and has researched, proofread and edited all of Jerry's books. Together, the pair has investigated crimes. They have, on occasion had to check their car for bombs each morning and were almost involved in a shootout with a pair of hoods.

The Books

All books were published by Jove Books:

1. *Surgical Strike*, 322 pages, 1988
2. *Assault on the Empress*, 185 pages, 1989
3. *Infiltrator*, 185 pages, 1990

THE TAKERS (JOSH CULHANE & MARY MULROONEY)
Three books by Jerry Ahern with Sharon Ahern

Josh Culhane is the author of the best-selling the Takers adventure books starring Sean Dodge, who draws upon his adventurous lifestyle to write his novels. While adventuring, Culhane will frequently make quips about Sean Dodge such as, "Let's see Sean Dodge do this" or "eat your heart out, Sean Dodge." When his identical twin brother Jeff, a CIA agent, is murdered by rogue ex–CIA agent Jeremiah Steiglitz, Josh continues his brother's job hunting down the Gladstone Log, a ship's log that leads to incredible power.

Unknown to everyone, the log had been sent to Mary Francis Mulrooney, Culhane's ex-girlfriend and paranormal investigator. Mulrooney is the author of several nonfiction books on the topic. The couple reunites to find the Gladstone log, which leads them to an alien base in Antarctica, racing and fighting Steiglitz to claim the alien technology. After the defeat of Steiglitz, Culhane and Mulrooney resume their relationship and adventures, investigating paranormal phenomenon such as El Dorado and voodoo cults, as well as tackling more mundane crimes such as a terrorist attacks.

Behind the Scenes

Jerry Ahern is the author of the Survivalist and the Defender post-apocalyptic series as well as **Track** and **Surgical Strike** and, under the name Alex Kilgore, **(They Call Me) the Mercenary** series. Ahern has also written more than 600 articles for various magazines and is the former president of Deutronics Firearms. Sharon Ahern is Jerry's high school sweetheart and wife. She has provided all the photos to Jerry's articles and has researched, proofread and edited all of Jerry's books. Together, the pair has investigated crimes. They have, on occasion, had to check their car for bombs each morning and have almost been involved in a shootout with a pair of hoods.

The Books

Books 1 and 2 were published by Gold Eagle Books; the final book in the series was not published by Gold Eagle Books and is only available in e-book or audio book format:

1. *The Takers*, 382 pages, 1984
2. *River of Gold*, 378 pages, 1985
3. *Summon the Demon*, 2001

Cameos and References

Both Josh Cullhane and Mary Francis Mulrooney both appear and take an active part in Track #4: *The Hard Way*. In Track #7: *Master of D.E.A.T.H.*, Dan Track recalls the events of the earlier crossover working alongside Josh Cullhane to fight off Malina terrorists in Los Vegas. Track mentions Cullhane's signature phrase, "Let's see Sean Dodge top this."

TERMINATOR (ROD GAVIN)

Six books by John Quinn

Rod Gavin was a Marine serving in Vietnam when he was recruited into the CIA's Terminator program. The Terminator project was to train a team of freelance operatives to perform clandestine missions. In return for their training, members of the Terminator unit are required to undertake eight missions for the CIA. Gavin was a reluctant participant in the program and when he inquired if he could get out of his contract, he was informed that if he wanted out he would be returned to the military and serve the remainder of his military service as a prisoner in Leavenworth. The series begins with Gavin being given his eighth and final mission for the CIA.

For his final mission Gavin is sent to the Central American nation of Costa Bella to eliminate the man responsible for the murder of several missionaries. On arrival, it is discovered that the man is on death row and, after eliminating the target, Gavin discovers that the true target of this mission is himself. Caught between the Costa Bella military and Mafia hit men, Gavin must use all of his training and skills to survive.

After surviving his final mission, Gavin retires and tries to settle down for a quiet life in Colorado but his former life keeps dragging him back. Friends and their family members often contact Gavin to help them when they are in trouble. Luckily for Gavin, he is able to be hired by various government agencies such as the Justice Department, NSA, DEA and FBI.

Gavin often discovers that his friends have stumbled on much larger conspiracies, such as the Yakuza attempting to steal top-secret encoding machines, secret assassin training camps, drug smugglers and terrorists.

Behind the Scenes

John Quinn is the pen name of Dennis Rodriguez. Rodriguez was editor of pornographic magazines for Pendulum Press where he worked with Ed Wood Jr. Rodriguez was the author of *Pachuco*, a novel set in the barrios of Los Angeles. While director Ed Wood Jr. also used the John Quinn pen name, there is no evidence that he wrote any of the books in this series.

The Books

All books were published by Kensington Publication Corporation:

1. *Mercenary Kill*, 186 pages, 1982
2. *Silicon Valley Slaughter*, 208 pages, 1983
3. *Kill Squad*, 199 pages, 1983
4. *Crystal Kill*, 208 pages, 1984
5. *Chameleon Kill*, 184 pages, 1985
6. *Checkmate Kill*, 1985

.357 VIGILANTE (BRETT MACKLIN)

Three books by Ian Ludlow

Brett Macklin is a helicopter pilot who renovates classic cars as his hobby, living a peaceful and quiet life. But when his father, a Los Angeles police officer, is burned to death on duty that all changed. The street punks responsible were set free on a bogus technicality, which led Macklin to hunt these criminals with his father's .357 Magnum. Dubbed by the press as Mr. Jury for his vigilante acts, Macklin must avoid the efforts of his best friend, a police detective assigned to capture Mr. Jury.

Further complicating this is the deaths of several of Officer Macklin's friends, which

Mr. Jury discovers is part of a political conspiracy to bring about a gubernatorial contest.

After avenging the death of his father, Macklin is contacted by the police chief and mayor to tackle the criminals that have escaped justice, setting him against a child pornography mogul who recently escaped justice. After a failed attempt to capture the pornographer, Macklin's girlfriend is killed by a bomb meant for him. This death is the spur Macklin needed to fully commit himself to becoming Mr. Jury again. After eliminating the child pornographer, Mr. Jury takes to the streets to tackle a white supremacist group.

Behind the Scenes

Ian Ludlow is the pseudonym of Lee Goldberg and Lewis Purdue. Goldberg chose the name Ian in honor of James Bond creator Ian Fleming and Ludlow so that the books would be next to Robert Ludlum on the shelf. Goldberg went on to a career in screenwriting, writing scripts for *Spenser: For Hire*, *The Cosby Mysteries*, *Diagnosis: Murder*, *Martial Law* and *Monk*. Goldberg now writes tie-in novels for *Diagnosis: Murder* and *Monk*. In the novels *Diagnosis Murder: The Death Merchant* and *Mr. Monk and the Two Assistants*, Goldberg has a best-selling novelist Ian Ludlow appear and interfere with the investigations in those books. Lewis Perdue was Goldberg's lecturer in college and helped him launch his career. Perdue is the author of *The Da Vinci Legacy* (1983), which predates Dan Brown's *The Da Vinci Code*. A fourth book, "Killstorm," was written but Pinnacle Books declared chapter 11 bankruptcy before the book was due for release.

The Books

All books were published by Pinnacle Books:

1. *.357 Vigilante*, 214 pages, 1985
2. *Make Them Pay*, 150 pages, 1985
3. *White Wash*, 151 pages, 1985

The Movie

New Line Cinema did option the series to be made into movie; while scripts were written by Goldberg, the movie was never made.

TNT (ANTHONY NICHOLAS TWIN)

Seven books by Doug Masters

Anthony Nicholas Twin, a freelance reporter better known by his initials TNT, was caught in the eye of an atomic blast while covering American nuclear weapons test. Instead of leukemia, he was endowed with superhuman abilities including night vision, increased stamina, and increased sexual prowess. Twin had been in semi-retirement as a reporter to look after his daughter October, who was born mentally handicapped, only taking jobs to finance her treatment.

Twin is reluctantly drawn into adventures by Arnold Benedict, a broker of information. Benedict is a ruthless pedophile, using his resources to procure young boys. The broker has fear of germs and being touched. Benedict has promised to look after October and find her a cure; this promise alone is all that keeps TNT from killing his handler.

TNT is frequently aided by soldier of fortune Dawlish who has a pathological hatred of all Russians, even going as far to see all enemies as Russians. TNT has faced some unusual situations, including eight deadly identical dwarves, a death trap based on Dante's *Inferno*, an indestructible vehicle, and a deadly training arena. Often Twin is the only person who could survive these situations thanks to his unique physiology.

Behind the Scenes

Both Michael Borgia (French versions) and Doug Masters (American translations) are pseudonyms. The books were written by Pierre Rey and Loup Durand. Pierre Rey (1930–2006) wrote books about the rich and famous, fictionalizing the lives of Aristotle Onassis (*The Greek*), Grace Kelly (*The Rock*) as well as the Hollywood party scene (*Sunset*). His novel about the Italian Mafia (*Out*) brought death threats, causing Rey to hire bodyguards. This fascination with the rich and famous seems to have stemmed from his tenure as editor of *Marie Clare* magazine and informed the tastes of Benedict Arnold in the TNT series. Loup Durand (1933–1996) is the author several thrillers, including *The Ankor Massacre* (1983), *Daddy* (1988) and *Jaguar* (1990). He started writing late in life at age forty-three after working on a variety of jobs including dock worker and journalist and travelling extensively in the Far East.

The Books

The original books by Michael Borgoa were published in France by Editions Robert Laffont:

1. *Les sept cercles de l'enfer*, 1978
2. *Le grand congélateur*, 1978
3. *La bête du Goulag*, 1978
4. *Huit petits hommes rouges*, 1978
5. *Les jeux d'Hercule*, 1978
6. *Le grand chaperon noir*, 1979
7. *Les cobras de Lilliput*, 1979
8. *Terminus Eldorado*, 1979
9. *Les huit femmes de Barbe-bleue*, 1980

The English versions were published by Charter Books as by Doug Masters:

1. *TNT*, 216 pages, 1985 (*Les sept cercles de l'enfer*)
2. *The Beast*, 201 pages, 1985 (*La bête du Goulag*)
3. *The Spiral of Death*, 197 pages, 1985 (*Terminus Eldorado*)
4. *The Devil's Claw*, 184 pages, 1985 (*Huit petits hommes rouges*)
5. *Killer Angel*, 1986 (*Les jeux d'Hercule*)
6. *Ritual of Blood*, 185 pages, 1986 (*Les huit femmes de Barbe-bleue*)
7. *Kingdom of Death*, 185 pages, 1986 (*Le grand congélateur*)

The Comics

In 1989, Claud Lefranq Editions began a three-volume series of comic book adaptations:

1. *Octobre*, 1989
2. *Les 7 cercles de l'enfer*, 1991
3. *La horde d'ore*, 1992

TRACK (DAN TRACK)

Thirteen books by Jerry Ahern and Patrick Andrews

Daniel Hunter Track was born 21 June 1948 in Chicago, Illinois. When his parents died in 1956, he was raised by his sixteen-year-old sister, Diane. Dan eventually became like an older brother to his nephew George Beegh, born 1959 after his sister's marriage to Robert Beegh in 1958. Dan ran wild, dropped out of school and joined a gang and at age seventeen. He was hauled before a judge when a rival gang member died in a rumble. The judge advised Track that he would soon have a criminal record if he kept up this kind of behavior and offered him the opportunity to join the Army. Track accepted. Instead of serving in Vietnam, he found himself stationed in West Germany.

It was during this time that Track was encouraged to get his high school equivalency and start studying. Eventually, Track rose to the rank of Major in CID, investigating gunrunners and anti-terrorism activities. After retiring from the army, Track began teaching special weapons and tactics to police and military personnel.

Track's nephew George joined Air Force intelligence and retired to hauling nuclear material across America. It was during one of those runs, hauling one of four loads of twenty-five defective nuclear weapons, that George's truck was ambushed and all of the weapons were stolen. George was the only driver to survive the ambushes and he was a prime suspect in their disappearance. George reached out to his uncle Dan.

Dan was able to help his nephew and took a job as troubleshooter for a group of international insurance companies known as the Consortium. The nuclear weapons that had been stolen were a serious threat to many of the policy holders of the Consortium.

Working with the Consortium, through his contact, Sir Abner Chesterton, Track was able to do more than conventional law enforcement, with the Consortium picking up the bill and smoothing the way. Track is assisted by his nephew George in the field. Track also receives help from his lover and gunrunner Desiree Goth and her giant African bodyguard Zulu, an Oxford graduate. Track and his team chase stolen nuclear weapons, rescue kidnap victims, stop KGB plots, and take on the secret society D.E.A.T.H. (Directorate for Espionage, Assassination, Terrorism and Harassment) as well as escorting valuable archaeological treasures.

Behind the Scenes

Jerry Ahern is the author of the Survivalist and the Defender post-apocalyptic series as well as **the Takers** and **Surgical Strike** and, under the name Alex Kilgore, (**They Call**

Me) the Mercenary series. Ahern has also written more than 600 articles for various magazines and is the former president of Deutronics Firearms. Sharon Ahern is Jerry's high school sweetheart and wife. She has provided all the photos to Jerry's articles and has researched, proofread and edited all of Jerry's books. Together, the pair has investigated crimes. They have, on occasion, had to check their car for bombs each morning and have almost been involved in a shootout with a pair of hoods.

In book 11, there is a one-page introduction to Patrick Andrews, born in 1936, who has written westerns and action-adventure novels. An ex-paratrooper, he retired after twenty-three years of service and has written articles on military history for *Soldier of Fortune* and *Infantry* magazines. Andrews also mentions that he is friends with **Phoenix Force** author Gar Wilson. Under the pen name Patrick Lee, Andrews wrote several books in the Six-Gun Samurai western series. As John Lansing, he wrote the Black Eagles series set during the Vietnam War.

The Books

1. *The Ninety-Nine*, 220 pages, 1984 (Ahern)
2. *Atrocity*, 222 pages, 1984 (Ahern)
3. *The Armageddon Conspiracy*, 219 pages, 1984 (Ahern)
4. *The Hard Way*, 220 pages, 1984 (Ahern)
5. *Origin of a Vendetta*, 218 pages, 1985 (Ahern)
6. *Certain Blood*, 219 pages, 1985 (Ahern)
7. *Master of D.E.A.T.H.*, 219 pages, 1985 (Ahern)
8. *Revenge of the Master*, 219 pages, 1985 (Ahern)
9. *The D.E.A.T.H. Hunters*, 217 pages, 1985 (Ahern)
10. *Cocaine Run*, 219 pages, 1985 (Ahern)
11. *The Ghost Dancers*, 219 pages, 1986 (Andrews)
12. *Drug Runner*, 217 pages, 1986 (Andrews)
13. *Amazon Gold*, 218 pages, 1986 (Andrews)

TRACKER (NATHANIEL TRACKER)
Eight books by Ron Stillman

Major Nathaniel Tracker was a pilot in the Air Force. He also developed many new technological advances in the radar and tracking devices used in their planes. Driving home one night, Tracker swerved to avoid a dog and rolled his car. One of the bystanders lit a roadside flare, igniting the leaking petrol and, as a result of his injuries, Tracker was blinded.

Due to his injuries he was invalided out of the military. But Tracker was determined that he was not finished and, utilizing his expertise in radar and other tracking devices, began to develop OPTIC, essentially a new set of "eyes" which took the form of a pair of glasses. This allows Tracker to effectively see again. Over time Tracker refines his

OPTIC to a pair of contact lenses. During his missions Tracker is injured and loses body parts; a finger was replaced by a laser and his left shin was replaced by a generator.

Tracker then approached the government and was able to unofficially return to active duty as an operative. Tracker's control was Wally Rampart, an undersecretary of State and former Army major general.

Tracker was hired to be the government's tracker, the go-to guy when an agency loses something. In his first mission, Tracker is sent to retrieve an Air Force pilot lost in Libya.

Behind the Scenes

Ron Stillman was the pseudonym of Don Bendell. Bendell wrote the first six books in the series but was replaced when Bendell began to insist that the books be issued under his own name ("Don Bendell — The Author," 2002, http://chass.colostate-pueblo.edu/magazine/2002/wildapplause2.html). Bendell served in Vietnam from 1968 to 1969 and used his experiences to write a series of autobiographical novels. He is also the author of several westerns and the Criminal Investigation Detachment terrorist hunting series. Bendell is also a master martial artist.

The Books

All books were published by Charter Diamond:

1. *Tracker*, 187 pages, 1990
2. *Green Lightning*, 172 pages, 1991
3. *Blood Money*, 185 pages, 1991
4. *Black Phantom*, 184 pages, 1991
5. *Fire Kill*, 166 pages, 1991
6. *Death Hunt*, 166 pages, 1991
7. *Shock Treatment*, 184 pages, 1992
8. *Dynasty of Evil*, 182 pages, 1992

VEIL (VEIL KENDRY)

Two books by George C. Chesbro

When Veil Kendry was born, a brain infection nearly killed him. This also left him with the ability to dream through time and space and see into the minds of others. Veil served in Vietnam and Laos with the CIA. When a dangerous and illegal mission organized by his controller, Archangel, went wrong, Veil left the CIA and became a painter. Veil paints the landscapes he sees in his dreams and makes a career out of his paintings.

Eventually, Veil begins to investigate his unique abilities with the Institute of Human Studies and becomes involved in a top-secret Army project code-named the Lazarus People, which studies the experiences of people who have been declared clinically dead and resurrected. These experiences match Kendry's paintings. Someone wants Kendry dead and he fights to find why, taking the battle to the next realm.

After that battle, Kendry's past comes back to haunt him as his former CIA controller Archangel is about to be appointed as Secretary of State and Kendry is kidnapped. Warned by his dreams, Kendry hires private detective, Dr. Robert Frederickson better known as Mongo, to investigate his disappearance. Mongo's investigations uncover details about Veil's past with the CIA and allow Mongo to rescue Veil and expose Archangel's illegal activities.

Kendry's next exploit has him using his dream abilities to visit the mind of other men to track down the thief who stole an African tribal artifact from the gallery that displays Kendry's paintings. Kendry discovers that the warrior prince of the Kalahari tribe is responsible and that he is being hunted by corrupt police officers and the Cosa Nostra. The law of the jungle comes into play as Kendry and the warrior-prince fight their way through the evil men seeking the idol. Kendry is occasionally called to assist Mongo on cases, including tracking down the vigilante **Chant** Sinclair, and his dreams lead him to fight supernatural menaces.

Behind the Scenes

This series was written by George C. Chesbro, who initially wrote the first book under the David Cross pseudonym with the hero named Chant Kendry. The only thing the publisher liked was the name Chant, and so that novel was reworked and became the first novel in the Veil Kendry series published under his own name. For that publisher, Chesbro created John "**Chant**" Sinclair and wrote three books. Chesbro is also the author of the Mongo mystery series.

The Books

Both books were published by Mysterious Press:

1. *Veil*, 228 pages, 1986
2. *Jungle of Steel and Stone*, 200 pages, 1988

Related Works

Veil appears in the Mongo novel *Two Songs This Archangel Sings* (Atheneum, 249 pages, 1987). Both Chant and Veil Kendry appear in the Mongo novel *Dark Chant in a Crimson Key* (Mysterious Press, 217 pages, 1992). Two Veil short stories, "The Lazarus Gate" and "Unmarked Graves," appear in the collection *Lone Wolves* (Apache Beach, 245 pages, 2003). Both stories had previously published in *Ellery Queen's Mystery Magazine*.

VIGILANTE (JOSEPH MADDEN)

Six books by V. J. Santiago

Joe Madden was a veteran of the Korean War, who on his return to civilian life became an engineer in New York City. Happily married, Madden and his wife, Sara, had a weekly dinner date with Sara's sister and her husband for dinner. One night that Madden was called to an urgent meeting with a difficult client and Sara went to dinner on her own. On her way home Sara was murdered, her face slashed in the attack on the subway.

Madden did not react well to this and attempted to drink himself into oblivion. One night, while drunk out of his mind, Madden was attacked; the attacker stole his wallet and wedding ring and sliced open his face. It was then that Madden became a vigilante. Initially armed with a kitchen knife, Madden quickly upgraded his armament, taking weapons from the criminals he killed.

Unaware of his vigilante activities, his firm sends him all over the country troubleshooting major projects for them to help him get over his traumatic experiences. Everywhere he goes, Madden hunts down criminals and kills them. While Madden tackles street-level crime, he is able on occasion able to take down crime bosses. One of Madden's jobs was with a printing company and he was able to get several false identity documents made, which he puts to good use in his war on crime.

Behind the Scenes

This series, based on ideas by Lyle Kenyon Engel, was written by Robert Lory under the penname V. J. Santiago. Lory was also the author of the Horrorscopes and **Dracula** series under his own name as well as the several books in **the Expeditor** series as Paul Edwards.

The Books

The series was published by Pinnacle Books:

1. *New York: An Eye for an Eye*, 180 pages, 1975
2. *Los Angeles: Detour to a Funeral*, 182 pages, 1975
3. *San Francisco: Kill or Be Killed*, 166 pages, 1976
4. *Chicago: Knock, Knock, You're Dead*, 184 pages, 1976
5. *Detroit: Dead End Delivery*, 179 pages, 1976
6. *Washington: This Gun for Justice*, 178 pages, 1978

WARHAWKS, INC.

Six books by James Keith

This is about a team of mercenaries that were recruited by Col. Rhodes (he's not given a first name, just called either the Colonel or Rhodes), one of the most renowned mercenaries in the world before an unspecified illness prevented him from participating in field operations. Rhodes rescues a fellow soldier of fortune, Jeff Hawke, from certain death to help him create his own specialized mercenary force. Hawke had been captured by a South American dictator that he'd been fighting against. The dictator had tortured Hawke and was nearly ready to kill the Aussie mercenary. Hawke, who had worked with the Colonel earlier when he used another name, is offered the opportunity to form a specialized team known as Warhawks, Inc.

The six-man team consists of:
- Jeff Hawke: Australian team leader
- Dirk Paulus: South African soldier
- Mitch Devlin: ex-Marine and surveillance expert, a red-haired, freckled-faced giant
- Chick Larkin: English explosives expert
- Pepe Andre: French, the most experienced veteran on the team, and admits it's not his real name
- Dieter Hinkel: German killer
  The crew is joined by two women:
- Christina Rhodes: pilot and the Colonel's daughter
- Hanni Stein: Israeli who joined the team after avenging the death of her parents

The Warhawks, Inc., team is based out of Rhodes family estate, Palmyra, in Miami, which is a large estate, suitable for jungle training. Rhodes also owns a beach house on the coast of Florida which can be used for beach assault training. Rhodes' conception for the team is an elite strike force that can handle any high-risk assignment, including bodyguarding, bounty hunting, security, surveillance and military operations. Over the course of the series, they act as bodyguards for the son of an African president, storm a hijacked plane, fight a rogue mercenary group, stop a neo-Nazi group, and stop terrorist attacks.

Behind the Scenes

Cleveland Press is one of Australia's longest running pulp publishers, founded in 1953 and publishing primarily westerns. By 1984 they were seeking to broaden their output, adding the Cougar Book line for romance novels and starting the Warhawks, Inc. series. Both of these ventures were unsuccessful, with the axing of Warhawks, Inc. and the conversion of Cougar to a western reprint line.

Cleveland approached Keith Hetherington, one of their fastest writers, to create a non-western series for them and he created this soldier-of-fortune series. Hetherington had written westerns under many pseudonyms for Cleveland, including Kirk Hamilton, Brett Waring and Clint McCall. For other publishers, Hetherington turned out thrillers under the name Keith Conway and the boy's adventure novel *The Scuba Buccaneers* (1966) as James Keith. Hetherington also wrote scripts for the Australian television crime series *Homicide*, *Matlock Police* and *Division 4* for Crawford Productions from 1970 to 1975.

The Books

All books were published by Cleveland Press:
1. *Strike One*, 128 pages, 1984
2. *Rogue Merc*, 128 pages, 1984
3. *Birds of Prey*, 128 pages, 1984
4. *Yesterday's Hero*, 128 pages, 1984
5. *Kill Zone*, 128 pages, 1984
6. *Shadow Mission*, 128 pages, 1984

Keith Hetherington had written ten books for this series but, due to poor sales, only the first six books were published. The unpublished titles were:

7. "Passage of Arms"
8. "Wolves of War"
9. "Paycheck Soldiers"
10. "Warheads"

Related Works

It is strongly implied that Col. Rhodes could be Allen Faulkner from **the Wild Geese**, Hawke mentioning that he was unavailable for that mission.

WILD GEESE

Two books by Daniel Carney

Col. Allen Faulkner is considered to be one of the greatest mercenary commanders in the world. But his standing took a blow when his last contract was unable to be undertaken as African leader Julian Limbani was captured by a rival force before Faulkner arrived in Africa. After this, Faulkner is unable to get work until he is approached by merchant banker Sir Edward Matheson. Matheson is aware that Limbani is still alive and hires Faulkner to rescue him from the rebel forces. Faulkner is to form a force of fifty men and rescue the former president.

Faulkner quickly recruits his lieutenants:

• Rafer Janders: the best planner in the business but got into trouble with the Mafia when he shot the nephew of the London Don after being tricked into carrying drugs
• Jeremy Chandos: a young, reckless gambler who, after being disinherited by his father, became a mercenary
• Peter Coetzee: Rhodesian game warden who travelled to London to see the big city; his bush skills make him ideal for the mission
• Shaun Fynn: pilot for Mad Malloy in Biafra, who joined the mission for a love of adventure

The officers are joined by the training officer:

• Sandy Young: sixty-year-old sergeant major responsible for training the fifty men for this mission

The fifty-man team trains and eventually rescues the president but, due to a heavier military presence guarding Limbani than anticipated, the team is unable to take their plane and is forced to attempt to travel overland with heavy causalities. The second book has Faulkner training another team of mercenaries to rescue Rudolph Hess from Spandau Prison for an American television network.

Behind the Scenes

Daniel Carney was born in 1944 as the son of British diplomat. While educated in England, he grew up in the Far East. In 1963, Carney settled in Rhodesia (Zimbabwe) and joined the British South Africa Police. He divided his time between writing and defending the country's borders against guerilla attacks and passed away from cancer in 1985.

The Books

Both books were published by Corgi Books:

1. *The Wild Geese*, 302 pages, 1977 (originally titled "The Thin White Line")
2. *Square Circle*, 280 pages, 1982 (also published as *The Return of the Wild Geese* and *The Wild Geese II*)

The Movies

The Wild Geese was released in 1978 and starred Richard Burton as Col. Allen Faulkner, Roger Moore as Lt. Shawn Fynn (spelling changed from the book), Hardy Kruger as Lt. Pieter Coetze and Richard Harris as Rafe Janders. This all-star production was one of the biggest movies of the year. Producer Euan Lloyd was inspired by the earlier *Guns of Navarone*. The movie had several differences from the book, with the characters of Shawn Fynn and Jeremy Chandos amalgamated, and characters who died in the book surviving in the movie. In 1984, *The Wild Geese II* was released. Initially intended to be Col. Allen Faulkner leading a new group of mercenaries to free Rudolph Hess from Spandau Prison, with the death of Richard Burton, his role was recast with Edward Fox as playing Faulkner's brother Alex.

Related Works

Carney's book help popularize "wild geese" as a generic term for mercenaries. So, therefore, it is difficult to determine if any use of Wild Geese may be a related work or a merely a use of the generic term. Mike Hoare's memoir *Congo Mercenary* was re-issued by Corgi books as *Mercenary: The Classic True-Life Account of Mercenary Warfare by Mike Hoare, Technical Adviser for the Film The Wild Geese* in 1978 with a similar cover to their edition of *The Wild Geese*. The 1984 Italian movie *Geheimcode: Wildganse (Codename: Wild Geese)* is a generic use of the term.

Kouta Hirano's manga *Hellsing* (1997) features a team of mercenaries called the Wild Geese; their leader Pip Bernadotte is a sixth-generation member of the Wild Geese, suggesting this is a reference to the original Irish Wild Geese rather than to this version. Hirano's earlier hentai (pornographic manga) *Coyote*, set during World War II, also features a mercenary named Pip Bernadotte who may be the grandfather or father of his namesake in *Hellsing*.

In the **Warhawks** series by James Keith, Australian mercenary Jeff Hawke mentions to Col. Rhodes that he was on the way to the Wild Geese jump when that mission was aborted. While Col. Rhodes could potentially be Col. Allen Faulkner, this is likely a reference to the generic term.

Marvel Comics' New Universe line of comics featured *Mark Hazzard: Merc*. One of Hazzard's team is Sgt Major Peel. Peel is introduced in issue #7: *Incentives* but in #10: *Iran Slam*, Peel is asked to gather some of the Wild Geese to assist in a rescue mission. This would seem to be a generic reference but in Annual #1: *A Matter of Lives and Death*,

Peel recounts how he came to be a mercenary after the Vietnam War with the group "they called the Wild Geese. Although I always thought that Richard Burton was wrong for the part in the film." This is a clear reference to the Wild Geese film where Richard Burton played Col. Allen Faulkner.

Z-COMM
Four books by Kyle Maning

Z-Comm is another group of mercenaries. The Z-Commandoes are "mean muthas, sick bastards. America's Best."

The group consists of a group of Vietnam veterans:

- Logan Cage: team leader
- Frank "Bear" MacBeth: giant, bald, ex-Special Forces
- Harry Zabriske: thief and acquisitions specialist
- Sam Proffit: martial artist and weapons whiz
- Domino Black: sex appeal

Oddly, Domino is depicted on the covers as sporting an eye patch, a fact not mentioned in any of the books. Similarly, Bear MacBeth is described as being completely bald in the books but the cover illustrations of the team have all team members with hair.

When the situation is hopeless, the solution is Z-Comm. When neo-Nazis try to enslave America, Z-Comm goes undercover and stops their plans. Z-Comm has also protected world leaders, tackled terrorist groups, hunted down kiddie porn snuff filmmakers and searched for soldiers listed as missing in action in Vietnam. The team liaison in Washington is Peter Quartermaine, who gets the jobs too dirty for other agencies for this team. Peter Quartermaine was one of the greatest mercenaries the world has ever seen but, after making his fortune, he retired to strategically manage his own mercenary team, Z-Comm.

Behind the Scenes

Kyle Maning was the pen name of action adventure author David Alexander. The *Richmond Observer* called Alexander "The King of Action-Adventure Fiction" and he is the author of the post-apocalyptic series Phoenix, the near-future Nomad series and several novels based on the adventures of the United States Marine Corps, set in a world where America fights both the war on terror and the Cold War at the same time. Alexander has an interest in the future developments in warfare and has written several books and articles on the future of warfare. He is also the author of several nonfiction works on conspiracies and coverups as well as the history of the Pentagon.

The Books

The series was published by Leisure Books:

1. *Swastika*, 285 pages, 1988
2. *Killpoint*, 273 pages, 1989
3. *MIA*, 279 pages, 1989
4. *Blood Storm*, 280 pages, 1990

Appendices

1. Crossovers, References and Parodies

The serial vigilante genre is one that has been influenced by the dime and pulp novels that preceded it. Other scholars such as Jess Nevins (2003) have pointed out that the characters in those stories would often meet, interact and refer to each other. This is certainly true of the serial vigilantes who also make reference to and meet characters from the pulps and earlier.

PULP REFERENCES

Of course, the serial vigilantes were directly inspired by the hero pulps that preceded them but this section is not about that but rather where the characters of the hero pulps are directly referenced or appear in the serial vigilante texts themselves. The first reference to pulp heroes in the serial vigilante genre comes, appropriately enough, in the first **Executioner** novel, *War Against the Mafia* where two Mafia goons compare Don Pendleton's Mack Bolan, the Executioner to the Phantom and the Shadow. In later adventures Mack compared a villain to Doc Savage and faced K'tulu (Cthulhu). In 1975, Don Pendleton was asked to write an introduction the Ballantine Mystery Classics reprint of *Hound of the Baskervilles*. In that essay Pendleton opens with a dream where Mack Bolan visits 221B Baker Street and interacts with Sherlock Holmes.

In the **Destroyer** #4: *Mafia Fix*, Remo Williams meets James Bond, Hercule Poirot and Mr. Moto. Bond reappears in Destroyer #8: *Summit Chase*, Remo goes on to meet in later books Fu Manchu, and a man who may be the Green Hornet's partner Kato (Destroyer #83: *Skull Duggery*), and Khadhulu/Sa Mangsang (Cthulhu) (Destroyer #77: *Coin of the Realm*, #100: *Last Rites*, #139: *Dream Thing*, #141: *Frightening Strikes*) and discovers he was buried next to Danny Colt, the Spirit in Wildwood Cemetery (Destroyer #69: *Blood Ties*). In the same adventure he meets members of the Cranston family (from the Shadow series) and a mercenary named Brock Savage. Destroyer #102: *Unite and Conquer* has references to the Phantom and Zorro. Edgar Rice Burroughs' Pellucidar series and Jules Verne's *Journey to the Centre of the Earth* are referenced in Destroyer #136: *Unpopular Science* and #137: *Industrial Evolution* when the villain escapes in a mechanical mole into a cavern system deep in the earth.

Lara Croft, Tomb Raider, encounters a cult that worships Uhluhtc (Cthulhu) in *The Lost Cult* and makes reference to her ancestor, Roger Croft, serving in the Napoleonic wars with Greystoke, Holmes, Templar, Quatermain, and Bond (implicitly ancestors of Tarzan, Sherlock Holmes, Simon Templar, Allan Quatermain and James Bond) in *The Man of Bronze*. In the novelization of the first Tomb Raider movie Lara compares a portrait of her father to Arne Sacknussem. Arne Sacknussemm (note the slightly different spelling) made the original discovery of the path to the Earth's centre during the 16th century in Jules Verne's *Journey to the Centre of the Earth*.

Mark Hardin, **The Penetrator**, compares himself or is compared to Superman and Robin Hood in several of his adventures and fights Vlad Dosadan Magarac, a vampiric descendant of Count Dracula in Penetrator #45: *Quaking Terror*. In several books, Hardin uses the alias of John Savage. Philip Jose Farmer's Greatheart Silver meets a parody version of nearly every hero pulp character in his first story *Showdown at Shootout*. Similarly, Lin Carter's **Prince Zarkon** also interacts with more serious versions of these characters at the Cobalt Club from the Shadow series in all but the first of his adventures. Jake Speed, when told that Doc Savage used the type of jeeps that he is forced to use, reminds his assistant that Savage had been retired for years. Tom Brannon from **Invasion USA** read Doc Savage novels back when he was a boy.

Less obviously, in **The Hitman #2**: *L.A. Massacre*, Dirk Spencer lives up to a reporter's wish for an "old-fashioned vigilante," showing his hero-pulp inspiration even more than his fellow serial vigilantes, being a wealthy playboy turned vigilante. Jesse Mach (Street Hawk), in his first adventure, joked about leaving a silver bullet so they would think he was the great-grandson of the Lone Ranger. The classic detective Ellery Queen is mentioned by the Vigilante (Adrian Chase) in Vigilante #13: *Locke Room Murder* and Annja Creed of **Rogue Angel** is a regular reader of *Ellery Queen's Mystery Magazine* as mentioned in Rogue Angel #1: *Destiny*. In *Dexter in the Dark*, **Dexter** is on honeymoon in Paris and considers making a pilgrimage to Rue Morgue, referring to the *Murders in the Rue Morgue* by Edgar Allan Poe. Mr. Chapel of Vengeance Unlimited stays at motels in the Paladin Motel chain. This is reference to Paladin from *Have Gun Will Travel*.

COMIC BOOK UNIVERSES

Just as the influence of pulp heroes such as the Green Hornet, the Shadow and Doc Savage can be seen on the comic book pages with the Crimson Avenger, Batman and Captain America, we see the same influence coming to play with the serial vigilantes on a new generation of comic book heroes such as the Punisher, the Vigilante and the Huntress. Stemming from the 1940s super teams like the Justice Society and the Invaders, both DC and Marvel Comics created interwoven universes where their characters could and often did interact.

With the introduction of serial vigilante–derived characters in comics, there operated a generation gap between the older characters and these new characters. Perhaps the character that best exemplifies this is the Huntress. In her original incarnation, the Huntress was Helena Wayne, the daughter of Batman and Catwoman, who operated as a female Batman, adopting the role of Gotham's protector after the death of her father. But in 1986, DC had the universe-shattering *Crisis on Infinite Earths*, which rebooted continuity and erased Helena Wayne and the Huntress. In her place, a new Huntress,

Helena Bertinelli, daughter of mob boss Guido Bertinelli, seeking to avenge the death of her family, appeared. In the final story arc of her nineteen-issue series, *Days of Rage*, she encountered Batman — the pair of them dealing with a gang war from different perspectives. At the end of the story, as Helena is packing up her belongings, implicitly retiring from crime fighting, she ruminates that she expected Batman to accept her as a kindred spirit but he rejects her and her methods. In subsequent stories, Helena has moved to Gotham City and is continuing to try to earn Batman's approval — something he won't give, as he sees her as too violent and unpredictable.

When Adrian Chase became the Vigilante, his methods for taking out the members of the mob family who killed his family bring him into conflict with the New Teen Titans, who disapprove of his methods. When the Vigilante finally encounters the man responsible for the death of his family, Batman's partner Robin attempts to dissuade the Vigilante from taking the law into his own hands and allowing the justice system to take care of the mobster.

The Punisher, in many of his early appearances, battles established superheroes like Spider-man, Daredevil and Captain America. In Captain America #241: *Fear Grows in Brooklyn,* Captain America encounters the Punisher; these two war veterans come into conflict over how to deal with a meeting between two mob bosses. Captain America wishes for the mobsters to be taken into custody but the Punisher uses a bomb to kill these men. Captain America in the end declares that he and the Punisher are similar, both waging a personal war, but next time they meet Captain America will stop the Punisher — this difference in methods will cause them to clash in the future, just as his methods cause the Punisher to clash with the other superheroes he encounters; they view his methods as too violent and extreme. In the Punisher's encounter with Batman, Batman refuses any assistance and tells the Punisher to get out of Gotham.

Serial vigilante–inspired characters are not team players, and their interactions in a larger superhero universe are often tense, due to their conflicts with other superheroes. The Punisher has never been part of a superhero team, although he was part of the loose alliance called Marvel Knights. When the Punisher found a job too large to handle alone, he gathered other heroes such as Daredevil, Black Widow and Shang Chi, referring to these other heroes as "do-gooders." The so-called do-gooders immediately decide to hunt him down after the threat is over. Similarly, the Huntress was invited to join the Justice League so they could keep an eye on her; Maxwell Lord had to use his mind-control powers on her to get her to agree. So we see that serial vigilante–inspired characters do not work well with more conventional superheroes. This is because these superheroes' moral code (largely forced on the publishers by the Comics Code Authority) makes them an extension of the justice system that the serial vigilantes are working outside of.

CROSSOVERS AND REFERENCES

Just as the serial vigilantes draw on their pulp roots as seen above, the various series often refer to each other. Direct crossovers where one series character meets and interacts with another series character are fairly uncommon outside of the Executioner and its spinoffs. More commonly, another hero will be mentioned or referenced in the course of an adventure. This often serves as a cross-promotional tool, using the popularity of series such as the Executioner or Knight Rider to build an audience for a newer series.

The crossovers and references between the Executioner and its spinoffs are far too many to catalog here, but the key crossovers are Executioner #2: *Death Squad* where Carl Lyons, Rosario "Pol" Blancares and Herman "Gadgets" Schwarz are all introduced. In Executioner #39: *The New War* all three are invited to join Mack in his war on terror, thus leading to **Able Team** #1: *Tower of Terror*. Mack Bolan also hand-selected the five men of **Phoenix Force**, meeting all of them in Phoenix Force #1: *Argentine Deadline*. The Executioner, Able Team and Phoenix Force all fought together for the first time in *The Stony Man Doctrine*.

Mack Bolan had met Niles Barrabas in Vietnam and cleared Barrabas' name of charges of massacring innocent civilians in "Incident at Hoi Binh" in Executioner #63: *The New War Book*. The favor was returned in **Soldiers of Barrabas** #3: *Butchers of Eden* when Niles Barrabas recalls another meeting in Vietnam with Mack Bolan, although Barrabas refers to the other hero as John Macklin Bolan.

The Penetrator is more subtle in its references. In Penetrator #11: *Terror in Taos*, Mark Hardin is asked to translate a page of a book about a "white guy and a gook running around snuffing people for the government" and "television sets and soap operas," clearly a reference to the Destroyer books. Mark Hardin uses the alias Mack Colan in Penetrator #8: *Northwest Contract*. In Penetrator # 5: *Mardi Gras Massacre*, Hardin is nearly captured by a security guard who had been reading Executioner novels.

Destroyer #8: *Summit Chase* has Remo asking if anyone has seen Mack Bolan. The Sword of Sinanju from Destroyer #3: *Chinese Puzzle* was referenced by Lara Croft in Tomb Raider #3: *The Man of Bronze*. Jake Speed refers to Mack Bolan, the Executioner and Remo Williams, the Destroyer.

In **Track** #4: *The Hard Way*, Dan Track teamed up with Josh Cullhane of **The Takers** to battle gangsters in Las Vegas. In Track #7: *Master of D.E.A.T.H.*, Track remembers this team up. In **Home Team**'s *Undeclared War*, one of the team, bounty hunter Max Warrick, has stark white hair and smokes cigars and it's suggested that he must be on the jazz, just like that A-Team character (Hannibal Smith) he looks so much like.

The Wild Geese by Daniel Carney has been influential enough that Col. Rhodes in **Warhawks** #1: *Strike One* is strongly suggested to be Allen Faulkner of the Wild Geese. One of Marc Hazzard's men, Sgt. Major Peel, was also part of the Wild Geese as revealed in Marc Hazzard: Merc #10: *Iran Slam* and expanded on in Annual #1: *A Matter of Lives and Death*. A group of mercenaries called the Wild Geese appear in volumes 2, 6 and 7 of the manga *Hellsing*.

In the 1980 film *The Exterminator*, Det. James Dalton, who is hunting the Exterminator, has a slip of the tongue and says, "the Exec... the Exterminator," which suggests that Dalton is aware of the Executioner.

In **C.O.B.R.A.** #1: *The Heroin Connection*, Jon Skul makes reference to Richard Camellion, **The Death Merchant**. Senator Harriet Clayton appears in **Black Ops**: *American Jihad* and in **Codename**: *Extreme Prejudice*, tying the two series by William Johnstone together. Implicitly, she is the female president seen in Johnstone's **Stark** and **Invasion USA** series. Barry Rivers, **The Rig Warrior**, adopts the CB handle Dog after reading a book about **The Dog Teams** when he was a boy. Both Jarrod, the Pretender, and Robert McCall, the Equalizer, are referenced in Star Trek: *The Eugenics War: The Rise and Fall of Khan Noonien Singh Volume 1* by Greg Cox.

In his interview for *A Study of Action Adventure Fiction: The Executioner and Mack Bolan*, Don Pendleton points out that he created the Mafia slang term "turkey meat" for people who have been tortured by the Mafia. The term is used by Lionel Derrick (Chet Cunningham) in The Penetrator #2: *Blood on the Strip* and by Chet Cunningham in **The Avenger #1**.

In the season two episode of Knight Rider, "The Mouth of the Snake" (1984), Michael Knight and KITT encounter David Dalton. Dalton then appeared in the television movies *Code of Vengeance* (1985), *Dalton: Code of Vengeance II* (1986) and the two-episode series *Dalton's Code of Vengeance* (aka Code of Vengeance) (1986). Knight Rider had several later spinoffs and the television movie *Knight Rider 2000* (1991) and television series *Team Knight Rider* (1997). The 1994 television movie *Knight Rider 2010* only used the name and did not have any connections to the original series or other spinoffs. In the Amazing Stories episode "Remote Control Man," which first aired December 8, 1985, a man through his remote control is able to materialize characters from his television; among those he conjures are KITT from Knight Rider and Templeton "Face" Peck from the A-Team.

Kim Newman's short story, "Andy Warhol's Dracula: Anno Dracula 1978-79," set in an alternate reality where Dracula won, features a group of fearless vampire killers which includes Travis Bickle (*Taxi Driver*), Thana (*Ms .45*), an architect on a crusade to avenge his family (Paul Kersey, *Death Wish*) and the exterminator with a skull on his chest and a flame thrower in his hands (a dual reference to the Punisher and to the Exterminator who wielded a flame thrower).

PARODIES

Most of the crossovers and references listed above have treated the "guest" in a serious light. However, the guest stars may be distorted and shown in less favorable light, either as a figure of fun or menace. The Destroyer #38: *Bay City Blast* sees Remo Williams and Chuin protecting a deep-cover federal agent buried deep in the Mafia. This agent has taken over Bay City, New Jersey to allow the Mob to centralize, thus making it easier for law enforcement to take out a large slice of the Mafia in one raid. Certainly without the complication of the undercover operation, such a setup might well have appeared in an adventure of the Executioner, **The Butcher** or any of the other mob fighters. So Sapir and Murphy used this opportunity to make fun of three rival series also published by Pinnacle at the time.

In *Bay City Blast*, weapon designer Samuel Arlington Gregory adopts the alias of the Eraser and forms his three-man Rubout Squad consisting of:
• Mack Tolan, the Exterminator: A parody of Mack Bolan, the Executioner, which emphasizes the violent side of the character and ignores the compassionate aspect, "Sergeant Mercy," that Pendleton imbued his character with. Tolan is totally kill-crazy and ready

to kill any and everything. The Exterminator is what someone might have expected to read in an Executioner if they were totally unaware of the character.

- Al Baker, the Baker: A parody version of the Butcher, Al Baker is a former numbers runner, who claimed to be much higher in the mob than he actually was. He sells Gregory information about the workings of the mob, all of which he has made up.
- Nicolas Lizzard, the Lizard: The Death Merchant, Richard Camellion, gets the parody treatment. Camellion's mastery of disguise is the main element parodied here as the alcoholic Lizzard frequently disguises himself as a woman with his three day growth still intact. Lizzard believes that his disguise is so good that every man he meets has fallen madly in love with him.

The Destroyer takes most of the novel to catch up with the Rubout Squad, but when he finally confronts them, all four members are very quickly dispatched by Remo and Chuin.

In *Bay City Blast*, the parodies are played mainly for laughs, but parodies can also be used to air a grudge with a rival series. Mike Newton revealed in an interview for *A Study of Action Adventure Fiction: The Executioner and Mack Bolan* that NBC was allowed access to Able Team files for a potential television series in 1982. In 1983, NBC produced *The A-Team*.

In 1986, Gold Eagle published Able Team #24: *Blood Gambit* where Able Team comes into conflict with the Gun Team, an evil parody of the A-Team. The Gun Team is a crack Commando unit court-martialled after developing a taste for flesh, eating those killed in napalm attacks. The Team escapes and develops a Robin Hood image in the press, although they act as a troubleshooting force for Armageddon Arms, a weapons manufacturer. The Gun Team is lead by Col. Carruthers "Cannibal" Jones—the team leader who appears in a bad disguise and is a play on Col. John "Hannibal" Smith. Templeton "Face" Peck is parodied as Francis "Feces" Forthingham, a six-foot-six baby-faced conman. Orville Daemmeus "O.D." Yus is the ebony-skinned stoner pilot. O.D.'s appearance and name suggests a parody of B.A. Barracus, although his skills and British accent suggest a parody of H.M. Murdock. "Slaughter" Smith, the thin, gangly team member with a wild shock of red hair and a vicious temperament, is a similar combination of H.M. Murdock and B.A. Barracus, sharing the latter's dislike of flying. The Gun Team is completed by Doris Drane, a homicidal reporter who is as likely to kill you with a hat pin as write up a story. Doris parodies the roles of Amy Amanda Allen and Tawnia Baker in the A-Team.

In 1996, in Destroyer #102: *Unite and Conquer*, Remo and Chuin encounter Blaise Fury, the Extinguisher. The Extinguisher was a Green Beret in Vietnam who discovered that his family of firefighters was killed by Mafia arsonists and had a series of novels published about him. Remo revealed that he had read the early Extinguisher novels during his tours of Vietnam. Eventually, it is revealed that the man is not really the Extinguisher but rather Remo's son, Winston Smith, posing as the Extinguisher. Winston had also been reading Extinguisher novels including #221: *Hell on Wheels* and #214: *Deadly Death*. At one point, the young Winston Smith is questioned about how the Extinguisher can still be so young and have served in Vietnam. Winston's answer is that the Extinguisher is eternal and will be alive as long as there is injustice. The Extinguisher and the Executioner are similar: Both have achieved similar numbers of volumes in a similar period and both have been questioned about the age of the hero given his history in the Vietnam War.

As a popular culture phenomenon, the serial vigilante has been the subject of a more general parody. *Mad* Magazine ran parodies of movies and television series: *Billy Jack*, *Death Wish*, *Death Wish 2*, *Knight Rider*, *The A-Team*, *Hardcastle and McCormick*, and the *Equalizer*. The satirical online paper *The Onion* ran an article in 2004 describing how the A-Team was finally pardoned. The article parodied a number of conventions of the series, such as where the team was frequently imprisoned with items that allowed them to escape. The article can be found at http://www.theonion.com/content/node/30660. In comic books, the Punisher has frequently been parodied in such publications as 1992's *The Pummler* from Parody Press and the Pulveriser in Marvel's *What the...?!*, or the more pornographic Punish-her Score Journal and the Paddler. Punisher parodies also appear in Monster in My Pocket #2 as the Exterminator, and Boris the Bear appeared as the Punishbear in issues 13 and 21 of his own title.

2. Precursors to the Serial Vigilante

It has been pointed out that popular fiction has had a long tradition of avengers, men and women who take the law into their own hands, seeking to avenge the wrongs done to them or bringing law to a lawless land. Both Turner (1977) and Kittredge and Krauser (1978) express the view that the serial vigilante forms part of this cycle of justice figures. It is possible to examine the earlier incarnations of the justice figure and look at how these genres and the characters they spawned have led to the development of the serial vigilante. The justice figure can be traced through the pulp hero, the British outlaw, the dime novel, the penny dreadful, and back into the realms of folklore, myths and legend.

Perhaps the earliest known example of the justice figure is Robin Hood. The earliest versions of the legend of Robin Hood had Robin and his men as simple thieves, but as the story grew, elements were added such as Maid Marian, Friar Tuck and the fight against corrupt and unjust governments of the Sheriff of Nottingham and Prince John. More modern retellings added that Robin had been in the Crusades with King Richard. Robin's fight against injustice and tyranny became the model for the justice figure.

The English penny dreadfuls and their American counterparts, the dime novels, took historical and contemporary outlaws such as Dick Turpin, Jesse James and Billy the Kid and gave them much more noble characters and showed them entering a life of crime in response to the unjust treatment handed them by corrupt authorities. Many of the dime novels were written after the American Civil War and the outlaws returned from the war only to be unfairly treated by the carpetbaggers forcing them into a life of crime. These outlaws robbed the rich and corrupt carpetbaggers and gave the money to the small farmers and ranchers in danger of losing their properties.

The pulp heroes of America and the characters seen in Thriller and competitors in England showed the next evolution of the justice figure with men returning from World

War I and fighting against crime. These criminals ranged from the mundane gangsters inspired by Al Capone through to villains wreaking havoc and destruction with super-scientific weaponry.

We see the modern revamps of pulp heroes such as *The Saint* television series (1962–69). The Shadow was revived for a series of nine novels starting with *The Return of the Shadow* in 1963, then the 1964 revamp of dime and pulp novel hero Nick Carter as Nick Carter, **Killmaster**. Also in 1964, Bantam Books began reprinting the Doc Savage series. In 1966, there was the revamp of the Green Hornet in the television series starring Van Williams and Bruce Lee and the revamp of Bulldog Drummond in *Deadlier Than the Male*, which was followed by 1969's *Some Girls Do*. The popularity of these revamps and reprints paved the way for the serial vigilante.

THE BRITISH OUTLAW

Thriller magazine and its rivals were the British version of the pulps and spawned a number of characters who operated outside of the legal system to seek justice for those unable to help themselves. Many of these characters served in World War I, which left these characters with a thirst for adventure.

- **THE JUST MEN** (1905): The debut novel of Edgar Wallace featured the Four Just Men — Leon Gonsalez, George Manfred and Raymond Poiccart, with the fourth member killed during an earlier adventure. The Just Men fight against injustice, threatening to kill a member of Parliament if an unjust bill is not withdrawn. The Just Men's recorded activities start back in 1899. The Just Men feel that the law is inadequate and set about killing those who have evaded the system. In 1959, a new group of Four Just Men appeared in a British television series that ran for one season. This new group of Just Men had served together in an Allied unit during World War II and as a promise to their commanding officer, Col. Bacon, Ben Manfred, a British MP; Tim Collier, an American reporter based in Paris; Jeff Ryder, a New York lawyer; and Ricco Poccari, a Roman hotelier; all promised to fight injustice around the world. Each man operated with a female assistant.

- **FU MANCHU** (1913): Sax Rohmer wrote fourteen novels featuring the villain Fu Manchu and his nemesis, Sir Dennis Nayland Smith. Smith originally encountered Dr. Fu Manchu in Burma and dedicated his life to stopping the devil doctor. Smith is a special agent for Scotland Yard. Fu Manchu was revived for the comic series Shang Chi: Master of Kung Fu with the title character as the son of Fu Manchu joining forces with Sir Dennis Nayland Smith and fighting his father.

- **RICHARD HANNAY** (1915): Starting with *The 39 Steps*, John Buchan's hero stumbles upon a German plot to invade England prior to the outbreak of World War I. Hannay's service during that war formed the basis of the next two novels, *Greenmantle* and *Mr. Standfast*. *The Three Hostages* and *The Island of Sheep* have Hannay fight against criminal conspiracies.

- **BULLDOG DRUMMOND** (1920): Sapper (H.C. McNeile) created Drummond, a former soldier in the Great War seeking adventure through an advertisement in the paper. This brought him into conflict with the master criminal best known as Carl Peterson. Drummond's adventures had him fighting against Peterson and his criminal empire as well as facing other criminals. After Sapper's death, the series was continued by Sapper's friend and partial model for Drummond, Gerald Fairlie.

- THE RINGER (1925): Another Edgar Wallace creation, Henry Arthur Milton is a master of disguise known as the Ringer. A veteran of World War I, Milton returned to England to discover that his sister had committed suicide after a con man left her penniless and pregnant. From that point, the Ringer kills this man and uses his skills to kill those who prey on the weak and vulnerable.

- THE SAINT (1928): Simon Templar, the modern Robin Hood, was the creation of Leslie Charteris. Templar was a veteran of World War I who, out of the thrill of adventure, took to fighting the ungodly. Initially, the Saint was very physical, often shooting the criminals he faced; in later adventures he relies more on cunning and guile to out-con the criminals he faces.

- TIGER STANDISH (1932): Created by Sydney Horler, the Hon. Timothy Overton Standish is an adventurer in the mold of Bulldog Drummond. Initially a freelance adventurer, with the outbreak of World War II, Standish became a freelance agent for section Y1 of British Intelligence, flushing out Nazi spies and saboteurs.

- THE TOFF (1938): The Honorable Richard "Rollie" Rollison, better known as the Toff, was the creation of John Creasy. An adventurer in the Saint mold, Rollison is a wealthy young man who decided to fight crime. Initially, working entirely outside the law, Rollison's successes led the police to tolerate and assist him in his adventures.

- PATRICK DAWLISH (1939): Another creation of John Creasy, who was writing under the pseudonym of Gordon Ashe, Dawlish is an adventurer in the mold of Bulldog Drummond. If it wasn't for his broken nose, left over from his boxing days, Dawlish would be handsome, standing at 6'3" with wide shoulders and an ease of movement seen in the physically fit. Dawlish is an implacable foe, fighting thieves, blackmailers, murderers and Nazis. Dawlish eventually became a special commissioner for Scotland Yard and headed the organization known as Crime Haters.

- THE FALCON (1940): Initially a single short story by Michael Arlen, the character was quickly translated to film by RKO with British actor George Sanders taking the title role of Gay Stanhope Falcon in 1941. Sanders, also portraying the Saint for the same studio, played the role for another four movies. Sander's final performance was in *The Falcon's Brother*, where Gay Falcon was killed and his brother Lawrence Falcon investigated, making this the first time a series character was killed on screen. Lawrence Falcon was played by Tom Conway, who was Sander's real brother, and appeared in a further ten films. Another three Falcon films were made starring John Calvert as Michael Waring. In 1954, the Adventures of the Falcon television series aired on ABC. The Falcon was now played by Charles McGraw and the Falcon's identity was Mike Waring. This Falcon was credited as an adaptation of the Falcon novels of Dexler Drake. Drake's novels started in 1936 featured Malcolm J. Wingate as the Falcon. Leslie Charteris attempted to sue RKO in 1945, alleging unfair competition and that the Falcon was a plagiarism of the Saint. RKO was paying less for the rights to the Falcon, dropped the Saint and avoided a lawsuit.

PRIVATE EYES

- **CONTINENTAL OP** (1923): This heavyset operative of the Continental Detective Agency was the creation of Dashiell Hammett. Hammett, a former operative of the Pinkerton Detective Agency, used his experiences as the basis of the cases of the nameless hero.

- **RACE WILLIAMS** (1926): Created by Carroll John Daly, this character was one of the first hardboiled private eyes. Race Williams sees himself as a halfway house between the cops and the crooks, able to walk in both worlds.

- **SAM SPADE** (1930): Dashiell Hammett's other private eye debuted in *The Maltese Falcon* and featured in several short stories. Hammett's blonde detective operated as the middle man between police and the criminals trading on his tarnished reputation to bring criminals to justice. Filmed three times in the decade after it was published, the 1941 version, starring Humphrey Bogart and directed by John Huston, is considered to be the definitive version.

- **PHILIP MARLOWE** (1939): Raymond Chandler was a writer influenced by Hammett and the Black Mask pulp writers. Initially writing short stories featuring various private eyes such as Johnny Dalmas, Chandler broke into novels with the character of Philip Marlowe in *The Big Sleep*. With the success of the novels, Chandler's short stories were reprinted and edited as Philip Marlowe stories. It was Chandler who defined the hardboiled detective in his essay "The Simple Art of Murder," describing a noble man able to walk down mean streets.

- **MIKE HAMMER** (1947): Initially conceived as comic book character Mike Danger, by Mickey Spillane. Mike Hammer first appeared in the novel *I, the Jury*. Tough and uncompromising, Hammer is single-minded in solving the cases he is hired to investigate. In the ultimate blurring of creator and creation, Spillane played Hammer in the 1963 movie adaptation of *The Girl Hunters*. Don Pendleton cites Mike Hammer as an influence on his creation of **The Executioner**.

- **TRAVIS MCGEE** (1964): Florida-based "salvage" expert Travis McGee retrieves stolen items for the fee of half the value of the items. Travis then takes parts of his retirement living off the money until the next job. McGee encounters a number of emotionally and psychologically scarred women during his salvage operations and his relationships with them heal their wounds. This character was created by John D. MacDonald.

HERO PULPS

The hero pulps can be considered to be closest relative to the serial vigilante. With skills forged in war, these heroes returned to America to fight against crime, operating outside of the law in the interests of justice.

- **NICK CARTER** (1886): Nick Carter was raised by his father Sim Carter to be a great detective. Sim's training gave his son great strength, a keen mind and the ability to be a master of disguise. Carter operates a private detective firm but has an open consultancy with the police. A popular character, he appeared in over 1000 exploits and was adapted and exploited all over the world. One of the first characters to be adapted to film, Carter appeared in four French serials between 1908 and 1912. In 1942, Carter made the transition to radio. In 1964, the Nick Carter name was revived and reinvented for the **Killmaster** series.

- THE SHADOW (1930): Initially the narrator for the radio program *Detective Story*, which dramatized stories from Street and Smith's magazine of the same name, the Shadow gained his own magazine when people began asking for that Shadow magazine. Street and Smith hired Walter Gibson to write the Shadow under the house name of Maxwell Grant. The Shadow pulp ran for 325 novels with Gibson writing the majority of those. The Shadow was quickly adapted to a radio program; the most famous of the voice actors for the character was Orson Welles. The Shadow also appeared in movies and comics. The Shadow was referenced in *War Against the Mafia*, the first **Executioner** book.

- THE SPIDER (1933): Initially written by R.T.M. Scott, the Spider was a nickname for Richard Wentworth, a World War I veteran who took an amateur interest in crime with his valet Ram Singh. After two books, Scott left the series and Norvell Page, using the house name Grant Stockbridge, took over writing and the series really took off. Page established the Spider as a costumed identity that Wentworth used to mete out the death penalty on the underworld. The treats faced by the Spider were apocalyptic: flights of vampire bats, hoards of cavemen, and super weapons that destroy metal. The Spider was adapted for two serials. Four books in the series were revised and updated as **Spider** in 1975.

- DOC SAVAGE (1933): As the followup to the Shadow, Street and Smith created Doc Savage. Under the house name Kenneth Robeson, the majority of the 181 novels were written by Lester Dent. Doc Savage and his five aides traveled the world righting wrongs. Doc had been raised from birth to be the ultimate superman for that purpose. Doc has been adapted into comics several times and Bantam Books reprinted the original pulp novels and several new books by Philip Jose Farmer and Will Murray. Richard Sapir and Warren Murphy acknowledge Doc Savage as an influence on the **Destroyer** series.

- THE AVENGER (1936): Another Street and Smith series also written under the Kenneth Robeson house name: this time Paul Ernst was the writer behind the name. The Avenger was adventurer Richard Henry Benson, whose wife and daughter disappeared during a commercial air flight. The shock of the disappearance left Benson's hair white and his face frozen and malleable like clay. This made Benson a master of disguise. Benson used his new skills to fight crime and formed Justice, Inc., with his band of assistants. After the *Avenger* magazine folded, the character appeared in several short stories in the back pages of *Clues*. The series was reprinted by Warner Books in the 1970s and several new Avenger novels were written by Ron Goulart.

- DOMINO LADY (1936): One of the very few mystery women of the pulps is the Domino Lady. Created by Lars Anderson, socialite Ellen Patrick became the Domino Lady to avenge the murder of her father, Owen Patrick. Clad in black mask and skin-tight white dress, this heroine was capable of clouding the minds of men.

- GREEN HORNET (1936): Strictly speaking not a pulp hero, but this radio serial hero was created by Fran Striker, creator of the Lone Ranger, as an updated version of that hero and shares many of the traits of the pulp heroes. Britt Reid, crusading newspaper publisher, adopts the costumed identity of the Green Hornet to fight crime with his chauffeur Kato. Britt is the great-nephew of John Reid, the Lone Ranger. Revived in 1966 by William Dozier as a companion series to Batman, the Green Hornet helped make a star of Bruce Lee.

COMICS

In the early days of comics, characters were a mix of pulp-influenced mystery men and super-powered beings. Many of the themes seen in serial vigilantes, such as the death of family members from criminals, can be seen in the comics.

- **CRIMSON AVENGER** (1938): Lee Travis was a newspaper editor who was distressed by the crime rate, donned a crimson mask, cape and fedora, and fought crime as the Crimson Avenger with his chauffer Wing. Later, the pair replaced their pulp-inspired costumes with more Superman-inspired tights and continued to fight crime.

- **BATMAN** (1939): As a child, Bruce Wayne witnessed the slaughter of his parents at the hands of an armed robber. His parents left Bruce very wealthy and he used his money to train himself to the peak of human ability. Realizing that criminals are cowardly and inspired by a giant bat, Bruce adopted the disguise of Batman. Joined a year later by his boy sidekick Robin, Batman became one of the greatest and best known superheroes of all time.

- **PHANTOM LADY** (1941): Socialite Sandra Knight gained a taste for adventuring after saving her senator father's life with only a rolled-up newspaper. After gaining a black light projector, which blinds opponents, Knight adopted a skimpy yellow and green, later blue and red, costume to fight crime. The character moved through several publishers, eventually settling at DC Comics where several younger characters have taken the name the Phantom Lady.

- **BLACK CANARY** (1947): Dinah Drake was the daughter of a police officer and dating a police officer, Larry Lance. Unable to join the police force, she created a secret identity to assist with the fight against crime; she worked as a florist during the day. At night she donned a blonde wig, fishnet stockings and the rest of her costume to infiltrate criminal gangs as the Black Canary. The character appeared as a supporting character in several titles. Later, Dinah's daughter Dinah Lance became the new Black Canary, gained the power of a sonic scream and began dating the Green Arrow.

WESTERN

Westerns have been a major influence on the serial vigilantes, with many of the serial vigilante authors also writing westerns. The western mythos of men like Bat Masterson and Wyatt Earp riding into a lawless town and single-handedly bringing law and order, or the romanticized legends of outlaws like Billie the Kid or Jesse James of men forced outside the law by the corrupt authorities, plays heavily into the idea of the serial vigilante. This can be seen by the frequent references and comparisons to the Lone Ranger that many serial vigilantes seem to invite. The western influence can be seen most clearly in the movie version of **Death Wish**: Paul Kersey travels to Arizona, where his client extols the virtues of the western lifestyle and how there is less crime. Kersey is given a six gun by a grateful client and returns to clean up the streets of New York City. At several points, Kersey asks the villain to "fill his hand" and is ordered to leave town at high noon, both references to the gunfighters of the old West. Marvel comics one-shot comic, *A Man Called Frank*, reimagines The Punisher in the old West, riding the range to avenge the death of his family.

- ZORRO (1919): Created by Johnston McCulley, Zorro is the costumed identity of Don Diego Vega used to fight against the corrupt government of the pueblo of Los Angeles. The character first appeared in *The Curse of Capistrano* in the August 1919 issue of *All-Story Weekly*. The character may have finished there but Douglas Fairbanks decided to adapt Zorro for his next film in 1920. Zorro appeared in a number of other novels, short story, films and television series. Several generations of Zorros have appeared throughout history always fighting injustice.

- LONE RANGER (1933): During an outlaw ambush, a troop of Texas Rangers is killed with only one survivor. This Lone Ranger is brought back to health by the Indian Tonto, who discovered the site of the massacre. Donning a mask made from the vest of his brother, who rode as commander of the Rangers, the Lone Ranger and Tonto ride the old West helping people and fighting crime. The Lone Ranger doesn't kill, preferring to shoot the guns out of outlaws' hands. Starting as a radio show, the Lone Ranger has been adapted to novels, movies, comics and television. The character of the Green Hornet is an update of the Lone Ranger and is revealed to be the great-nephew of the Lone Ranger.

SPY

The spy genre has a long history but gained popularity with the Cold War between America and the Soviet Union that emerged after World War II. This diplomatic war of words gave the scope for clandestine operations.

- JAMES BOND (1953): Arguably the most famous spy of all time. Created by Ian Fleming for *Casino Royale*, Bond is Agent 007, working for the 00 section, which gives him a license to kill. Bond travels the world fighting the plans of the Soviet agency SMERSH and the criminal/terrorist organization SPECTRE. Bond made the transition to film, where he has been played by Sean Connery, George Lazenby, Roger Moore, Timothy Dalton, Pierce Brosnan and Daniel Craig. After the death of Ian Fleming, the series was continued by Kingsley Amis, John Gardner, Raymond Benson, Charlie Higson and Sebastian Faulks.

- THE AVENGERS (1961): This television series featured secret agent John Steed and his partners as they hunt and avert threats against Great Britain. Initially assisted by Doctor David Keel, Steed was then partnered with Cathy Gale, followed by Emma Peel and Tara King. The series was revived as the New Avengers with Steed mentoring two new agents, Mike Gambit and Purdey.

- MODESTY BLAISE (1963): The head of a criminal organization known as the Network, when Modesty and her right-hand man Willie Garvin retired to England, they were hired by the British Secret Service on a freelance basis. This started as a newspaper strip written by Peter O'Donnell. O'Donnell then adapted the series for novels and short stories. Modesty's adventures have been the basis for three films.

- **THE MAN FROM U.N.C.L.E.** (1964): The television series features agents of the United Network Command for Law Enforcement and featured an American agent, Napoleon Solo and a Russian agent Illya Kuriarkin working against the terrorist group THRUSH. The show had a spinoff, The Girl from U.N.C.L.E., which had agents April Dancer and Mark Slate also fighting THRUSH. Both series had original tie-in novels.

- **MISSION IMPOSSIBLE** (1966): Another spy television series where the Impossible Missions Force create an elaborate con or sting to obtain vital intelligence from enemy agents. One of the longest running spy series ever, the series was revived in 1988 for another television series with a new team from the IMF. In 1996, the series made the transition to the big screen for three movies starring Tom Cruise.

- **CALLAN** (1967): David Callan works for the Section, a security department that monitors and eliminates traitors and other threats to security. Callan is the best operative but he is plagued by his conscience; he needs to know what his targets have done before he can eliminate them. *Callan* ran for four seasons and one 1981 television movie. Series creator James Mitchell wrote several novelizations. Star Edward Woodward played a similar character, Robert McCall, in *The Equalizer* (1985–1989).

3. Modern Pulp

Pulp Heroes from the 1930s and '40s were a major influence on the serial vigilantes of the '70s and '80s. The reprinting of pulp heroes like Doc Savage, the Shadow and **The Avenger** showed publishers the viability of series fiction. With this success of these reprints, all new adventures were written for these characters. Walter Gibson penned the Return of the Shadow before Dennis Lynds wrote several new Shadow adventures under the Maxwell Grant name. Pulp historians Ron Goulart and Will Murray wrote new adventures of the Avenger and Doc Savage respectively, under the Kenneth Robeson house name when the publishers ran out of stories to reprint.

Just as new adventures were written for pulp heroes, authors were creating new pulp heroes with adventures set in the pulp era of the '30s and '40s. These new characters appeared side by side with the serial vigilantes and offer a subset of the serial vigilante. Modern pulp characters can be seen in many different formats, including novels, film, television and comics.

- **COMPANY Z**: Western author J.T. Edson created this series about an unofficial company of Texas Rangers set in the 1920s and '30s, in homage to the works of Edgar Wallace. Company Z is unfettered by the rules that regulate the Texas Rangers and is able to tackle the crimes and criminals that fall through the cracks. In three of the books in this series, Company Z works with Edgar Wallace's Mr. J.G. Reeder to stop criminal genius Mad Jack Flack.

- **AGENT 13/13 ASSASSIN:** A companion piece to Orion, this series was created by Flinte Dille and David Marconi for the *Secret Agent S.I.* role-playing game as the basis of pulp style adventures in the 1930s. A young, talented child was kidnapped in 1907 by the Brotherhood, an organization that has existed from the dawn of civilization for the betterment of mankind. That was until Itsu, the Hand Sinister, seized power and is trying to take over the world. The child, known as Agent 13, was trained in disguise and other espionage arts, rebelled against the Brotherhood and fights to prevent them from taking over the world. The comic books series *13 Assassin* brings Agent 13 to the modern age, still fighting Itsu and the Brotherhood.

- **DOC SIDHE:** Starting in the modern world, Olympic kick boxer Harris Greene is transported into a parallel reality, where elves and fairies exist in a parallel 1930s. Zeppelins fly overhead and the greatest hero is Doc Sidhe, the elfin version of Doc Savage, and his team of adventurers.

- **NIGHT RAVEN:** The Night Raven's true identity is never revealed in these stories written for Marvel UK, as the cloaked vigilante dispenses justice on the mean streets of Canada. While many of the character's exploits were told in comic format, text stories appeared as back-up features in many titles accompanied by illustrations deliberately invoking the pulp novels that inspired it. Night Raven's equipment and headquarters were later discovered by the superhero Nocturne. The series makes both Night Raven and Nocturne British, contradicting the earlier stories.

- **THE MASKED AVENGER:** The series is set in 1930s New York and written by pulp historian Tom Johnson. The Masked Avenger is a mystery man fighting evil. He faces criminal masterminds like the Centipede.

- **THE ROOK:** Max Davies is a young man driven by visions of crimes yet to be. Emotionally scarred by witnessing the brutal murder of his father, Davies trained in every martial art and scientific discipline, becoming a scourge on evil. Set in 1930s Atlanta, the Rook battles supernaturally empowered villains. First published in 2006, the Rook series consists of two novels and several short stories and the Rook has met many original pulp heroes such as the Black Bat and Ascot Keane.

- **INDIANA JONES:** The most successful of the modern pulp characters, archaeologist Indiana Jones travels the globe searching for artifacts and treasures. The star of four movies, a television series, comic books and several series of novels, Indy's creators George Lucas and Stephen Spielberg were inspired by the serial and pulp heroes of the '30s and '40s.

- **TWILIGHT AVENGER:** Reece Chambers is the star player for Randolph College Tornados and an honor student in science. When his fiancée Dolores Herth is brutally run down and in a coma, Chambers and Dolores' father, Dr. Milton Herth, developed a number of scientific weapons and a costume to fight the man responsible, the masked criminal only known as the Centipede.

- **THE GLOOM:** Armed with supernatural guns that only shoot evil, millionaire Carson Kane fights crime as mystery man the Gloom. The Gloom teams up with fellow adventurer Doc Adventure and the sultry reporter Vixen La Fox to battle Nazis in 1940s New York.

- **THE ROCKETEER:** Dave Stephen's tribute to the Rocketman serials from the '40s, this comic series focused on the adventures of pilot Cliff Secord who discovered a rocket pack created by an unnamed Doc Savage and encounters the Shadow.

- **PLANETARY:** Warren Ellis' comic book series about a group of mystery archaeologists has as a group of pulp-analogues Doc Brass (Doc Savage), Hark (Fu Manchu), the Jungle Lord (Tarzan), the Millionaire Vigilante (a mix of the Shadow, the Spider and the Green Hornet), Jimmy (Jimmy Christopher Operator #5), the Aviator (G-8) and Edison (Tom Swift).

- **THE PROWLER:** This series of comic mini-series and a one shots has a mixture of stories from the 1930s and the present. The 1930s tales show the adventures of Leo Kragg, a Hollywood executive who adopts the costumed identity of the Prowler to fight gangsters, mad scientists and zombie masters. The tales in the present have Kragg coming out of retirement to train a new Prowler, Scott Kida, and fight terrorists and child pornographers. The 1930s exploits include "reprints" of a 1942 Sunday newspaper strip, records of Prowler novelty music, various items of Prowler memorabilia such as ads for war bonds, 1944 animated Prowler cartoons and stills from the Prowler serial.

- **ATHENA VOLTAIRE:** The adventures of a 1930s barnstorming pilot and adventuress. Athena is the daughter of World War I French flying ace Tristam Voltaire and Countess Anezka Sikorsky and raised on a ranch in Arizona. Fighting Nazis and hunting treasures around the world, Voltaire is in high demand from fellow adventurers and allied governments.

- **DOC DARE:** During World War II, Doctor Joanna Dare was working with the United States military researching the Gladiator serum used by Abednego Danner to create an army of super soldiers. Her research was interrupted by Nazi saboteurs and Joanna was forced to drink the serum. Whenever she orgasms the serum gives her heightened strength and speed to fight Nazis and Japanese threats.

- **CAPTAIN GRAVITY:** The Captain Gravity serials are the hottest properties in Hollywood and feature a flying hero. During a location shoot in Mexico for the latest Captain Gravity serial, Nazi agents take over the shoot and hold the film crew hostage. Joshua Jones, an African American working behind the scenes, discovers the mysterious element 115 which allows him to control gravity. Donning the Captain Gravity costume, Jones frees the crew from the Nazis and begins a heroic career as Captain Gravity.

4. Missing the Mark: Singletons, Police, Private Eyes, Criminals and Other Oddities

With the success of Don Pendleton's **Executioner**, many similar series were produced. However, other types of fiction tried to copy this success so we began to see characters and series that were not strictly serial vigilantes but utilized many of the themes and motifs of the serial vigilante. In many cases, they adopted the conventions of the serial vigilante, such as the numbering of the series, and were published alongside serial vigilante series, such as Warner Books' Men of Action series, which published the Dirty Harry original novels alongside serial vigilante series such as **Ninja Master** and **S-Com**. This section will examine a sample of some of the various series that for many reasons did not meet the criteria for the serial vigilantes. This listing is not exhaustive and does not examine the western and the science fiction post-apocalyptic series.

SINGLETONS

By its very nature a series requires more than one book, comic or movie. For a number of reasons these serial vigilantes never went beyond a single exploit.

- Fire Force One, *No Sanctuary*, by Jim Bowser (1987): After a terrorist attack by PLO splinter group, the Shield of Allah, which killed over 100 Marines, one of those Marines reacted. He was the son of Ret. General Headley DeFarge, multimillionaire owner of the DeFarge Foundation. The general hires a team of veterans from his time in Vietnam. Known as Fire Force One, they fight terrorism around the world.

- Deathwalker, *Rites of the Demon*, by Roman Castevano (1976): Billed as the first in a new series of non-stop action and unbelievable terror, this was the only exploit of Luke Paine. Paine was a journalist who was captured in the Vietnam War and was rescued through a prisoner exchange. Upon his return to America, he discovered that his girlfriend Donna Donofrio had become involved with strange cult.

- *Jake Speed* (1986 movie): Jake is the hero of a series of books written by Reno Melon and published by Gold Eagle with titles such as *Race through Hell*, *Dog Flight*, *Indochina Zoo* and *Zambezi Run* (this last title recounts the events recorded in the film). To the world at large, Jake is a fictional character and his exploits aren't real, just stories in a book like those of the Destroyer and the Executioner (whose books also appear in the film, implying a similar status, as does a reference to Doc Savage). But when white slavers kidnap Margaret Winston's sister, Margaret soon discovers that Jake and his partner Desmond Floyd are all too real, as is his powerful shotgun the Kid and car H.A.R.V. (Heavily Armored Raiding Vehicle) as he drags her along on his latest adventure. Reno Melon is the pen name the pair uses to record their adventures and the royalties are used to fund their war on crime. *Jake Speed* (1986) was written by Wayne Crawford and Andy Lane, directed by Andy Lane and starred Wayne Crawford as Jake Speed. The novelization of the film was published by Gold Eagle titled *Jake Speed* and the author was listed as Reno Melon.

- Black Ops, *American Jihad* (Art Jenson), by William Johnstone (2006): During a mission in Iraq, Art Jenson, the great-grandson of Smoke Jenson (hero of Johnstone's the Last Mountain Man series), shoots an unarmed insurgent and is crucified by the media, who make it appear that Jenson knew that the insurgent was unarmed. Jenson is court-martialled and sent to jail. The military decide to form a one-man Black Ops team who tackles the terrorists and criminals that can't be touched by conventional law enforcement. Jenson leaves an ace of spades at all of his kills. Senator Harriet Clayton appears in this book and in Johnstone's **Codename** series.

- *The Destroyers*, by A.W. Miller (1979): Inspector Buddy Wells fought the war on drugs in San Francisco for years. During that fight he was able to rescue Emily Conover, daughter of Michael Conover. Conover was a millionaire land developer and he offered

Wells the deal of a lifetime, to take a free hand in the destruction of the heroin pipeline. With Conover's backing, Wells picked five other frustrated lawmen from all over America and together they attacked the Mexican town of Culiacan, which was the main pipeline of heroin into America. The mission caused the deaths of half the team.

• Kung Fu Master: Richard Dragon #1: *Dragon's Fist*, Award Books, by Jim Dennis (Dennis O'Neil & Jim Berry) (1974): This novel tells the story of Richard Dragon, the son of a diplomat who wandered into a life of crime. Attempting to steal a scroll from a martial arts dojo, he is invited to train at the school and eventually becomes a master of kung fu. Dragon is dragged into the world of crime-fighting when the terrorist known as the Swiss kidnaps Carolyn Woosan, the daughter of his kung fu sensei. No second novel was published but Dennis O'Neil adapted this novel as the first four issues of the comic *Richard Dragon: Kung Fu Master*. The series ran for a further fourteen issues.

After the series finished, O'Neil used Dragon in his run on the Question as a sensei to the title character. Dragon was subsequently revealed to have trained a number of martial artists in the DC universe. Other characters introduced in Richard Dragon: Kung Fu Master have appeared in other DC comic titles, such as Batman, Birds of Prey and Suicide Squad. In 2006, Dennis O'Neil adapted the first year of his Question run into a novel titled *Helltown*. Richard Dragon appeared in that novel only referred to as Richard.

NOVELIZATIONS

When a television series or movie is successful, there will be a number of spinoffs and tie-ins. One such tie-in is the novelization where the events of a television series or movie are retold in prose form. There were novelizations for Darkman, the A-Team, Knight Rider, Streethawk, the Equalizer, and the Persuaders. In some cases, there were original adventures written for these series.

• *MacGyver on Ice*, by Mark Daniel (1987): The only novel based on the MacGyver series serves as a prequel to the television series, explaining how MacGyver became the troubleshooter for the Phoenix Foundation.

• The A-Team #6: *Operation Desert Sun: The Untold Story*, by Charles Heath (1985): This A-Team novel serves as a prequel to the television series describing how the team escaped from military prison and went on the run.

• Darkman: Following on from the novelization of the first movie, Randall Boyll wrote four original novels featuring Darkman:
  1. *The Hangman*, 1994
  2. *The Price of Fear*, 1994
  3. *The Gods of Hell*, 1994
  4. *In the Face of Death*, 1995

The novels have badly scarred research scientist Peyton Westlake using his synthetic skin to fight serial killers, rogue spies and other threats. The novels feature characters and places that originally appeared in Marvel Comics' six-issue mini-series.

• Tomb Raider: Lara Croft was created for the Tomb Raider computer game; the archae-

ologist character has been adapted into two films and several comic book series. The character has also been the basis for three original novels:
   1. *The Amulet of Power*, 2003 (Mike Resnick)
   2. *The Lost Cult*, 2004 (E.E. Knight)
   3. *The Man of Bronze*, 2004 (James Alan Gardner)

• Supernatural: This story is based on the television series where the Winchester brothers, Sam and Dean, travel America battling demons and other supernatural threats. The novels are:
   1. *Nevermore*, 2007 (Keith R.A. DeCandido)
   2. *Witch's Canyon*, 2007 (Jeff Mariotte)
   3. *Bone Key*, 2008 (Keith R.A. DeCandido)

• *Buckaroo Banzai*, Earl Mac Rauch (1984): The novelization of the cult 1984 movie contains so much additional material that it should be considered an expansion. While the movie dealt with Buckaroo's battle with John Whorfin and the Lectroids from the Eight Dimension, the novel also recounts Banzai's battle with the arch criminal Hanoi Xan.

• *Burn Notice: The Fix*, Tod Goldberg (2008): This book, based on the television series, features disavowed spy Michael Western helping people and trying to discover why a burn notice was issued for him.

POLICE

The serial vigilantes came from the notion that the police were either corrupt or too hampered by the rules imposed on them. In response we saw police officers who openly flouted the rules and were far more effective than their fellow officers.

• Dirty Harry: This tough cop debuted in 1971 with the film *Dirty Harry*; since then there have been four movie sequels as well as two video games and novelizations of the first four movies as well as twelve original novels. Despite Dirty Harry's unorthodox approach to crime-fighting, we see his opinion of serial vigilantes play out in the plot of the second movie, *Magnum Force* (1973), where Harry tackles a team of vigilante cops.

• The Headhunters, series by John Weisman and Brian Boyer: This series focuses on the tough internal affairs investigators of Detroit PD. Nicknamed the Headhunters, they are the toughest and hardest cops, given access to resources, weapons and methods not available to regular police. They tackle corruption not only of police but of other law enforcement officials, such as judges and district attorneys. This three-book series was published by Pinnacle Books.

• C.A.T. (Crisis Aversion Team), series by Spike Andrews: The Crisis Aversion Team is two super-elite cops, Detectives Vince Santillo and Stewart Wilson, who get the garbage cases that are too tough, too dirty, too touchy for the other police of the New York Police Department. The Crisis Aversion Team was part of Warner Books' Men of Action Books line along with the Dirty Harry original novels.

• Little Saigon, series by Nicholas Cain: This series of four novels deals with the Vietnam veterans turned police officers who patrol the streets of Little Saigon in California, the largest Vietnamese community in the United States. The Metro Asian Gang (MAG) is headed former military police officer Luke Abel.

PRIVATE EYES

The hardboiled private eye was one of the inspirations for the serial vigilantes and, in the wake of the serial vigilantes, several new series featuring tough and hard private eyes appeared.

- Dakota, series by Gilbert Ralston: This series of five novels features Native American private eye Dakota, who lives on his family compound in Carson Valley, Nevada. Dakota investigates various crimes, including murder, often getting involved in shootouts and fights. This series was published by Pinnacle Books, the original home of the Executioner and the Destroyer.

- Hardman, series by Ralph Dennis: Jim Hardman, a former Atlanta police officer, and his partner Hump Evans investigate crimes in Atlanta. Tough and uncompromising, the pair appeared in twelve books.

- Shannon, series by Jake Quinn: Patrick Shannon is the most expensive private eye in the world and the star of three books. Shannon is a tough guy and can be "as vicious as the worst Mafia thug who ever used a blowtorch on a stoolie." Shannon operates out of his Manhattan penthouse with his Magnum .44.

- Triphammer, series by Douglas Enefer: Another tough private eye that lasted for four books.

CRIMINALS

Just as the serial vigilantes openly flouted the rules and laws of society in their pursuit of justice, the criminal element in a similar way breaks the rules and laws of society in pursuit of a profit.

- Nolan, series by Max Allan Collins: A professional thief seeks to retire but is always lured back for one last score. This caper series has seven volumes.

- Quarry, series by Max Allan Collins: This seven-book series features a hit man known only as Quarry on his various assignments. Quarry initially worked for the Broker but, after being betrayed, went solo. Quarry operates on a code of honor, such as not becoming involved with victims.

- The Ms. Squad series, by Mercedes Endfield: The two-book series featured the Ms. Squad, a trio of women striking a blow for feminism by recreating great crimes unsuccessfully committed by men and then successfully pulling them off. The Ms. Squad is made up of Jacqueline Cristal, chemical genius; Denna Royce, singer and actress; and Pammy Porter, expert martial artist. The trio is chased by former super spy turned private eye James Stock, a parody of James Bond.

OTHER ODDITIES

There were several series, one-shots and anthologies which did not meet the guidelines for serial vigilantes.

• Rogue Warrior, series by Richard Marcinko: After the success of Richard Marcinko's autobiography *Rogue Warrior* (1992), he was banned from writing any further factual accounts of his adventures, so the former SEAL began to turn out fictional accounts of his team's adventures, currently at twelve volumes. Marcinko has also written three motivational books, *Leadership Secrets of the Rogue Warrior* (1997), *The Rogue Warrior's Guide to Success* (1998) and *The Real Team* (1999).

• SEAL Team Seven, series by Keith Douglas: This seven-man SEAL team led by Lt. Blake Murdoch travels the world fighting terrorists and other threats to world security.

• Scorpion Squad/Vietnam: Ground Zero, series by Eric Helm: Initially published by Pinnacle Books for four books, the series features Special Forces commander Anthony Fetterman and his team during their service in Vietnam. The series was then acquired by Gold Eagle Books, renamed Vietnam: Ground Zero and ran for twenty-one books and four super novels.

• Saigon Commandos, series by Jonathon Cain: The military police who patrolled the streets of Saigon were known as the Saigon Commandos. This series — part war story, part police procedural — follows Sergeant Stryker and the MPs of 716th as they tackle crimes during the Vietnam War. This series was the basis for the 1987 movie *Saigon Commandos*.

• TALON Squad, series by Cliff Garnett: The Technology Augmented Low Obstacle Networked (TALON) Squad is a high-tech strike force drawn from the various branches of the United States military. This seven-person force tackles the toughest and most dangerous missions.

• Soldier of Fortune/Mercenary, series: This series of twelve books published by British publisher 22 Books started as the Soldier of Fortune series but with book #10 it became the Mercenary series. This anthology series gave the adventures of mercenaries. Each book followed a different mercenary while many of the books were contemporary. Some, such as #5 *Action in the Arctic*, were set in World War II. The publisher also publishes series that focus on SAS (Special Air Service) and SBS (Special Boat Service)

• Soldier of Fortune Magazine Presents: This anthology series of action/adventure titles was produced by *Soldier of Fortune Magazine*. In the twenty-eight books in the series, there were adventures during the Vietnam War, stories of MIA hunters, cult crashers, revolutionaries, and terrorist hunters.

• Weird Heroes Anthology, series edited by Byron Preiss: This anthology of new pulp stories is a mixture of short stories and novels. This series introduced the adventures of Cordwainer Bird (Harlan Ellison), Greatheart Silver (Philip Jose Farmer), Guts the Cosmic Greaser (Byron Preiss), Doc Phoenix (Ted White) and Adam Stalker (Archie Goodwin).

• Blade, series by Jeffrey Lord: This series features British secret agent Richard Blade. Blade was drafted into a top-secret project to travel through dimension X to alternate realities. Blade starts off naked and unarmed and fights his way through the various worlds he finds himself in before returning to his home dimension.

• Cody, series by David Brierley: Cody was recruited by Britain's Secret Intelligence Service (SIS) and trained by the CIA. After completing her training, Cody went freelance. In this series of five novels, we follow Cody's adventures.

• Rambo, original novel by David Morrell: David Morrell's 1972 novel *First Blood* showed the conflict between Korean War veteran Sheriff Teasle and Vietnam War veteran Rambo (no first name was given) and ultimately Rambo dies. In the 1982 movie starring Sylvester Stallone, Rambo was given a first name, John, and he survived. This was followed by the 1985 sequel *Rambo: First Blood, Part II*, scripted by Stallone and James Cameron and novelized by Morrell. This was followed by the sixty-five episode animated series where Rambo heads the Force of Freedom against the evil forces of S.A.V.A.G.E. The year 1988 saw Rambo return in *Rambo III*, where he rescues his mentor, who has been captured in Afghanistan. In 2008, Stallone returned to the character in *Rambo*, where the hero helps a group of missionaries in Burma. Rambo ultimately is not a serial vigilante as he lacks the ongoing drive to continue fighting; he only acts when he is forced.

• Bodyguard series, by Richard Reinsmith: This series deals with the adventures of a bodyguard named Ray Martin. Martin is one of the best in the business and he gets many clients whose lives are in jeopardy. He often takes violent action to protect his clients. Martin also manages to bed many women while protecting his clients.

5. The Female of the Species

Traditionally, the protagonist of the action/adventure story has been male. But there have been exceptions. Within various mythologies, there have been very few heroic females such as the valkyrie of Norse myths and Amazons from Greco-Roman mythology. The valkyrie were low-level female deities who took slain warriors from battle to Valhalla and determined the outcome of battles and wars. In some cases they participated in the battles. Similarly, the Amazons were a nation of warrior women who were believed to have removed their right breasts to aid them in the firing of arrows, although many artistic representations did not conform to this and heightened the sexuality of these women. Throughout history there have been female heroines, such as Calamity Jane, Joan of Arc, Anne Bonny and Annie Oakley to name a few. These women operated outside of the cultural norms for the time and often were the equal to the men they worked alongside.

PULP MYSTERY WOMEN

After the introduction of the Shadow, pulp mystery men proliferated. Doc Savage, the Avenger, the Whisperer, the Spider, the Phantom Detective and many other crime-fighters quickly appeared. But mystery women were far less common with the pulps, introducing the Domino Lady and Senorita Scorpion. The Domino Lady was Ellen Patrick, socialite daughter of politician Owen Patrick, who adopted her mystery woman persona to avenge the death of her father. She continued to fight crime through the pages of *Saucy Romantic Adventures* for five adventures, with a sixth story appearing in *Mystery Adventure Magazine* during 1936. All stories were written by Lars Anderson.

For *Domino Lady: The Complete Collection*, James Sterenko not only provided title page illustrations for the pulp reprints but also wrote the story "Aroused the Domino Lady," telling the Domino Lady's origin in 2004. In 1991, Eros Comics published the three-issue mini-series Domino Lady, which heightened the sexual tension of the original pulps into the realms of the erotic, with the heroine frequently losing her clothes and having sexual adventures while battling a master criminal's attempt to take over the city with dinosaurs and mind control.

Senorita Scorpion was Elgera Douglas, who like the Lone Ranger rode the old West. Senorita Scorpion protected the lost Santiago gold mine against land-grabbers and other threats. The lost gold mine had been in the Douglas family for two hundred years after an Indian attack left George Douglas and an Indian woman trapped in the mine and the hidden valley near it. Elgera is described as a fast draw, able to outshoot the various hired guns she fights against.

FEMALE SUPERHEROES

However, it was the early superhero/mystery men comics and comic strips that brought forth a wave of female crime-fighters. Some like Wonder Woman were superpowered but the majority were not. Sandra Knight (the Phantom Lady), Brenda Banks (Lady Luck), Diana Adams (Miss Masque), and Marla Drake (Miss Fury) were all socialites who adopted costumes and fought crime. Similarly, actresses Linda Turner (the Black Cat) and Rita Farrar (Senorita Rio) became costumed crime fighters.

While Peggy Allen (the Woman in Red) was a police officer frustrated with the rules, Dinah Drake (the Black Canary), a police officer's daughter, was unable to join the force. Secretary Louise Grant became the Blonde Phantom to help her employer Mark Mason, originally an O.S.S. agent and later private eye. Socialite Jan Dodge became Rulah and was considered a Jungle Goddess during her adventures in Africa, joining other jungle queens such as Sheena, Tiger Girl and the nameless actress who played Princess Panther and became too involved in her role.

GIRL DETECTIVES

There were also juvenile detective series such as Nancy Drew, the Dana Girls, and Trixie Belden, where teenage girls became detectives. These girls became involved in mysteries but did not adopt new identities, instead operating as amateur detectives.

FEMALE SPIES

During the 1960s, there was a rise of the female espionage agent. This was best personified by Emma Peel but Steed's other partners, Cathy Gale, Tara King and Purdey, as well as Agent 99 from *Get Smart* and April Dancer (the Girl from U.N.C.L.E.) are other examples. The female spy in this scenario is partnered with the male spy, playing an active role, being an equal partner in the investigations of espionage matters. The female spy is either as competent as or more competent than her male companion.

SEXY SPIES

With the success of the spy genre, there were a number of soft-core pornographic spy series, most patterned after the Man from U.N.C.L.E. and its spinoff, the Girl from U.N.C.L.E., so there were men from O.R.G.Y., P.U.S.S.Y., T.O.M.C.A.T., S.T.U.D. and C.H.A.R.I.S.M.A. who were quickly joined by girls from P.U.S.S.Y.C.A.T., B.U.S.T., and H.A.R.D. as well as a lady from L.U.S.T. These sexpionage agents work in a world where capture meant depraved sexual torture and any mission offers the opportunity for as much sex play as there is gun play.

MODESTY BLAISE

It was Modesty Blaise who provided the template for many of the female serial vigilantes. Created by Peter O'Donnell for a newspaper strip in 1963, Modesty was a child left orphaned during World War II eventually becomes the leader of the criminal organization known as the Network. The story opens when Modesty and her right-hand man Willie Garvin retire from their life of crime to Great Britain and are offered the opportunity for occasional excitement working as freelance operatives for the British Secret Service under Sir Gerald Tarrant. O'Donnell then attempted to adapt his character to film but, when the studio rejected his script, he turned it into a novel, *Modesty Blaise*, which started a series of novels and short-story collections that ran parallel to the comic series.

FEMALE SERIAL VIGILANTES

With the models in place of Modesty Blaise and **The Executioner**, it was only a short time before female serial vigilantes were created. **The Sexecutioner** was the first series created, written by one of the writers of the Lady from LUST, and set the model of a freelance operative who trades on her sexuality and deadly skills. The Sexecutioner works for the New York Mafia Prosecution and Harassment Organization (N.Y.M.P.H.O.) fighting organized crime around the world. The Sexecutioner was quickly joined by **The Baroness, The Black Swan**, and Su-Lin Kelly of **The Girl Factory**.

TEAM PLAYERS

While the serial vigilante team would seem to be a male-only domain, many of the groups have female members. Their roles vary from tactical support such as April Rose and Barbara Price as seen in the Executioner and related series to active team members like Hanni Stein from **Warhawks, Inc.**, and Domino Black from **Z-Comm**. In every instance they are in a minority.

BLAXPLOITATION

The blaxploitation film genre introduced films featuring African-American protagonists such as Shaft. The genre had several female leading characters such as Coffy, Foxy Brown, Cleopatra Jones and TNT Jackson. Cleopatra Jones was the only character to feature in more than one film, also appearing in *Cleopatra Jones and the Casino of Gold*. *Foxy Brown*, originally titled *Burn, Coffy, Burn*, was intended as a sequel to Coffy with the same director and star, but the studio did not wish to make a sequel and ordered a quick rewrite to make an original character. These characters were parodied in Austin Powers in *Goldmember* by the character Foxxy Cleopatra.

FEMALE PRIVATE EYES

In 1977, Marcia Muller published *Edwin of the Iron Shoes*, featuring the first hard-boiled female private eye, Sharon McCone. It was not until 1982 that Sue Grafton and Sara Paretsky were able to add their female private eyes, Kinsey Milhone and V.I. Warshawski, and they were followed by many other female eyes.

EROS COMIX

During the 1990s, Eros Comics introduced two new sexy crime-fighters, Marcia Bolens, the Sexecutioner II, and Razmataz. Like Cherry Delight, the new Sexecutioner used her sexuality and fighting skills to bring down organized crime.

DISTAFF VERSIONS

The 1990s saw several new incarnations of older serial vigilantes and, in an attempt to do something different, made female versions of male heroes.

• Knight Rider: The television movie *Knight Rider 2000*, which was to serve as pilot to the series had Michael Knight passing the car on to Shawn McCormack, a female police officer who had one of KITT's computer chips inserted in her head. The movie was never picked up as a series.

• Vigilante: In the comic series Deathstroke the Terminator, policewoman Patricia Trayce discovered the uniform and equipment of the earlier Vigilante, Adrian Chase, and adopted the identity. Trayce remained a supporting character in several series. Since the conclusion of those series two new male Vigilantes have debuted.

• Punisher: During the Punisher story arc "Suicide Run," Frank Castle was believed dead and several characters adopted the costume and name of the Punisher. One of those was ex-police officer Lynn Michaels; in Punisher War Journal #62 she officially became Castle's successor. Within a year, all of the Punisher's titles were cancelled and all relaunches have featured Frank Castle as the Punisher again.

• Femme Fatale: In 2003, Gold Eagle's sister company Silhouette published a collection of three connected novellas with references to the Executioner and **Stony Man** series. Each novella introduced a female operative of the Stony Man Farm chasing down a terrorist mastermind and finding love. There has not been a second collection.

All of these distaff serial vigilantes were ultimately unsuccessful and short-lived before other attempts to revive these characters were implemented.

ADVENTURING ARCHAEOLOGISTS

In the 1990s, we saw the rise of girl power with shows like *Xena, Buffy the Vampire Slayer, Charmed, VIP* and *Alias,* all of which featured strong female lead characters. At the same time, the Tomb Raider video game was being developed and featured the adventures of Lara Croft, a tomb raider in the Indiana Jones mold. This was the first time a video game was designed exclusively around a female character and didn't give players the option of playing a male character. The game and character were a success and the franchise has expanded from video games to comics, movies and novels. The success of the game inspired the television series *Relic Hunter,* which featured archaeology professor Sydney Fox and her assistant Nigel Bailey traveling the world searching for relics. The 2006 novel series Rogue Angel featured another female archaeologist, Annja Creed. In this instance, Creed has found the sword of Joan of Arc and is now fighting evil around the world.

BACK TO THE STREETS

The 2005 movie *Hard Candy* offered a more streetwise take on the vigilante — a pedophile hunter. Haley meets men online with the screen name thonggirl14 and arranges meetings with the ones who sexually proposition her. Through psychological mind games, the pedophiles are persuaded to commit suicide, believing that it is the only way to avoid exposure.

Academy award winner Jodie Foster played the vigilante Erica Bain in the 2007 movie *The Brave One.* Bain was viciously attacked and left for dead. After her recovery, Bain buys a black market gun and begins to kill criminals, eventually hunting the gang that attacked her. Also released in 2007 was the independent release *Juncture,* which offers a female vigilante diagnosed with terminal cancer seeking to make the world a better place.

These vigilantes offer a throwback to the earlier street-level vigilantes such as those seen in **Death Wish** by Brian Garfield and **The Vigilante** series by V.J. Santiago, with the new twist of a female protagonist.

CONCLUSION

As can be seen, the female characters in action fiction have evolved from a largely supporting role to taking center stage. These characters have been frequently sexualized, with skimpy costumes and a focus on their physical beauty. This came to a peak with characters like Su-Lin Kelly, the Baroness and the Sexecutioner, who were nymphomaniacs bedding nearly every male and many females who came across their paths. This trend was reversed somewhat with the debut of the female private eye and attempts to create female versions of male characters, focusing on their skills and abilities. This trend continued with the adventuring archaeologists, all of whom were successful in their field and capable of handling any situation. However, their physical beauty is still a factor. With the streetwise vigilantes of the new millennium, the focus became less on the physical beauty and more on the psychological state of the vigilante.

6. The Future of the Serial Vigilante

The serial vigilante did not emerge from a vacuum and forms part of a continuum of justice figures from many different strands of literature and folklore. We can see elements of the serial vigilante in the tales of Robin Hood, William Tell, Jesse James, Billy the Kid, Spring-heeled Jack, the Just Men, the Shadow, the Saint, the Lone Ranger, the Scarlet Pimpernel and numerous other characters. These characters have appeared in legend, folklore, penny dreadfuls, dime novels, thrillers, pulps and comics. These terms have defined and placed these characters in socio-political contexts often defined by major world events.

Alice Turner (1977), in her essay "The Paperback Hero," argues that several societal conditions in 1969 led to the rise of the serial vigilante — the assassination of Bobby Kennedy, the Chicago trials, My Lai massacre, Altamont following Woodstock, the president's "secret plan" for peace in Vietnam, anger, frustration and a deep division. Turner then suggests that we may never see the like again but she does point out that there have always been macho heroes dispensing frontier justice.

This last thought has been echoed by other scholars such as Cawelti (1975), Kittredge and Krauser (1978), and Ruehlmann. Since the highpoint of the 1980s, there has been a marked decline in the serial vigilantes. The Executioner, the Destroyer and the Punisher are the only characters from the founding decades of the 1960s and 1970s still being published. None of the characters who debuted during the 1980s are still in production.

What can we predict about the next wave of justice figures? By examining the trends seen in serial vigilante fiction — such as the recent reprints and revivals, trends seen during the '90s and beyond, the effect of the September 11 terrorist attacks, the rise of the female serial vigilante and the supernatural serial vigilante — it will be possible to predict something of the nature of this next wave of justice figures.

REPRINTS AND REVIVALS

One of the factors that led to the advent of the serial vigilantes were the reprints and revivals of the pulp heroes during the 1960s, as evidenced by the reprints of Doc Savage, the new adventures of the Shadow and television shows based on the Saint and the Green Hornet. Today, the pulps seem to undergoing another revival with the new adventures of Captain Hazzard as well as new reprints of Doc Savage, the Shadow and the Phantom Detective. Paul Malmont's *The Chinatown Death Cloud Peril* takes pulp creators William Gibson (the Shadow) and Lester Dent (Doc Savage) and sets them on an adventure worthy of their creations.

Has there been a similar revival for the serial vigilantes? Ignoring British editions of series like the Executioner, the Destroyer, and **The Death Merchant**, which were licensed to British publishers within a few years of original publication, there are very few reprints. Leisure books reprinted Chet Cunningham's first eight **Penetrator** novels in 1991, which, by coincidence, was the same year as the unauthorized film *The Firing Line* starring Reb Brown as Mark Hardin. In 2000, Eagle One Media offered the Penetrator series as e-books. Pinnacle Books reissued William Johnstone's Rig Warrior series in 2001.

The collection *The Best of the Destroyer* was printed in 2007 by Tor Books to help promote their original Destroyer novels and reprinted three early Destroyer novels. The Tor Destroyers novels, billed as the New Destroyer, can be considered a revival of the Destroyer series which had been seen as mishandled under the former publisher Gold Eagle and ignored many of the later books in that publisher's run.

There have been several other revivals of serial vigilante franchises. Knight Rider went through several failed revivals with the torch-passing *Knight Rider 2000*, the irrelevant *Knight Rider 2010* and the short-lived series Team Knight Rider and a new television movie in 2008 with Michael Knight's son, a former Army Ranger, taking a new car and continuing the fight for justice.

The Punisher, after the cancellation of his three series in 1995, went through several unsuccessful revivals including making the Punisher the head of a Mafia family (Marvel Edge imprint) and an angelic demon hunter (Purgatory mini-series) until Garth Ennis took over the character with the Welcome Back Frank mini-series in 2000 for the Marvel Knights imprint. Ennis returned the character to his street-level roots and added a dark humor to the character which revived the character's popularity and spawned a two new series and several specials and served as a partial basis for the 2004 movie. The 2004 movie updated the character's origin from serving the Vietnam War to serving in the first Gulf War in Kuwait and further expanded the character's popularity.

Other recent movies have followed the trend of updating the character's back stories so that Bob Lee Swagger's Vietnam sniper experience in the novel *Point of Contact* was updated to black ops sniping in Africa for the movie version *Shooter*. A similar transformation took place with **The Specialist** movie and the novel series that inspired it, with Vietnam veteran Jack Sullivan becoming explosives expert Ray Quick, who served in Nicaragua. Similarly, the entire plot of the movie *Death Sentence* was updated and the characters changed to move away from the *Death Wish* film series. The novel *Death Sentence* was a sequel to the novel *Death Wish*, which formed the basis of the film series. How a proposed remake of *Death Wish* will update and alter the movie is to be seen. With Hollywood's tendency to turn old television series into movies, it is expected that many serial vigilante television series will make the jump to the big screen. It remains to be seen what, if any, changes these movies make to the original series.

FEMALE SERIAL VIGILANTES

During the 1970s, we saw many female serial vigilantes in series such as **The Baroness** (Baroness Penelope St. John Orsini), **Black Swan** (Shauna Bishop) and the **Girl Factory** (Su-Lin Kelly). The movie industry was not far behind with the adventures of blaxploitation heroines such as Coffy, Foxy Brown, TNT Jackson and Cleopatra Jones. In more recent times we have seen the rise of female serial vigilantes such as Tomb Raider (Lara Croft), Black Scorpion (Darcy Walker), Relic Hunter (Sydney Fox) and **Rogue Angel** (Annja Creed). The 2007 film *The Brave One* offers us a female version of the serial vigilante, starring Jodie Foster as Erica Bain, a DJ who lost her fiancé in an attack.

In recent world conflicts such as both Gulf Wars and Afghanistan, women have been in combat situations; as a result there are more women with combat training and experience in society. As current fiction shows, more characters with modern combat experience may see more female characters taking on a serial vigilante role.

THE 1990s

After the high point of the 1980s, many of the characters that debuted during that period stopped publication, but new serial vigilante series continued to be created and published.

Kasner's **Black Ops** and Johnstone's **Codename** series debuted in novels during this time. Both series offered teams funded by elite groups to tackle worldwide terrorism and other unpunishable crimes.

But the 1990s saw many more serial vigilante television series such as *Hack, Pretender,* and *Soldier of Fortune/Special Ops Force* (SOF). *Black Scorpion, Relic Hunter* and *Vengeance Unlimited* also debuted. This was also the decade that saw three attempted revivals of the Knight Rider franchise the television movies *Knight Rider 2000* and *Knight Rider 2010* and television series *Team Knight Rider.*

Perhaps the most influential of the serial vigilantes from that decade didn't originate in any of those formats but debuted in a video game. Lara Croft, Tomb Raider, started as a video game but quickly spread into other media with a comic book series, two movies and several original and adapted novels. The character paved the way for other female adventuring archeologists, such as Sydney Fox Relic Hunter, Annja Creed, Rogue Angel, and Abbey Chase of Danger Girl.

SEPTEMBER 11, 2001

It may have been expected the terrorist attacks of September 2001 might have launched a new wave of serial vigilantes avenging the deaths of their families at the hands of terrorist attacks. But this didn't happen.

One factor in the rise of the serial vigilante during the 1960s was the belief that the system wasn't working. The events of September 2001 made the police and firefighters of New York City heroes whose efforts showed that the system did work. To go outside of that would be seen as an insult to the men and women who gave their lives in this crisis. Mack Maloney's **Superhawks** were created in response to the September 11 attacks and featured a team of ex-military personnel, all of whom had lost loved ones in those attacks, tracking down and killing the people responsible for September 11 and preventing further attacks.

Often heroes have military background. Many western heroes served in the Civil War; the pulp heroes had a similar background with World War I. Most spies of the Cold

War started in either World War II or the Korean War. Many serial vigilantes started out in the Vietnam War.

We see this trend continue with the military crime series *JAG* and *NCIS*. Detectives such as Elliot Stabler and Robert Goren from the *Law and Order* franchises *Special Victims Unit* and *Criminal Intent*, Colby Granger from *Numbers*, Det. Bobby "Fearless" Smith from *Boomtown* all have prior military service. Perhaps our new wave of serial vigilantes will find their training grounds in the war on terror, and the frustration of hunting terrorists who remain elusive despite the large-scale manhunts.

We only need to look at how earlier heroes were updated to suggest the origins of new serial vigilantes. When the Pulp hero **The Spider** was updated and slightly revised to become the serial vigilante known as Spider, his military service changed from World War I to the Korean War. In a similar fashion the origins of the various incarnations of the Punisher have similarly updated the various conflicts. In the original conception, Frank Castle was a Vietnam veteran. The 2004 movie updated this and had Frank Castle serving in Kuwait during the first Gulf War and then later joining the FBI. The Kuwait back story was removed from the original release of the Punisher movie but was retained in the novelization and restored in the extended cut of that film.

The latest batch of serial vigilantes had similar new origins. **Home Team**'s members served in both Bosnia and the first Gulf War. Two of Kasner's Black Ops team members also served in the first Gulf War. William Johnstone's one-man Black Ops team, Art Jenson (a direct descendant of Johnstone's western hero, Smoke Jensen), had served in Iraq. While **Invasion USA**'s Tom Brennan is a Vietnam veteran, many of those who have assisted him had fought in Desert Storm and the Afghanistan conflicts.

Additionally, we have seen the rise of the revenge film, *Man on Fire*, *Kill Bill Vol. 1 & 2* coming out at the same time as the 2004 Punisher movie. Interestingly, these can be seen as a harkening back to the earlier period. The *Kill Bill* movies are Tarantino's homage to the spaghetti westerns and martial arts movies of the 1970s. *The Punisher* is a version of a '70s comic book character and a remake of a 1989 film. *Man on Fire* is based on A.J. Quinell's 1980 novel of the same name and is also a remake of the 1987 movie, which was also based on the book.

This trend has been continued with revenge/vigilante films such as *The Marine*, *The Brave One*, *Shooter*, *Death Sentence* and a new Punisher film, *Punisher War Zone*. While *The Marine* and *The Brave One* are original movies, the other films were adapted from older literary sources. *The Punisher* has been covered above; *Death Sentence* is adapted from Brian Garfield's 1975 sequel to *Death Wish* of the same name; *Shooter* is based on Stephen Hunter's 1993 novel *Point of Contact*.

PRIVATE SECURITY FIRMS

In both Iraq and Afghanistan, there has been an increased reliance on private military contractors, such as Blackwater Worldwide, to provide security and military forces. These private military forces may form the basis of new series where members of these forces fight terrorism and crime. Private military forces have appeared in fiction but primarily in the role of villains, such as in the 2008 pilot movie for Knight Rider where operatives from Darkwater Security are trying to steal the new Knight Industries 3000, or in *CSI Miami* episode, "Guerillas in the Mist," where Paragon Security has been hired by the government to kill gunrunners with a weapon called "the Vaporizer"; the CSI team must track and bring these killers to justice.

SUPERNATURAL SERIAL VIGILANTES

Often, the fight against the evil that humanity does has not been enough; several serial vigilantes have taken the fight from the natural realm to the supernatural. During the 1970s and 1980s, there were several series devoted to supernatural serial vigilantes. In these cases, supernatural horrors replaced the mundane Mafia and terrorists. In some cases, our hero may have mild supernatural abilities; in others, he may be able to harness the supernatural for his ends, but often these are battles of the natural against the supernatural. These can be seen in series such as Lory's **Dracula, The Satan Sleuth, Chill, Sabat** and **Night Hunter.**

In 1998, the Punisher went through a supernatural phase in a four-issue Marvel Knights mini-series titled Purgatory. In the story Frank Castle has committed suicide and is sent back with blessed guns to hunt demons. This supernatural version included a revision of the Punisher's origin where a skull-faced demon gets all the souls of the people the Punisher has killed. This supernatural aspect has largely been ignored in the current incarnations of the character, although Garth Ennis did allude to it in his Punisher Born mini-series. This appeared at the same time as the television series *Buffy the Vampire Slayer, Charmed* and *Angel.* While the supernatural version of the Punisher was not successful, it was not until 2005 that we saw new supernatural serial vigilantes. *Supernatural* gave us the adventures of Sam and Dean Winchester, brothers traveling America and fighting supernatural forces that they were trained by their ex–Marine father to fight. The Rogue Angel series combined the female adventuring archaeologist with fighting the supernatural.

CONCLUSION

Injustice will always exist in society, and art will always seek to explore the issues of society. In recent years there has been an increased interest in serial vigilante characters, with a number of revenge/vigilante films. Just as the success of various revivals of pulp heroes showed there was a market for the serial vigilante, the success of these revivals of serial vigilantes shows that there is a market for a new breed of justice figures. This new breed will likely be bred in combat for the war on terror as the situation in Iraq and Afghanistan has several similarities to Vietnam and its role in the war on communism.

This new breed may include a higher proportion of women, as women have taken on larger roles in both the military and the police in the last forty years, including service in combat zones, although just how big this proportion will be is dependent on how successful the first few of these female new breed are.

If the trend seen in the '90s continues, the new breed's adventures will most likely be recorded in either film series or television series; there will be a few new paperback series as well as comic book series. It may be that the more successful film or television series will be adapted in the other mediums. We can see this happening now as the Rogue Angel novel series has been adapted into the comic format.

The origins of the new breed will be similar to their serial vigilante predecessors. Some will lose loved ones in a terrorist attack; others will find that their loved ones will die at the hands of street gangs. Others will find themselves attacked personally either in the form of a physical attack or having their reputation attacked through trumped-up charges. All will begin a personal war.

The foes fought by the new breed will range from street-level criminals such as muggers and drug dealers through to terrorists. While the Mafia has become a spent force, organized crime in the form of prostitution rings and drug cartels is still a major force in criminal circles. Some of the new breed will venture into fighting the supernatural.

The new breed will be as different from the serial vigilantes as the serial vigilantes were from the pulp heroes that preceded them. They will share elements of the justice figure. Some series, like the President's Man and Invasion USA, will be regarded as transition series where the Vietnam era serial vigilante hands over the fight to the war on terror's new breed.

Bibliography

Cawelti, J. (1975a). "Myths of Violence in American Popular Culture." *Critical Inquiry*, 1(3), 521–541.

Cawelti, J. (1975b). "The New Mythology of Crime." *Boundary 2*, 3(2), 324–357.

Contemporary Authors On-Line (2007). Retrieved September 20, 2007, from http://infotrac.gale-group.com

Coogan, P. (2006). *Superhero: The Secret Origin of a Genre*. Austin, TX: Monkeybrain Books.

"Don Pendleton vs. the Mafia." (1973, Nov-Dec). *Mediascene*, 7, 8–10.

Kittredge, W., and Krauzer, S. (eds.). (1978). *The Great American Detective*. New York: Mentor.

Kraft, D. (1975). "The Executioner Speaks Out!: An Exclusive Interview with Don Pendleton." *Marvel Preview*, 2, 46–58.

Lynds, G. (1998). "The Strange and True Story of a Woman Who Wrote Pulp Fiction." In J. Grape, D. James, and E. Nehr (Eds.), *Deadly Women: The Woman Mystery Reader's Indispensible Companion* (pp. 143–145). New York: Carroll & Graf Publishers.

Nevins, J. (2003). *Heroes & Monsters: The Unofficial Companion to the League of Extraordinary Gentlemen*. Austin, TX: Monkeybrain Books.

Newton, M. (1989). *How to Write Action-Adventure Novels*. Cincinnati, OH: Writer's Digest Books.

Philips, G. (2006). "Death of a Pulp Writer." Retrieved November 12, 2008, from http://www.gdphillips.com/death_of_a_pulp_writer.htm

Pringle, D. (1996). *Imaginary People: A Who's Who of Fictional Characters, from the Eighteenth Century to the Present Day*. Brookfield, VT: Scolar Press.

Rovin, J. (1994). *Adventure Heroes: Legendary Characters from Odysseus to James Bond*. New York: Facts on File.

Ruehlman, W. (1974). *Saint with a Gun: The Unlawful American Private Eye*. New York: New York University Press.

Server, L. (2002). *Encyclopedia of Pulp Fiction Writers*. New York: Facts on File.

Simkin, J. (1998). *The Whole Story: 3000 Years of Sequels and Sequences*, 2nd ed. Port Melbourne, Vic., Austr.: Thorpe.

Talbot, P. (2006) *Bronson's Loose: The Making of the Death Wish Films*. New York: iUniverse.

Turner, A. (1977). "The Paperback Hero." In D. Winn (Ed.), *Murder Ink: The Mystery Reader's Companion* (pp. 144–147).

Young, W. (1996). *A Study of Action-Adventure Fiction: The Executioner and Mack Bolan*. Lewiston: Edwin Mellon Press.

Index

Entries in **bold** denote main entries.